American Military Vehicles
of World War I

American Military Vehicles of World War I

An Illustrated History of Armored Cars,
Staff Cars, Motorcycles, Ambulances,
Trucks, Tractors and Tanks

ALBERT MROZ

McFarland & Company, Inc., Publishers
Jefferson, North Carolina, and London

LIBRARY OF CONGRESS CATALOGUING-IN-PUBLICATION DATA

Mroz, Albert.
American military vehicles of World War I : an illustrated history of
armored cars, staff cars, motorcycles, ambulances, trucks, tractors
and tanks / Albert Mroz.
p.   cm.
Includes bibliographical references and index.

ISBN 978-0-7864-3960-7
softcover : 50# alkaline paper

1. Vehicles, Military—United States—History—20th century.
2. World War, 1914–1918—United States.
3. Armored vehicles, Military—United States—History—20th century.
4. United States—Armed Forces—Transportation—History—20th century.
5. World War, 1914–1918—Transportation.   6. Vehicles, Military—
United States—History—20th century—Pictorial works.
7. Armored vehicles, Military—United States—History—20th century—
Pictorial works.   8. United States—Armed Forces—Transportation—
History—20th century—Pictorial works.   I. Title.
UG618.M76   2009   623.7' 47097309041—dc22   2009022079

British Library cataloguing data are available

On the cover: *clockwise from top left* White armored car built in 1916;
Militor standardized 4 × 4 truck being tested by
U.S. Ordnance Department in 1918;
Indian motorcycle with machine gun sidecar and crew of three

Manufactured in the United States of America

McFarland & Company, Inc., Publishers
Box 611, Jefferson, North Carolina 28640
www.mcfarlandpub.com

To Edward and
Teresa Mroz

TABLE OF CONTENTS

CREDITS AND ACKNOWLEDGMENTS

American Truck Historical Society, Art Archives at Imperial War Museum, Autolit.com, Tom Berndt, Cadillac Factory Literature, Fred Crismon, Bev Davis, Peter Debski, Paul DeLucchi, Ralph Dunwoodie, Ford Factory Literature, FWD Museum, David Gallagher, Al Garcia, General Motors Factory Literature, Bryan Goodman, A. W. Hays, Don Hays, Elayne Hurd at Autopaper, Johnson's Auto Literature, Arthur Jones, James V. Lee, Library of Congress, Jacques Littlefield, Mack Factory Literature, McLellan's Auto Literature, Medical College of Pennsylvania, Military Vehicle Preservation Association, Edward Mroz, Nash Factory Literature, National Archives, National Automotive Museum, Pacific Northwest Truck Museum, Bill Powk, Dirk Roberts, Ed Roberts, Peter Roberts, Randy Shapiro, Society of Automotive Engineers, Society of Automotive Historians, Stanford Hoover Library, U.S. Patent Office, Roger Viollet, Western Front Association, White Factory Literature, Geoffrey Wintrup, Greg Wintrup, World War I Museum at Kansas City, Peter Zappel.

Published articles by the author of this book used in part throughout the text, including some photographs and illustrations, have appeared in the following magazines: *American History, American Iron, Antique Power, Army Motors, Auto Moto, Autoweek, Automotive History Review, Hard Hat, Militaria International, Old Time Trucks, Old Truck Town News, SAH Journal, Steam Traction, Tractor and Machinery, Transport Topics, Turning Wheels, Vintage Truck, VTFE Monthly,* and *Wheels.*

ABBREVIATIONS

AEF American Expeditionary Forces
ALAM Association of Licensed Automobile Manufacturers
CEF Canadian Expeditionary Forces
cc cubic centimeters
cid cubic inch displacement (as specified by SAE)
hp horsepower (brake, SAE or ALAM)
mm millimeter
MVPA Military Vehicle Preservation Association
NLWS Nation League of Women's Service
rpm (RPM) revolutions per minute
SAH Society of Automotive Historians
SAE Society of Automotive Engineers
WCTU Women's Christian Temperance Movement

PREFACE

Although the internal combustion powered motor vehicle was invented nearly three decades before World War I exploded in Europe, it was in the crucible of war that various forms of mechanical, self-propelled conveyances were greatly improved, and mass production became the norm rather than the exception in the evolution of America's motorization. As an outgrowth of the Industrial Revolution during the 1800s, American manufacturing capabilities, along with the abundance of natural resources, became a dominant force among nations around the world, and America's entry into World War I became a turning point in the defeat of the Axis nations and those that joined the aggressors in that far-reaching conflict.

I've always been fascinated with vehicles of all types, partly because they have made our world smaller in a sense, allowing long-distance, rapid and efficient travel, and they have changed nearly every aspect of our lives around the globe, sometimes defining us individually, in many ways for the better, but also in vast ways to the detriment of our environment. In terms of military power, motor vehicles and aircraft were the most influential inventions of the early 20th century, followed by the advent of electronics, computers and complex weapons systems. World War I was the culmination of knowledge in the production of steel through advances in metallurgy and in the development of new and enormously powerful weapons through chemistry, aspects of which are delineated in a separate chapter about the Industrial Revolution and its influence on the war.

That my father, Edward Mroz, Ph.D., was an automotive engineer surely sparked an enthusiasm in me for an appreciation of cars, trucks, motorcycles and all forms of vehicles on and off the road. But how and why the trappings of this ubiquitous form of transportation raised the efficiency of destruction, most likely subverting our ecology or even our very existence on Earth is a subject for another book. So is the commentary on the moral deficiencies of those involved in making and carrying out warfare.

In 1991 I had the good fortune of discovering the truck collection of A. W. Hays in Woodland, California, which became the Hays Antique Truck Museum, now part of the Heidrick Ag Center. Having already done some years of research and printed some articles, I wrote and published *The Illustrated Encyclopedia of American Trucks and Commercial Vehicles* (Krause, 1996), which also included military vehicles. During the course of collecting material, I concentrated on photography and was very fortunate to purchase several personal albums from the war era from which I gleaned a number of previously unpublished photos. As much as World War I has been considered a precursor to the Second World War, and as much as attention has also been given to the political, strategic and social underpinnings of the subject at hand, despite the numerous references that are made to these important general elements, they are not covered in depth in this book, in order to stay on the subject of vehicle development and history in a limited number of pages.

There are countless books and collections of information about World War I, but few if any of them treat American motor vehicles as a separate subject, let alone include such eventually diverse creations as motorcycles, ambulances and tanks. In an attempt to organize the topic of American motor vehicle production of this specific era into a cohesive discussion, and at the same time to assuage the thirst for general knowledge, I have perhaps created a certain irony in attempting to expand and narrow the subject at the same time by including armored cars, staff cars, motorcycles, ambulances, trucks, tractors and tanks in one book. Surely, a book on each type of vehicle could and in some cases may have been written. Yet, as wide a category as this may seem to be collectively, many if not most of the individuals and companies involved in manufacturing in America prior to 1919 built several types of motor vehicles and were engaged in developing a wide array of machines and mechanical devices, eventually for the war effort. This still allows me to exclude ships, railroads, aircraft, cavalry and numerous modern weapons, although it would be impossible not to make mention of their overlapping technology and strategic importance alongside motorization.

The subject of Pancho Villa and the Punitive Expedition of 1916–1917 is inherently intertwined in the history of America's involvement in World War I as it developed overseas. Because the United States was basically sidelined by Pancho Villa's attack on Columbus, New Mexico, or perhaps it chose to have its military operations diverted in that way (with Mexico as a nation in the throes of a revolution), a chapter is dedicated to this episode. This is included in part because it was also America's first experience with motorized ground transport and the first use of aircraft for military operations at a time when aviation technology was derivative of motor vehicle technology, and both the civilian industry as well as the military had yet to learn the value of standardization as the industry further adopted mass production. As the Punitive Expedition ended, America entered the war and began sending the nation's entire effort overseas.

In the early days, the design of vehicles powered by an internal combustion engine emanated from the minds of engineers, the technical drawings of draftsmen and the components made by machine shop craftsmen. This required versatile individuals who had to be well versed in building related mechanisms and devices before specialization narrowed each field and each designer's degree of know-how and responsibility.

In order to collect information pertaining to the abundance of American-made motor vehicles built during World War I, I have delved into a wide variety of sources. My membership at the Hoover Library at nearby Stanford has been invaluable, as has been my docent membership with the Behring Museum at Blackhawk. So has it served me well to have received very generous help from Fred Crismon, an expert on the subject if there ever was one, as well as having had access to the excellent collection of the late Ralph Dunwoodie (one of my mentors and a founding member of the Society of Automotive Historians as well as Bill Harrah's researcher and purchasing agent). In addition, I received information from SAE, of which I am a member, as well as numerous photos from the Library of Congress, among the sources that I document in more detail in the bibliography as well as the credits and acknowledgments section. Perhaps by expanding on the subject of American motor vehicles from this era, I have simultaneously narrowed it down for the open-minded reader.

INTRODUCTION

In 1900 the nations of Europe were at peace, following almost a century of relative quiet. In the post–Napoleonic era, local uprisings and upheavals demanded autonomy in the new spirit of liberalism and republicanism—the former favoring freedom of the individual from overreaching government control and the guarantee of basic civil rights, the latter dismantling the power of monarchy in order to base governments on written constitutions.

Several of the economies of the European "Great Powers" had been vastly bolstered by colonial empires around the globe. The Industrial Revolution had rapidly accelerated technological progress, attributed largely to the mechanization of industry through steam

Soldiers mustering out at Camp Dix, New Jersey, on a 1918 Dodge military staff car. Note seven-bolt clincher wheels.

An illustration by Gayle Porter Hoskins published in October 1918 shows an artist's conception of an Allied motorcycle dispatch rider (D.R.) running into German cavalry along a dirt road near Landrecies, France.

engine power in the late 1700s, especially in England. Here, and in the Continent, cities were churning out products and wealth for the new middle and upper echelons of society. Mass production was giving millions of people access to what was once only available to the wealthiest classes.

But as marvels in chemistry, metallurgy, electricity, mechanical engineering and medicine continued to improve everyday life for so many people, militarization increased at a tremendous pace. The large-scale development and production of armament and weaponry of all types was intense and widespread. At this juncture, any major conflict would have to involve this new industrialization, which included inventions such as aircraft, diesel-powered submarines, high explosives, and poison gas—in addition to the cars, trucks and motorcycles being mass produced by hundreds of independent companies in Europe as well as in the United States.

The assembly line system became common practice in the manufacturing of firearms before Henry Ford adopted those methods for producing automobiles. And the notable improvement in steel production allowed factories and shipyards to build railroads, firearms, artillery and gargantuan ships-of-war, while some corporations constructed utilitarian bridges and busy skyscrapers.

By 1906 not only did the Wright Brothers make heavier-than-air flight a reality, but

A destroyed tank from the Third Battle of Ypres in August 1917.

it was also the year Britain built its first dreadnought battleship. A fleet of these enormous battleships were to be powered notably by oil instead of coal, due to the direct involvement of then First Lord of the Admiralty, Winston Churchill, who strategically insisted the British government would become a major stockholder in the Anglo-Persian Oil Co. (British Petroleum) in what is now Iran.

At the same time, both Germany and France were developing enormous military might, including huge artillery. Construction of a fleet of submarines was begun in Germany, also in 1906, directly following such developments in Russia and France. Only two decades earlier, after some development in France, the internal combustion engine was invented in Germany, along with the first motorcars that were powered by this type of propulsion. The vulcanization of rubber, discovered by Charles Goodyear, was common practice in the first decade of the 20th century. Through their inventions, men such as Thomas Edison (light bulb and light power station of 1882), Alexander Graham Bell (inventor of the telephone, inaugurated 1892) and Guglielmo Marconi (wireless telegraph patented in 1900) changed the nature of illumination and communication, helping to create a plethora of electrical and electronic devices on which we depend to this very day.

With the discovery of oil and development of fuels derived from petroleum, motorization would rapidly change the landscape of the modern world. But all these great inventions had also become a part of the expansion of the military as tensions continued to grow between political regimes across Europe and in the U.S. Those tensions were based on age-old conflicts over territory and differences in culture, language, tradition and political and social philosophy. Both the Spanish-American War of 1898 and the assassination of President William McKinley in 1901 were manifestations, and a spill-over effect, of this conflict in America, which had also enjoyed peace and prosperity in the decades after the Civil War.

Among the people who were famous during this era, Sir Arthur Conan Doyle began publicizing the imminent possibility of war after an event involving the automobile in 1911. That year he was part of the International Road Competition organized by Prince Henry of Prussia. This was known as The Prince Henry Tour, in which the owners of motor vehicles from England and Germany competed in order to improve quality and show off superiority. Participants traveled from Hamburg, Germany, to London, England, by way of roads and ferryboat Channel crossing.

Conan Doyle and his wife were on one of the British driving teams. Each of the nine cars in the competition carried a military observer from the opposite team. Doyle noted the hostility of the German observers and the fact that they openly discussed the inevitability of war.

That prediction, or perhaps self-fulfilling prophecy, came true fewer than three years later, but the "war to end all wars" had its inception in a place men such as Conan Doyle and his Prince Henry Tour military observers had not anticipated.

Chapter I

BULLETS, BLOOD AND GASOLINE

Gavrilo Princip was a young Serbian ultra-nationalist who belonged to the Black Hand, a group that was part of a larger organization called Union or Death. He was the assassin of Archduke Franz Ferdinand in Sarajevo, Bosnia, which was annexed by Austria-Hungary in 1908. The Archduke was there to supervise the Habsburg army's maneuvers during the summer of 1914. On the commemorated day of the year when Serbia had been defeated by the Turks in 1389, Gavrilo Princip was visiting Sarajevo on this June 28 with several associates at the same time as the Archduke.

After three of his associates failed in the attempt on Franz Ferdinand's life using thrown explosives, which bounced off his car, it took three shots of a revolver by the assas-

Archduke Franz Ferdinand and his wife in Sarajevo on June 28, 1914, just before the assassination.

sin to kill the Archduke along with his wife as they were being chauffeured in an open automobile, after the driver took a wrong turn and slowly backed up the vehicle. It was an ominous portent of the significance of motor vehicles and their development at a time when such technology was in its infancy.

The Austrians decided that the Serbian government was behind the assassination and made various demands at seeking justice with those possibly complicit in the crime. Within the next two months, the nations of Europe declared war on each other, and World War I exploded across the continent, spilling over into the Middle East when Turkey threw itself into the conflict on the Axis side. The war extended into North Africa and what was then called Mesopotamia (now partly Iraq), where such westerners as Lawrence of Arabia became famous for their involvement in the war. The war also spanned Asia as far away as Japan, which sided with the Allies in World War I.

The war on the Western Front was instigated by Germany, following an official written plan devised by General Alfred von Schlieffen, chief of the general staff, who died in 1913 before the war began. Albeit ill-conceived, his plan envisioned an attack on France through Belgium and Holland, bypassing the fortresses and mountains along the Franco-German border. Schlieffen proposed to concentrate on a massive northerly invasion that would encircle Paris from the north and east. However, the new chief of staff, Helmuth von Moltke (the younger), watered down the original plan, avoiding Holland and throwing a large contingent of his army to the south. This allowed the French to outflank the Germans without ever having to rely on Plan XVII, France's own attack strategy adopted in 1913.

In the battle of the Marne, the French Sixth Army under General Michel-Joseph Maunoury rushed troops to the front in September of 1914 using every possible vehicle that was available in Paris and vicinity. This became the legendary "taxi-corps," in which soldiers were driven to the battle by commandeered cabs, trucks and private vehicles of all types and makes, within a 72-hour period, successfully outrunning the German army. It was an extemporaneous effort that would again truly foreshadow the significance of motor vehicle transport during World War I, and notably thereafter.

The reliability, versatility and speed of motor vehicles was put to an acid test and would be relied upon by the Allies once it was realized that Germany outgunned the French, British and, later, American forces. This was especially proven after August 1914 when the Belgian Liège Forts were decimated by such huge guns as the 420 mm Big Bertha, or other huge Krupp howitzers, and guns from Skoda, such as the 305 mm.

In the 1800s the flow of technology tended to be mostly from Europe. World War I would change all that. But before the U.S. was fully mobilized, it would take quite a lot of improvisation to transport French and British armies as the situation changed on the ground.

In France, buses were quickly transformed into troop carriers, with the only visible difference that glass windows were replaced by canvas. These troop carriers had a speed of 14 mph, whereas ordinary trucks did not usually run higher than 12 mph. It was possible, however, to achieve on a commercial average of 10 mph for troop-moving operations under normal conditions. The length of trips in moving troops from point to point varied from 20 to 100 miles.

To take one specific example, when the Germans were making their attacks on Verdun, in February of 1916, all fresh troops were brought from Bar-de-Luc to Verdun by

In September 1914, before the Battle of the Marne, the French used every available vehicle, forming what was known as the "taxi corps," to successfully outrun the German army.

means of automobiles and trucks, rather than trains which were considered vulnerable to enemy bombardment. Primarily with the use of 1,250 3½-ton trucks, 30,000 men were taken to the front, in just 4 hours' time. The rapidly organized convoys were a mix of ordinary trucks and troop-carrying vehicles. One advantage of vehicle transport was that a gravel or dirt road was much easier to repair than a rail line.

On numerous occasions in France, the French and Allies shifted huge numbers of troops parallel to their front and in a direction at right angles to all the main railroad lines. Under such conditions the availability of the motor vehicle was considered not only superior but essential. Using special signs to mark off sections of about 6 miles in length, every group was in "telephonic communication with the others," as explained by frontline journalists after the initial German attacks.

Durable, reliable, versatile, and mass produced, the motor vehicle proved superior to

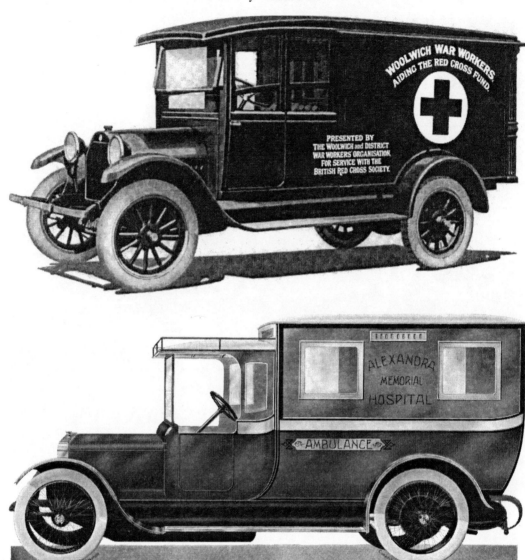

Top: This ambulance built on a 1-ton Studebaker truck chassis in 1917 represents the numerous improvised vehicles used for medical emergency use that were sent by a multitude of U.S. and British civic organizations and private companies as a show of camaraderie during the war. *Bottom:* A standard, enclosed ambulance design by Cooper's Motor Coachwork, 1915. Many ambulances were donated to be shipped to France before the United States entered World War I.

the ultimate vulnerability of men and mules on foot, to distant ships in deep oceans, and to heavy railroad cars and locomotives easily derailed by explosives on their steel tracks. The motor vehicle's four-wheel drive and grinding toughness in the face of bad weather eventually made it essential in war.

The dawn of the aircraft industry saw rapid advances in aeronautics, aerodynamics and internal combustion engine design; soon, dominance of the sky would become crucial in any large-scale military conflict.

Armies all over the world had relied on infantry and cavalry up until World War I.

The motor ambulance became crucial in battle. Shown here is a Ford Model T with British soldiers being loaded from hand-drawn carts and stretchers. Without fast transport back to medical care, soldiers had little chance of surviving wounds and injuries.

But as the war plodded on, trench warfare became the drudgery of death along the Western Front. It eventually became clear during the slow course of such combat by shear attrition that soldiers, horses and mules were barely effective in a landscape filled with machine guns, barbed wire, mire and endless trenches. Fortresses were now useless against massive artillery. It was finally dawning on military leaders that equestrians, pack animals and horse-drawn wagons were too slow and easily attacked to be relied upon for transporting men and materiel.

One of the crucial elements in the standoffs and stalemates between armies amid miles of trenches separated by a no-man's-land was the use of another new killing mechanism: the machine gun. Rushing the enemy with a large number of soldiers was no longer a reliable tactic. The adoption of the machine gun resulted in the mowing down of countless men on foot or horseback before they even got near their objective. In addition, French generals forbade the use of new uniforms, so for the first few months French infantry still wore bright red trousers, making them easy targets.

It could be said that the forerunner of the machine gun was the Gatling gun, invented by American dentist Richard Jordan Gatling in 1861 (patented in 1862) and bought by the U.S. Army in 1865. The early version had six rotating barrels and was followed by a ten-barrel version used in the Spanish-American War. It had the capability of firing 1,000 rounds per minute. The somewhat similar Gardener two-barrel rapid-fire gun followed in 1872. These early weapons were heavy and too complex, but they proved the effectiveness of rapid, high-caliber firepower.

Developed in 1884 and demonstrated the following year, Hiram Maxim's machine gun is considered the first true machine gun. It was belt-fed and water-cooled. First adopted by the British in 1889, the machine gun was considered a novelty by the American military, which delayed its purchase. The British first used the Maxim machine gun in the field in 1893.

Another revolving-barrel machine gun was invented by Benjamin Hotchkiss in Watertown, Connecticut, in 1872. The machine gun was named after him, and he was also responsible for the design of an improved cannon shell and a bolt-action rifle that appeared in 1875. John Moses Browning was another inventor in this technology, and his piston gas-driven Browning machine gun of 1890 was adopted by the U.S. Navy by 1895. In 1901 he patented a gun that used a short recoil. His inventions were used in the American M1917 water-cooled and M1919 air-cooled machine guns, often mounted on armored cars, in addition to use by infantry and adoption of the air-cooled type on aircraft, once synchronization with the propeller was accomplished.

Although Hiram Maxim wanted to develop a weapon for the sole advantage of the Allies, every major country used the Maxim-Vickers and similar Vickers Mark I–type machine guns. The Vickers machine gun was adopted by the British in 1912 and was mounted in aircraft. Additionally, an American colonel, Isaac Lewis, developed a reliable gas-operated machine gun, which was adopted by the British in 1915 and produced in large quantities there.

Once the war began, but before the United States was directly involved by shipping men and equipment to Europe, some American companies and organizations began sending wheeled vehicles across the Atlantic. At first these were primarily ambulances. But the motor vehicle industry as a whole, just barely 20 years old, was in disarray and in fact quite primitive in the second decade of the 20th century. There were countless manufacturers, and quality varied even if it appearances were outwardly very similar.

Moreover, it was even still quite uncertain whether vehicles would be powered by steam, electricity or gasoline, or whether the horse would prevail. At the time, most people thought that motor vehicles were a passing fad, or that motor vehicles would only fill a narrow niche in transportation as taxis, buses and "playthings of the rich." The military was particularly slow to change over to motorized transport. The "old brass" continued to put their faith in the centuries-old concept of cavalry.

Among the military ranks there were a few who could see the future quite clearly. In America, Major General Nelson Miles foresaw the need for self-propelled transportation

This 1917 Hudson was transformed into an open-side ambulance, as were many other miscellaneous vehicles, before being sent to European battle zones.

even before he retired as head of the Army in 1903. He recommended that at least five cavalry units be superseded by motor truck regiments after seeing a Duryea machine gun car in 1901, which had been built under the supervision of Major Royal P. Davidson (not related to the second partner in Harley-Davidson). This recommendation met with hostile indignation among the cavalry brass and his suggestion was ignored. Although some experimental partially armored cars had been developed before World War I, it was the invention of the heavy machine gun that led to the invention of the armored car as a countermeasure and as an attack vehicle.

The pioneer in this continuing development was Major Royal P. Davidson, professor at the Northwestern Military and Naval Academy at Lake Geneva, Wisconsin. His first design of 1898 was a three-wheeled vehicle carrying a Colt Model 1895 .45 caliber machine gun protruding through a split armor plate. Davidson used a standard 6 hp Duryea tri-car and the vehicle carried a crew of three. The machine gun could fire 480 rounds per minute and had a range of 2,000 yards.

The following year, Major Davidson developed two similar vehicles based on a Duryea quadricycle. In 1900–1902 he built two steam cars at the academy that carried Colt machine guns and were sturdier than the quadricycle. These vehicles were shown in St. Louis that year, but the United States War Department showed little interest.

Only the Army Signal Corps was using trucks by that time. This small branch had bought three Woods Electrics in 1899. In 1904 the Signal Corps bought two Winton touring cars that carried "wireless" radio equipment. Additionally, in 1905 they bought a handful of Winton and Cadillac cars that were converted to staff cars and light trucks. In 1906 the Signal Corps also bought a White steamer and two Model D Franklin cars. Before the war, the U.S. Army also acquired a few staff cars, including Buick, Reo and Studebaker. (During the 1906 San Francisco earthquake, the Army used eleven Cadillacs for relief operations in and around the city.)

"Wireless" communication was a state-of-the-art technology based on newly devel-

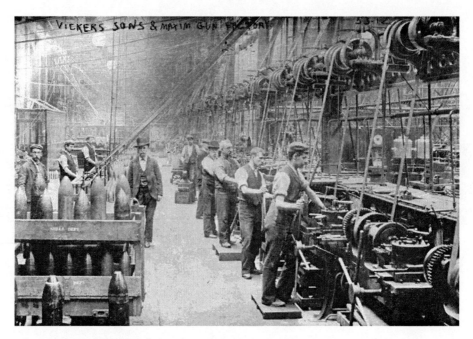

Top: Inside the Vickers and Maxim machine gun factory in 1915. Note lathes are all powered by belt pulleys from the ceiling and the Shell Dept. at left. *Left:* Ambulance fleet of the Red Cross composed of numerous types and makes assembled at the Court of Honor, Hôtel des Invalides, Paris, in May 1917.

oped shortwave radio. It had its limitations, including very bulky equipment, and it required large antennas. The communications could be even more easily intercepted than through the also newly developed telephone. Coded communication became of paramount importance.

Better known for their participation in World War II, American Indians were involved as "code talkers" during World War I as well. Choctaw soldiers on the western front were used for this purpose after being overheard speaking in their truly native language. The unidentified officer who overheard the Choctaw soldiers realized that none of the Germans would

Buicks at the Front

B UICK CARS maintain their pre-war leadership in Active Field Service at the Front. They are "doing their bit" for the Allied Cause in all the War zones.

Buicks stand up to hard usage, and the Buick valve-in-head motor delivers the power needed in war's emergencies.

Buick ambulances were common in France, as this 1916 ad shows. The swastika border was purely decorative and coincidental as the Nazis were not in existence yet.

understand their language, and several of these Native American Indian soldiers became the first code talkers for the U.S. Army. Their family members were honored at Camp Mabry, Austin, Texas, in 2007 by the Texas National Guard's 36th Infantry Division.

In addition to the Indian men who served in battle during World War I, 42,000 African-American men also served alongside French forces in a segregated military. It should be noted that conscription policy was enforced through the Selective Service Act of 1917 (developed by Brigadier General Hugh Johnson), which created a separate agency that was not part of the military services. Civic leaders were used to choose local men, who all had to register up to the age of 30, and some were set aside as manpower for essential production, especially in vital factories.

So-called "slackers" who resisted military duty were often rounded up in miscellaneous available trucks and transported to local offices for conscription or rejection for medical reasons or by profession. Unlike the Civil War era, when the Draft Act of 1863 was enacted, there were no violent draft riots and no provisions for buying substitutes, and there were no payments to recruit bounty hunters. During World War I, ads pronounced, "Don't Be Caught Napping. Every man registered under the Selective Service Law must carry his registration card at all times. Obey the law and save embarrassment." In one

Top: After the turn of the century transport by motor car became a matter of prestige. The Russian envoy is shown here visiting Washington, D.C., in 1905. Automobiles were considered the playthings of the rich at that time. *Bottom:* One American pioneer in the development of military motor vehicles was Major Royal P. Davidson at the Northwestern Military and Naval Academy at Lake Geneva, Wisconsin. His designs included this steam car with a machine gun, shown here with cadets.

roundup at the end of 1916, 1,500 "slackers" were sent to military camps for compulsory duty.

Within the next four years, the Northwest Military and Naval Academy in Lake Geneva, Wisconsin, became the center for motor vehicle experimentation. The experimental work continued under Major Royal P. Davidson. His three-wheeler experiment was too unstable. The first three vehicles were not used in combat but only for training purposes, yet they became the inspiration for further development, especially in light of the fact that the newly invented machine gun developed by Hiram Maxim could spray a hail of powerful bullets at any group of unprotected soldiers. Speed, range, reliability and armor became the key ingredients to any combat vehicle.

In 1911 there were approximately 25,000 trucks in America, out of which fewer than 30 were owned by the U.S. Army. A few of these were custom-built as "escort wagons" by Alden Sampson. There were also "officer's roadsters" from Autocar. The Society of Automotive Engineers, headed by Howard Coffin, and the Quartermaster Corps formulated detailed specifications for a standardized U.S. Army truck in 1913, but the plans were put aside and lay fallow during this period of technological awakening.

The cavalry still held a prominent position in the hierarchy and was the primary factor in resisting modernization. Military men still firmly believed that battles would be fought on foot and on horseback, even if armies were transported from one general area to another by trains and across oceans by ship. But in the brutal competition for conquest, technology changed rapidly and many advances were made during World War I, especially in motor vehicle development.

By 1912 one Hupmobile open touring was allocated to the 26th Infantry and used by Major Dickson as a "liaison and scouting vehicle." On maneuvers and camp exercises it

Before World War I, the Army tested a few "escort wagons," very similar to the factory illustration of this 1912 Alden Sampson.

Top: The 1915 Jeffery seen here, being tested with smooth solid tires and tire chains for traction in sand, became the Nash Quad when the company was sold in July of 1916 after Charles Jeffery survived the sinking of the *Lusitania* on May 7, 1915. *Bottom:* The Four Wheel Drive Company of Clintonville, Wisconsin, was the builder of this vehicle dubbed "The Battleship" before the pioneering enterprise built their well-known FWD trucks.

was used to carry senior officers, and also to deliver rations, tow a trailer and carry photographers. The Hupmobile did not break down and showed very little sign of wear. Major Dickson was so much impressed by this that he personally wrote to the Hup Motor Co., Detroit, which led to the acquisition of a few more cars of this type.

Early Autocar officer's roadsters in 1909 were quite unusual in that they were powered by an opposed two-cylinder 159 cid motor that remained in production until 1926. The first such Autocar had a body built for the military that was used in the Massachusetts Maneuvers for training in 1909. The Autocar featured seating for six and had a pedestal mounted .30 caliber machine gun. Reliability of the small Autocar "boxer" engine was the main advantage over larger trucks at a time when mechanical breakdown was an all-too-common feature of the internal combustion engine. Autocar built its reputation on durability, and its marque existed for a full century. It was absorbed by General Motors and then phased out completely as a name in the automotive industry a hundred years after its inception.

Another more progressive military leader emerged in the person of Captain Alexander E. Williams. He persuaded Quartermaster General James B. Aleshire into approving an elaborate test in off-road military convoy conditions in 1912. He went to visit the factories of Alden Sampson, Ford, Garford, Mack and White.

The first two trucks to be purchased for such experimental purposes were a 1¼-ton Alden Sampson and a 1½-ton White. Then Captain Williams noticed a small ad in a newspaper that would eventually lead to one of the most poignant success stories in truck development and production.

What Captain Williams discovered was a fledgling vehicle builder located in a small Wisconsin town named Clintonville. Ottow Zachow and his brother-in-law, William Besserdich, had patented the first double-Y universal joint encased in a drop-forged ball-and-socket, which was the basis for their four-wheel-drive concept. Other earlier designs using chain had failed or were so limited in steering capability they were essentially useless in any road conditions.

Captain Williams took a train to Clintonville and was given a ride in the second vehicle that the Four Wheel Drive (FWD) Auto Company had built. It was a large touring car later transformed into truck iteration. The all-important test drive, which included wheeling through plowed fields, mud holes and sand pits and even up the steps of the local Lutheran church, so impressed Captain Williams that he purchased an FWD car for $1,900. (To be precise, some records show $1,904, others $1,940.) It was equipped with an army escort wagon box for military use.

Wisconsin has been called the "badger state," and the Badger Four Wheel Drive Auto Company of Clintonville, Wisconsin, revolutionized motor vehicle design one century ago. (The Badger name had been dropped in 1911 and the company became known as FWD.) FWD trucks of World War I, along with Nash Quads, made a very significant impact transporting soldiers and materiel in a widespread theater of war at a time when there were very few paved roads and four-wheel drive was essential to slog through mud and snow across Europe.

Four-wheel-drive trucks had been built before those manufactured by FWD, but aside from the Jeffery Quad (Nash Quad, per subsequent purchase), earlier designs were very crude, inefficient and flimsy.

The patent in 1901 for four-wheel drive by Gustave Hoffman in England was not

This FWD truck was part of the Army's "road test" in 1912, which began in Washington, D.C., and continued as far as Fort Benjamin Harrison in Indiana over more than 1,500 miles, most of which was not road.

viable, nor were a number of other patented designs, primarily due to engineering deficiencies regarding chain drive, durability, torque transfer and other mechanical disorders.

It was Ottow Zachow with his brother-in-law, William Besserdich, who finally got it right. They owned a machine shop in Clintonville that had been started in 1891. The patents they filed in 1907 and that were granted the following year proved to be truly functional, and their two-man shop would become one of the great success stories in American ingenuity and productivity.

One of the patents they obtained was for the above-mentioned double-Y universal joint encased in a drop-forged ball-and-socket (U.S. Patent No. 882,986), in addition to another patent for a transfer case (U.S. Patent No. 907,940), which evenly divided the power to both front and rear axles.

The company started out on a shoestring budget and was further helped along in 1909 with the financial help of a local doctor whose name was W.H. Finney. He lost faith in the venture early on and withdrew his $1,800 investment.

The company's first vehicle, called the Z&B, was powered by steam and was not a success. The second vehicle, made in 1910 and dubbed "The Battleship," proved itself worthy of being called "four-wheel drive," and Joe Cotton, editor of the *Clintonville Tribune*, predicted, "If the recently patented drive lives up to expectations, it will revolutionize the

882,986. AXLE. OTTO ZACHOW and WILLIAM BESSER-
DICH, Clintonville, Wis. Filed Aug. 1, 1907. Serial No.
386,612.

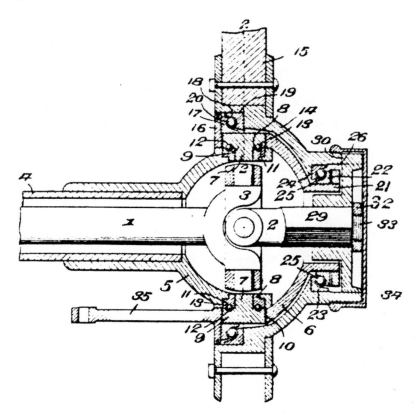

907,940. POWER-APPLYING MECHANISM. OTTO ZA-
CHOW and WILLIAM BESSERDICH. Clintonville, Wis.
Filed July 17, 1907. Serial No. 384.197.

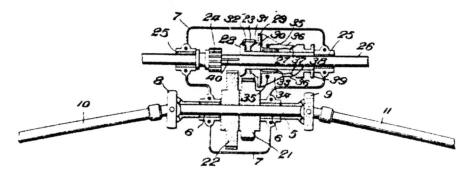

Top: With this patented double-Y joint in a drop-forged ball, the FWD Company became one of the most important builders of 4×4 trucks during and after World War I. *Bottom:* Working in their small machine shop in Clintonville, Wisconsin, Otto Zachow and William Besserdich obtained one of the most significant automotive patents of all time for building four-wheel drive.

automobile business and place inventors, Zachow and Besserdich, on easy street." Only the first part of that statement was true.

In 1910 the company was reorganized after Dr. Finney changed his mind. As the company's main promoter, Walter A. Olen stepped up to be head of sales and marketing. Olen had settled in Clintonville and gave up his law practice to dedicate himself to the new company.

The Clintonville Advancement Association, also formed that year, held a competition in which dozens of automobiles competed against an FWD in a sand pit. The list of contenders included a Brush, Buick, Cadillac, Ford, Halloway, Hudson and Imperial. All were humiliated when they had to be towed out by the FWD as a crowd of 7,000 cheered, "mad with enthusiasm" according to the local *Tribune*.

Excitement of the day spilled over into investment by the onlookers, and sufficient capital was raised to build a small factory in Clintonville very near the original machine shop, which has served as the FWD museum in later years.

Once Walter Olen became general manager, he surmised correctly in 1911 that the future of both the company and four-wheel-drive would be in commercial and military vehicle production. Olen persuaded the skeptical stockholders that among the first seven FWD vehicles the company was to build, at least one should be a two-ton capacity truck, even though FWD number three was a 4 × 4 touring car sold to the Pinkerton Detective Agency in Chicago.

Olen's gut feeling was correct, primarily due to the progressive outlook of Captain Alexander E. Williams, who was a graduate from West Point. He believed that the horse and mule were becoming obsolete and that it was time to adopt motor vehicles, according to a piece he published in the *Infantry Journal*. His four-year assignment with the Quartermaster Corps gave him time to develop his theory.

Although a rarity among Army brass, Williams was not the only officer to believe in modernizing the military. Major General Nelson A. Miles, who was a veteran of the Civil War and Indian campaigns, took command of the U.S. Army in 1895. Despite his senior status he was quite imaginative, even forming a bicycle troop in 1897. He took note of the use of trucks by European armies while the military in the United States remained stodgy and conservative.

In 1902 the Ordnance Department bought a forge and battery wagon from the U.S. Long Distance Automobile Company, and the following year the surgeon general asked the White Sewing Machine Company of Cleveland to develop an experimental ambulance.

When Major General Miles retired in 1903, he recommended that at least five motorized regiments be organized to replace standard cavalry units. He foretold that "self-propelled transportation will be utilized in the next war" and recommended the improvement of roads across the nation. But the intransigent cavalry officers were only offended by such recommendations.

Captain Williams continued with his efforts at mechanization, and after buying the Alden Sampson and White trucks, he also visited various truck factories such as Mack and Garford where he did not find an appropriate vehicle for off-road use. However, both Mack and Garford were later to become of paramount importance during the war.

The FWD became part of a planned "road" test that had been devised during 1911 by the Army brass. The road test course of winter 1912 started in Washington D.C., tra-

Top: One of the best ads FWD used during World War I was illustrating that four-wheel drive was like the four legs of a horse. *Bottom:* This 1918 FWD ammunition truck was equipped with all the basic tools for crossing terrain where there was only a muddy path.

Top: The FWD Model B was used extensively in World War I. This one with a later cushioned seat may have helped with the stiff ride, but original seats prompted some drivers to wear kidney belts. *Bottom:* Ohio-built Garford trucks introduced a cab-over-engine (COE) 5-ton model, shown here transporting troops on a test in the U.S. The company also built half-tracks.

versed across muddy dirt roads, trails and open land south to Atlanta, and then back up north to Fort Benjamin Harrison at Indianapolis, a total of 1,509 miles. The only trucks that were finally used in the test were an Autocar, the earlier bought Sampson, a White and the FWD. Each was loaded with a ton of supplies plus a ton and a half of sand ballast. To say that proving out the trucks in this way was grueling would be an understatement. The Sampson's engine's connecting rod bearings burned out, so it was left behind.

The other three trucks finally made it to Fort Benjamin Harrison on March 28, having started out February 8, 1912.

Even though all the trucks in the test had broken down at various points and had to be repaired along the way, Captain Williams proved that such vehicles could be used in the back country in certain situations. A second test from Dubuque, Iowa, to Sparta, Wisconsin, using the same trucks along with the repaired Sampson, plus a Kelly-Springfield, Kato, Mack, Saurer, Velie, Packard and a Graham, involved supplying a provisional regiment during the long practice march. All were two-wheel-drive except the FWD and the Kato.

Captain Williams proved that trucks could be very useful to the Army, provided certain design deficiencies were overcome. The primary trouble was that all the trucks were required to amble along at the speed of the marching infantrymen, which was about 3 to 4 mph. This tended to overheat almost every motor. The three trucks that were selected out of the whole group for further use were the Mack, White and FWD. The Kato, although four-wheel-drive, had major power distribution problems due to inadequate transmission/transfer design. Although the rest of the "Army grey beards," as *Automobile Topics Magazine* called them, were still uncertain of moving forward with mechanization, Captain Williams had broken the ice and opened a few minds to new ideas.

As war exploded across Europe in 1914, it soon became clear that motorization would become a major factor in the new century. The first momentous turn of events occurred when General Gallieni's famous "taxi-corps" army saved Paris in the first Battle of the Marne, outrunning the approaching German infantry by using every available motor vehicle to arrive ahead of the enemy. Some 12,000 taxis and sundry vehicles hurried 4,985 troops 28 miles in that all-important battle. This should have been a wake-up call for the U.S. military, but somehow it was overlooked.

By the end of World War I, over 15,000 Model B three-ton FWD trucks had been built, and many survived to continue work for road building, snow plowing, construction and many other applications.

Meanwhile, since the American military brass were still experimenting, FWD had to find its own civilian markets to continue its tentative existence. No assembly line meant that FWD cars and trucks were hand-built one by one, resulting in a very narrow profit margin. In 1912 FWD trucks were sold to the Silver City Beer and Ice Company of Denver, Colorado, and other 1½-ton and 3-ton trucks were sold in 1913. The trucks were powered by a 36.1 hp Wisconsin engine and were capable all of 16 mph when shod with the standard 42-inch hard rubber tires.

Financial uncertainties plagued FWD's first years, and Walter Olen became master at convincing the people of Clintonville not to relinquish the small but reputable FWD factory. He feverishly pursued his quest to meet the capitalization needs of a quarter million dollars in a town of about 2,000 inhabitants. The nearby city of Appleton tried to lure the FWD company away, but Clintonville citizens and the company directors resisted.

Once the war began in Europe, the firm of Gaston, Williams and Wigmore bought two FWD trucks and shipped them to England. Within four weeks an order for 50 more arrived, and the company was doing business like never before. The single order for 50 trucks was more than all the vehicles the company had built up to that time.

By the end of 1915, the factory output capacity had to be doubled and then doubled again, with a new building added. Orders came in from Argentina, Brazil, England, France, Portugal, Russia, Spain and elsewhere. For that year 400 trucks were shipped with a standing order of 200 per month from the military alone.

After Pancho Villa crossed the border and attacked Columbus, New Mexico, on March 9, 1916, the Quartermaster Corps ordered 147 FWD trucks. The U.S. government demanded shipment under the National Defense Act, and trucks painted gray for shipping to England, already loaded onto trains, were unloaded and repainted green as U.S. Army vehicles (although there was little greenery in New Mexico and northern Mexico in which to be camouflaged with those colors).

With FWD trucks proving themselves in the pursuit of Pancho Villa (although he was never caught), another order came for a trainload of FWD 3-ton trucks to be shipped to Honolulu for the 8th Regiment of the Artillery, which became the first unit of the U.S. Army to be completely equipped with motor transport.

Then in 1917, FWD received the largest contract for trucks ever ordered by the U.S. Army: 3,750 trucks to be shipped at a rate of 175 per month at a total contract of $12 million. The company struggled to keep up with production quotas. Because so many men went off to war, many women worked at the factory in assembly and as test drivers.

Although FWD was striving valiantly to fill their orders, mishaps, damage and even sabotage dogged shipments. A few trainloads of FWD trucks were sabotaged by German sympathizers, who poured sand into the crankcases and transmissions. This came as quite a shock to the American public when the news hit the headlines, and backlash soon followed. As an example, Kissel Kar dropped the "Kar" during World War I because it sounded too German, according to a statement by a company official after the war. Also, in 1918 seven FWD trucks fell into the hands of the enemy when the ship *Suchan* was captured by the German navy, and another shipment fell victim to German submarine torpedoes.

On the home front, while FWD prospered, the two key founding figures did not fare well at all. Ottow Zachow had cashed in his original 350 shares early on, assigned to him for his patent rights. He had received $9,000 and went back to his machine shop. William Besserdich had sold out by 1913, but along with several other impatient stockholders, who had become disillusioned early on, he brought a lawsuit against Walter Olen and the company directors. The plaintiffs charged that Olen's group had conspired to defraud them by concealing the British orders in the summer of 1914, but the courts settled in favor of the defendants. Consequently, Besserdich organized a rival company to build 4 × 4 trucks called Oshkosh in the nearby city by that name. It turned out to be one of the largest manufacturers of off-road and specialty vehicles for the U.S. military. The soundness of the 4 × 4 design could not have gotten a more certain tribute than by having the U.S. Army buy out the basic patents of the Four Wheel Drive Auto Company for the sum of $400,000 just before the end of World War I. These patents were used to build numerous other 4 × 4 vehicles through World War II.

With many hundreds of FWD trucks shipped to New Mexico for the Punitive Expedition against Pancho Villa, and thousands across the Atlantic during World War I, and many more doing duty at home, the FWD company's strategy after the war was to begin a large program of manufacturing spare parts for the glut of surplus trucks already out in the field. Many of the FWD trucks were disbursed by the government for road building, snow plowing, construction, fire fighting, oil drilling, logging and other applications. A second factory at Kitchener, Ontario, Canada, was opened in 1919, and FWD purchased one of two companies named Menominee in 1921, yet another Wisconsin firm.

By the end of World War I, FWD had built 15,000 Model B trucks for the military, making the company the largest producer of 4 × 4 trucks in the world. Most of them had been shipped to Europe and most of them were shipped back. That number was astounding in that it was such a large proportion of an estimated total of 35,000 trucks shipped from the U.S. to Europe once America was directly involved in the "war to end all wars." Of that number, 24,000 were engaged in supply and general cargo, and about 4,200 were involved in supplying ammunition. The Kahn-Wadsworth Bill after World War I allowed for the distribution of thousands of surplus trucks such as FWD for road building in America.

Sergeant E.V. Rickenbacker, who had been a famous pilot and was also a chauffeur for General Pershing, testified after the war about FWD trucks:

> I can only say, and will be backed up by some of the most eminent engineers of Europe and America, that it was one of the greatest factors in the defense of Verdun, Chateau-Thierry and even Paris. The FWDs were found everywhere, hurrying supplies of all descriptions, where most needed, and at the right time, frequently turning the tide of battle, for without it our armies in the field would have been nothing for want of ammunition and supplies.

By the end of the war, production had risen to $48 million. The 3-ton Model B FWD's 56 bhp motor powered all four wheels through a central three-speed transmission that had a transfer shaft driven by a 5-inch Morse silent chain splitting the power to front and rear shaft drive. The use of vanadium steel in the ladder-type chassis with straight channel-section side members was quite advanced. The truck could carry its own weight in load. Some of the FWDs shipped to the front were FWD–built artillery supply trucks, artillery repair trucks and ordnance repair trucks, which carried ammunition, gun spares, lathes, welding equipment and other machining equipment that could be carried into the field. It was one of the most useful trucks of World War I. With so many orders to fill for the military, FWD contracted other companies—Peerless, Kissel, Premier and Mitchell— to build the Model B.

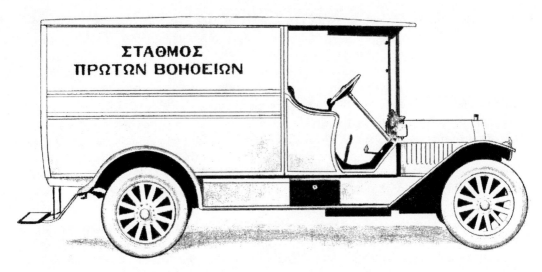

ΣΤΑΘΜΟΣ
ΠΡΩΤΩΝ ΒΟΗΟΕΙΩΝ

Kissel Kar, another vehicle builder in Wisconsin, received orders for ambulances in 1914 and 1915, such as this one, which was sent as part of a fleet to the Serbian government.

Among those that assembled the FWD Model B was Kissel Kar, as it was known before World War I. The company was a significant contributor to the war effort in Europe during this period, representing American automotive engineering even if it was on a small scale. Ironically, Kissel Kar was organized by the newly transplanted German family of L. Kissel in Hartford, Wisconsin, with sons George and Will, who began in farming and soon built their first automobile in 1905. The first Kissel Kar featured a four-cylinder motor and shaft drive, quite advanced for the time. By 1908 Kissel light trucks were also being built on passenger car chassis.

Perhaps through a historical accident that year, Herman Palmer, a graduate engineer, was on a tour of Wisconsin, playing cello with a small orchestra. When the train departed from Hartford, the orchestra had one fewer musician. Palmer enthusiastically joined Kissel Kar to pursue a career in automotive engineering. The Kissels were also fortunate to attract J. Frederich Werner to their employment ranks. Werner was an experienced auto designer who had worked for Opel Motor Works in Russelheim, Germany.

This was the period when Austria-Hungary was occupying Bosnia-Herzogovina, Croatia, Slovenia and northern Serbia. The Balkan Wars at the time took their toll during 1912–1913. When Austria-Hungary proclaimed war on Serbia in 1914, Kissel Kar was one of the first U.S. companies that began obtaining contracts from European countries for truck-based ambulances. There were connections through Werner who still had contacts back in Germany. Kissel obtained at least six orders for ambulances, including one for 30 such vehicles from the Serbian government. The ambulances featured "pneumatic tires to provide easy riding for the wounded soldiers," as company literature stated.

The "Kar" portion of the name was dropped to draw focus away from the German background of the company owners and engineers, especially after pro–German sympathizers poured sand into the transmissions of a trainload of FWD trucks, among other vehicles. But the small Kissel company's high-quality vehicles were sought out at least in small numbers as an early representation of help from America, especially after it was discovered that the Kissel "All Year Car" of 1913 featured a completely enclosed cab, which

There was such a demand for the Model B FWD trucks that they were built under license, such as these assembled at the Kissel factory.

was also adopted for Kissel trucks, and was available the following year with a removable winter cab mounted with plate glass windows. The severe Wisconsin winters were undoubtedly one source of inspiration for this design, also adaptable within the rainy terrain of northern Europe.

Kissel also featured dashboard lights in 1914, which was another innovation just starting to be adopted at that time by manufacturers. After using Beaver engines manufactured in Wisconsin, Kissel developed its own 48 hp six-cylinder L-head motor, which remained in production for 15 years. The Weidley V-12 engine was briefly adopted for some of Kissel's heavier trucks. After producing ambulances, trucks and a few staff cars, Kissel resumed production for the civilian market after the war and continued to stay in the automotive field until the company's final demise in 1931 during the Great Depression.

Thomas Jeffery made an equally important contribution regarding military trucks used in World War I. His company had built the Rambler automobile in Kenosha, Wisconsin, and it also introduced the Jeffery Quad 4 × 4 truck in 1913. The company built 3,096 Quads in 1914, but that year was marred by the sudden passing of Thomas Jeffery from a heart attack. His son Charles took over and continued to lead the prosperous enterprise.

When Thomas Jeffery died suddenly in 1914, his son Charles began experimenting with armored cars. This was "Armored Car No. 1," which was finished in 1915.

One of the first revolutionary purpose-built vehicles the Jeffery company built for the military would be Armored Car No. 1. It has been considered by military vehicle historians to be top-heavy and clumsy. It was basically a large quantity of .20-inch armor plate riveted at right angles to a square cage made of structural steel on a 4 × 4 Jeffery truck of 1914, probably completed in early 1915.

Despite its real shortcomings, the Jeffery armored car would be a platform from which further development continued. However, as impressive as the vehicles appeared, the issue of armor for armor's sake would be complicated by the problem of speed, maneuverability, steering, traction and visibility for the driver. Lack of good roadway, pavement or even solid ground precluded most armored cars from being at all effective in real combat situations until these problems were solved with deflection shape for lighter materials, large tires with heavy tread pattern, periscope vision and bullet-proof glass, multiple-drive axles and wheels, and other utilitarian features.

At the beginning of the war in 1914, American sentiment was largely neutral regarding the conflict in Europe. But Germany's tactical use of submarines began to take its toll on many American lives that were lost in the ruthless torpedoing of merchant and passenger ships, which was officially and publicly sanctioned by the German government.

Top: The second version of the Jeffery armored car of 1915 had two turrets and weighed six tons. It was nine feet tall and had .20-inch armor plate. *Bottom:* Once the war began, France bought a number of Jeffery Quad trucks, but even the tough 4 × 4 could get mired in mud, as shown here at the front in 1916.

History took a dramatic turn when on May 7, 1915, a German submarine torpedoed the *Lusitania*. Charles Jeffery was on board escorting some Nash Quads to Europe. He was one of the 761 survivors on the day 1,198 others perished in the North Atlantic. Isaac Trumbull, accompanying 40 Trumbull cyclecars, perished among the other passengers. After returning to the U.S., Charles Jeffery sold his company to Charles Nash by July of 1916, and the Jeffery-Quad became the Nash-Quad. Therefore, before America entered the war, numerous submarine attacks on ships crossing to England, and the sinking of the *Lusitania*, helped truly galvanize public sentiment in the United States to enter World War I.

From a larger perspective, so, too, did the exposing of bungling German propagandists and saboteurs in America, such as Dr. Heinrich Albert, whose misplaced briefcase in July of 1915 contained a stack of half-hatched plans, involving numerous spies and saboteurs. Then a coded message was intercepted from the German foreign secretary, Alfred Zimmermann, to the new Mexican government inviting them to wage war against the United States in exchange for the "return" of New Mexico, Texas and Arizona once the war was over. All this material was quickly published to the amazement of the public around the world and to the chagrin of the German government.

The sinking of the British passenger ship *Laconia* and the subsequent sinking of the American ships *City of Memphis* and *Illinois* prompted President Wilson to abandon his pacifist posture and convene a special session of Congress. Two days later on April 6, by overwhelming vote the resolution was passed to declare war against Germany. Other atroc-

A Mack AC tows a captured German submarine in 1918 to be placed for public display in Central Park, New York.

When Charles Nash bought the Jeffery Company in 1916, the trucks became known as Nash Quads, shown here on a road in France in 1918.

ities committed by German troops against civilians, such as the execution of British nurse Edith Cavell on October 12, 1915, further enflamed public outrage.

At that time, the 13th Artillery Regiment of the French Army was equipped with just ten Jeffery-Quad trucks used as tractors. The well-known 75 mm guns were carried on the trucks' platforms and off-loaded using ramps. Two more regiments were formed in July of 1916 and then April 1917. By 1918, 33 such motorized artillery regiments were organized using 8,600 vehicles and involving 44,000 personnel.

It was Jerry De Cou, superintendent at the Jeffery Company, who spearheaded the construction of the armored car on a Jeffery-Quad 4 × 4 chassis. Subsequently, two more were built, each with slightly different turret configurations. At the same time, a fourth version of the Jeffery-Quad armored car was built in series for the British Army.

These had bars protruding from the engine cover for cutting barbed wire. All the Jeffery-Quad trucks and armored cars had solid rubber tires. A 40 hp Buda engine allowed 20 mph. The armored cars weighed 6½ tons. At least sixty-two were known to have been shipped overseas eventually. Armored cars were to become a stepping stone to the development of the ultimate military motor vehicle—the tracked armored tank.

A very out-of-the-ordinary armored car of the time was the Jeffery-Quad double-ender. These not only had four-wheel drive and four-wheel steering but also had a driver at each end of the chassis. In the May 15, 1915, issue of the *Commercial Vehicle* it was announced, "The First American Reversible Battlecar Chassis ... was originated by Franco-

Top: Originally inspired by smugglers, the double-ended Jeffery was designed for narrow paths and roads where there was no room for a U-turn to escape gunfire. Only a few prototypes were built in 1915. *Bottom:* Another view of the Jeffery double-ender shows there are two drivers, each with a steering assembly and full controls of the vehicle with one engine and four-wheel drive.

Once Nash acquired Jeffery, the company continued to build armored cars using the 4 × 4 chassis such as this vehicle circa 1917. Note barbed wire cutters in the front. The helmets worn indicate this armored car was being used in Africa or the Middle East.

Belgian smugglers, who used this type of vehicle to avoid traps set by customs officers in narrow lanes of the border country." Three such Jeffery-Quad chassis were fitted with armored bodies, but not much more development took place during the war along these lines, and the double-ender concept was abandoned.

In addition to FWD and Jeffery/Nash, by the beginning of World War I there were only a few manufacturers in the field of four-wheel-drive vehicles. Around the turn of the century there had been only three notable patents awarded for four-wheel drive—to Gustave Hoffman in England during 1901, and in the U.S. to William Bard in 1904 (in addition to the third being Zachow-Besserdich at FWD).

As World War I ignited in Europe, among the competitors building four-wheel-drive vehicles were Couple-Gear, C.T., Duplex, Morton, Nevada, Walter and Ware. To be more specific, C.T. (which stood for "commercial truck" at one point) only built battery-powered trucks. Morton, the predecessor of Hurlburt, lasted only until 1916, and its biggest customer was the Russian government. Hurlburt lasted until 1927 but did not build 4 × 4s. Nevada built trucks under license from Four Wheel Traction Automobile Company, which became Kato. All were defunct by 1913. Couple-Gear built battery-powered as well as gasoline-electric hybrid trucks and buses before World War I.

By that time, the Four-Wheel-Drive Wagon Company, the American Motor Truck Company, Cunningham Engineering Company, Aultman & Company, the Four Traction Automobile Company (Kato) and the Cleveland Motor Truck Manufacturing Company had each tried their hand at building 4 × 4s and had not succeeded.

One out-of-the-ordinary exception was Golden West Motors of Sacramento, Cali-

A photograph from 1914 shows the first Golden West four-wheel-drive and four-wheel-steer truck chassis in front of the small, obscure Sacramento factory.

fornia. In addition to being a vehicle manufacturer on the West Coast, among only a very few at the time, the company was founded by an inventive engineer named Edward Robinson and several wealthy investors. However, they could not agree on the company's direction or proper management. Robinson had obtained four patents by 1914, including one for four-wheel steering.

At the time of the genesis of Golden West Motors in 1913, Sacramento and vicinity were growing rapidly. Nearby Stockton was also developing as an industrial deep-sea port city via canal to San Francisco. Sampson had started to build farm equipment, including tractors in Stockton, and Holt of Caterpillar fame also had its origins there, along with Best of crawler tractor fame in nearby San Leandro.

In 1911, Sacramento, which adjoins San Joaquin County where Stockton is located, annexed land to triple its area. Another basis for industry had been created by the Southern Pacific Railroad, which had established a large maintenance and repair facility along with its depot at Sacramento's "Old Town."

The first two Golden West trucks were both four-wheel drive and four-wheel steer. They were both powered by a Continental engine mounted on a subframe. The transfer case included Whitney silent chains, another innovation. All in all, Golden West Motors was a "golden goose" for Sacramento and its new industry. Cross-country tests were undertaken for 7,500 miles and a truck polo match was organized in front of the capitol for publicity.

However, due to stockholders' discontent and much wrangling among the key players, by 1916 the company was now called Robinson. That year the 8th Artillery Regiment in Honolulu, Hawaii, bought 36 four-wheel-drive trucks, but they were all built by FWD in distant Wisconsin. A group of Sacramento businessmen associated with the Globe Iron Works began negotiating with the federal government to assemble the Curtiss JN-4 "Jenny" airplane. This did come to fruition and Mather Field opened just outside Sacramento city limits as a flight training center. But because of further internal strife at Golden West, the company faded away, missing an enormous opportunity whether or not they would contribute to the military needs of the U.S. Army during World War I. There was also much need for this type of vehicle in the enormous California Central Valley agricultural fields.

The Golden West four-wheel-drive was well engineered and the four-wheel-steering feature was great for open terrain, but very problematic when in the city next to a building, curb, tree or other object, as the vehicle's aft turned inward, colliding with any adjoining obstacle. The next iteration of the company, named Big Four, abandoned four-wheel steering, but it was too late and the entire enterprise completely faded out soon after the war.

The Marine Corps Quartermaster used Mack trucks by 1913, which exemplified the gradual acceptance of motor trucks by the United States military. Mack became the most famous make, primarily with its 5½-ton AC model, which started out as the E2 prototype of 1915. It had a 471 cid four-cylinder engine that produced 40 hp under a Renault-type hood with radiator behind the engine. There were advantages of having the radiator behind the engine, including the protection of the radiator itself from damage, and airflow

Golden West Motors organized a game of truck polo as a publicity stunt in downtown Sacramento in 1915 after assembling its first two trucks. Aside from the unique chassis and engine subframe, the other major components were bought from Sheldon Axle and Continental Motors.

Top: Motor polo had already been popularized using Ford Model T cars, but not with trucks, such as the new Golden West four-wheel-drive, four-wheel-steer trucks in Sacramento during the winter of 1915. *Bottom:* Another event for the sake of publicity was a parade through Sacramento with two Golden West trucks and children on bicycles photographed next to the Capital Hotel.

Top: This prototype of a Mack AC from 1915 was photographed towing a 3-inch field gun, travel-ing from New York City to Plattsburgh Camp for Army Reserves training. *Bottom:* The Mack AC "bulldog" could carry a Renault tank directly on its own chassis without trailer, as shown here in 1918.

was controlled by fans at a time when very low vehicle speeds added little to the wind-chill cooling effect.

Although the reference to Renault comes up here, the idea of having a radiator behind the motor was used by such companies as International, Kelly-Springfield and Lippard-Stewart, using similar tapered front hoods (or bonnets), which were not intended to cre-ate aerodynamics, although they were quite distinctive.

In total, 2,500 Mack AC trucks served during the war. The Mack AC was sturdy enough to carry an FT-17 Renault light tank, heavy cranes for the Army Engineer Corps, as well as other heavy equipment such as generators and searchlights, blacksmith shops, machine shops, carpenter shops and mobile printing presses.

This became the truck for which Mack was nicknamed "bulldog." At that time, Mack was the largest builder of the largest trucks in America. As heavy-duty and mechanically advanced as Mack trucks were at this time, all of these used chain drive. Chain drive was prone to disrepair due to the tremendous amount of friction wear and need for adjustment, as the chain literally stretched before breaking, but most drivers and mechanics understood the relatively simple technology of the chain. Differentials using bevel or worm gear drive were still a hidden mystery to most of those involved in truck repair and required a higher degree of sophistication in manufacturing, especially in metallurgy and machining of gears. Nevertheless, the true advantages of mechanical precision and the durability of new steel alloys made chain drive obsolete within a decade.

While war blazed on the European continent and in North Africa, Doroteo Arango (better known as Pancho Villa) decided to attack Columbus, New Mexico, on March 9, 1916. This came as a complete surprise since Villa had been allied with the U.S. against the tyranny of the Mexican federal government, even though President de la Huerta had been officially recognized by President Woodrow Wilson.

President Wilson ordered General Pershing to lead the "Punitive Expedition" into Mexico in order to capture Pancho Villa. Naming this conflict an "expedition" was ironically appropriate in the sense that, despite an incursion deep into sovereign Mexican territory by the American Army using cavalry and new technology, very little of the warfare actually involved American forces. The tens of thousands of casualties were almost entirely in Mexican armies of several warring factions during the historically and politically com-

President Woodrow Wilson used Pierce-Arrow Open Touring cars as his personal transportation as shown here in 1918 reviewing a Liberty Bond parade near the White House.

plex Mexican Revolution that pitted the Mexican federal government against the so-called peons who had joined Villa (also called Villistas) amid various factions (see Chapter III).

However, the use of aircraft, motorcycles, staff cars, ambulances, tractors, trucks and a few armored cars under General Pershing was a profoundly appropriate, if not exactly deliberate, dress rehearsal before entering the war already raging across Europe, part of the Middle East and as far away as Africa.

By way of overview, it should be noted that in 1912 356,000 motor vehicles were built in the U.S. By 1916 the number had risen to 1,526,000, which reflected the fastest growth of any manufacturing sector in history. Overall registration for 1916 in the U.S. was 3,513,000. Rural areas had more vehicles per capita at the time than urban areas, which reflected the widespread use of mass transportation.

Another early milestone of the era was set on January 12, 1914, when Henry Ford raised the minimum wage to the unheard-of $5.00 per day. He more than doubled it from $2.34, setting a new industry precedent at a time when factory workers across the country were being paid an average of 30 to 40 cents per hour.

It was also the first year of a complete, fully automated assembly line at Ford. And now additional Ford assembly plants were located in Cleveland, Ohio; Dallas and Houston, Texas; and more significantly in Bordeaux, France, as the war began in Europe. Overall Ford production surpassed 300,000 for the period August 1914 to August 1915.

In 1915 there were 119 different officially listed auto makers in the United States in addition to even more commercial vehicle builders. Major components such as motors, transmissions, and axles were often built by "original equipment manufacturers." Entrepreneurs could purchase parts as independently built components, including clutches, wheels, tires, brakes, lights, carburetors, and wiring, along with all the nuts, bolts and other fasteners in order to create vehicles simply by fabricating a chassis and adding their own sheet metal and upholstery.

Aside from sales and marketing, for most people there was an engulfing mystique in the secrets of a properly assembled motor vehicle, its efficient use, and its maintenance and repair. More importantly, how could it serve better than a bicycle, horse-drawn conveyance, train, tram, boat and other more acceptable modes of transportation?

That motor vehicles were still very primitive and their use still poorly understood is illustrated by the following entry in A. L. Dyke's tome of 1915, describing a common ailment associated with the new technology:

AUTOMOBILE HEADACHE—Ask the druggist to put up a few number one capsules filled with three-fourths acetanelid and one-fourth citrated caffeine. Two of these capsules half an hour apart will relieve almost any automobile headache quickly if the stomach is not full of food. While not harmless in overdoses, two may be taken inside of one hour with perfect safety. Large doses will make the lips turn blue, and this effect is to be avoided.

When the British entered World War I on August 4, 1914, their first major shipment to France was 60,000 horses and 1,200 trucks. Later the same year, Canada shipped 7,000 horses and 133 trucks. Clearly, the motor truck was yet to become a truly recognized means of viable transport for troops, ammunition, artillery and equipment.

There were six primary reasons why motor transport was not in the forefront at the beginning of World War I:

(1) The motor truck was considered unproven and unreliable as a mode of transportation.

Top: Although Pierce-Arrow was known for its excellent passenger cars, the company also built trucks, such as this 1918 2-ton flatbed. *Bottom:* The enormous need for fuel to power motor vehicles soon led to shortages for civilian use during World War I. In some areas such as Norway, town-gas made from coal was used, as shown here with a 1915 Hupmobile carrying its own balloon of the volatile vapor.

(2) Nobody was certain which would be the best fuel to choose—electricity, steam or gasoline power (or combinations thereof).

(3) Roads were primitive or nonexistent. Battles took place in muddy fields criss-crossed with deep trenches.

(4) Hundreds of small manufacturers offered a confusing array of machines and components that were not interchangeable.

(5) Reliable railroads already crisscrossed the European continent and elsewhere.

(6) People were familiar with the equine and the iron horse, but not with motors, which required hand-crank starting, constant maintenance, repair work and driver training, in addition to transporting fuel and oil in huge quantities.

Shortages of oil and gasoline appeared early on as the war progressed in Europe, especially for civilian use. In northern Europe some automobiles, such as the Hupmobile, were converted to use town-gas, as it was called, as early as 1915. Vehicles that used natural gas carried enormous balloons on top of their roofs in order to make up for the low density of gas, which was not compressed. Within the first two years of the war each country developed its restrictions for civilian gasoline use. In Italy all private motoring was stopped to the extent that motor vehicle factories in Turin (Fiat, Lancia, Itala, Isotta-Franchini, etc.) were not even allowed to test run their vehicles for a time. Fiat was building about 100 trucks per day and testing them on the open road. Because this decree seriously interrupted supplying the military, the regulations regarding testing were quickly rescinded.

In England the police enforced strict regulations in the event a civilian managed to obtain some gasoline. In France the supply of gasoline was controlled and limited but available to some extent in a formal method of rationing. Many people across Europe protested they had to pay taxes on vehicles they could not use. The few private retailers that got tiny allotments had to pay $2.00 per gallon, which was nearly ten times the usual price prior to the war. The managers and officials in government were given special tags that exempted them except on Sundays. Taxis were widely removed from service and the drivers placed as laborers in factories.

In 1917, *Automobile and Automotive Industries* editorialized:

> Science Will Prevent Fuel Famine. Undreamed possibilities lie in scientific research for preventing fuel famine, and alleviating other supply shortages that the war and the increased population of the world may bring about.... Gasoline may give out, but it is altogether possible that alcohol may be used as a substitute, being manufactured in sufficiently large quantities to bring down the price. Furthermore new methods of manufacturing the former fuel may be introduced, such as have been demonstrated in Alberta, Canada, where gasoline has been extracted from natural gas fields in commercial quantities.... A hundred years of industrial research has at last transformed that laboratory method into a commercially operative process, by which thousands of gallons of high grade ethyl alcohol are made from yellow pine sawdust.... A cord of sawdust costing 50 cents yields 10 gallons of 95 percent alcohol. By this process any vegetable waste which can be collected cheaply and in any quantity becomes raw material for alcohol and releases for their proper use as food the corn and molasses now diverted to alcohol production ... it removes substantially all menace of a possible failure of the gasoline supply, since alcohol is equally available as a motor fuel.

However, the technology and infrastructure required to create a motorized society (and military) that used a large percentage of alcohol in fuel for motor vehicle engines was a dream that came through only in bits and pieces and only later in some countries, as it was discovered that the standard internal combustion motor could only function efficiently using alcohol mixed in large proportion with gasoline. This depended on the working design of the components that had to withstand much higher octane, alcohol's oxidation and lubrication problems, in addition, supplying ethyl alcohol in the amount of tens of millions of barrels was particularly challenging, since it was derived from agricultural production and still needed fermentation and distillation. Underground oil fields, on the other hand, still seemed, even in a fantasy of optimism, endlessly plentiful and inexpensive to

In what was called the "gasoline war," tankers, such as this 1918 FWD, were a necessity at the front and behind the lines to supply motor vehicles with the needed fuel that was considered of nearly no use just two decades before World War I.

drill, especially at the beginning of the 20th century. Ethyl alcohol as fuel along with bio-diesel were fuels of the future in 1917.

Despite local and sporadic shortages, especially when the front line moved up and tankers had to be quickly mobilized to supply gasoline and oil, petroleum-based fuels were made available through additional production and refining. This often meant the exploitation of various areas across the United States where oil had still not been depleted from underground sources such as Pennsylvania, Oklahoma, Texas and California, and later in Alaska.

The discovery of vast underground oil fields in the Middle East made the superpowers that much more aggressive in attempting to dominate and control certain regions of the world hitherto left to their own skirmishes, uprisings and strife not particularly related to oil production until then. As oil became a primary commodity this sort of apathy would change dramatically.

However, the horse was still relied upon to tread through the mud and snow, carrying soldiers or pulling a wagon or artillery piece. An entire support system of personnel provided care for the horses: shoeing, branding, feeding, grooming, harnessing, sheltering, and veterinarian services, in addition to breeding and training. In view of this complexity, the military command gradually, if begrudgingly, saw the advantage of the steel-and-gasoline machine over the flesh-and-blood animals, who were prone to exhaus-

Opposite, top: **The versatility of the newly invented motorcycle was proven out by mounting two stretchers for emergency use in 1916 by the Red Cross, calling the type of work "hero land."** *Bottom:* **Harley-Davidson called its first motorcycle "The Silent Gray Fellow" in 1916 and the U.S. military began buying them by the thousands.**

U. S. MOTORCYCLE CORPS, SHOWING ARMOURED MOTORCYCLE WITH MACHINE GUN.

Top: The U.S. Motorcycle Corps, showing armored motorcycle with machine gun in 1917. *Bottom:* This 1917 Indian motorcycle was used as a tow vehicle, shown here in a parade with a specially attached machine gun trailer.

tion and sickness, stubbornness and panic, of which the machine was entirely bereft despite its need for maintenance and repair.

With the development of the American motorcycle and the beginning of production of Indian in 1901 and Harley-Davidson in 1903, there was now a motor vehicle that would also have a saddle, not always but in many ways superseding the horse. A decade after the founding of Harley-Davidson, the most enduring bike built in the U.S., it became apparent the motorcycle would have many uses for the military, which began buying both Indian and Harley-Davidson in numbers by 1916, in addition to a few Excelsior and Reading-Standard, among others, for testing.

The invention of the side-

GMC contributed thousands of trucks that were transformed into ambulances by various groups and companies in America and abroad.

car gave the motorcycle a degree of road stability as a light carrier platform and tremendous versatility for work such as dispatch, light delivery, stretcher carrier, ammunition car, officer's car, light tow vehicle, reconnaissance and scout vehicle or even to be armed with a machine gun. As long as there was a decent road surface of some type and a few gallons of oil and gasoline, the motorcycle was more durable and faster than the horse. As with other motor vehicles, it never got frightened or sick and required very little "grooming."

Automobile and Automotive Industries explained the more advanced "Motorcycle Side Car Gun Mount" in the following note:

A motorcycle side car gun mount, operated by Lieutenant S.T. Kellog of a motorcycle platoon at Bridgeport, Connecticut, has recently been inspected by War Department officials. The entire outfit weighs 750 lbs. The gun works on a double pivot. The operator sits on a saddle, which is on a pivot, while the machine gun is mounted on a second pivot, one being independent of the other. There is also another pivot for pointing the gun upward for aircraft. The gun is so mounted that provision is made for an armor plate on the front to protect the operator of the gun. The gun can be fired from the front of the side position, of the rear, if necessary. This is accomplished by raising the arm that swings it over the side car wheel. The machine also carries an extra regulation tripod for trench work or arm which can be detached and carried on the platform and a gun-mount set on a pedestal for long-distance travel. A Colt automatic gun is used.

Although the U.S. was not directly involved in the first three years of the "Great War," American factories began manufacturing significant numbers of trucks, cars, ambu-

Top: GMC trucks made excellent ambulances for the war effort, such as this 1917 Model 16. *Bottom:* Of the multitude of truck makes in the World War I era, this 1917 Menominee 1-ton Model HT Express was made in yet another company located in Wisconsin.

lances and motorcycles specifically for the war effort. Between August 1914 and August 1915 the United States shipped approximately 16,000 trucks across the Atlantic. Many were transformed into ambulances as a gesture of humanitarian camaraderie, keeping a semblance of neutrality, and many were funded in Europe by private firms.

America exported 80,000 motor vehicles of all types in 1916, mostly to Europe as the

An unusual truck built during World War I was this 1918 Fulton, manufactured by Clyde Motor Truck Company at Long Island, New York. Note the military spotlight.

war continued in full force. Ford alone would donate approximately 1,000 ambulances over three years as well as give $500,000 to the Red Cross.

The Federal Road Act of 1916 brought $75 million dollars to improve America's roadways, which were lagging far behind in development as motor vehicle manufacturing accelerated rapidly. At the same time, Americans had their worries about the extensive war in Europe, and with few exceptions the alliance and sympathy was with France, England and Russia against the aggressors Germany, Austria-Hungary and Turkey. There would also be many smaller, but not necessarily lesser, players.

At the outbreak of war it was estimated there were 1,000,000 motor vehicles operating in the United States, 250,000 in Great Britain, 90,000 in France, 70,000 in Germany and 10,000 in Russia.

Chapter II

THE HUNT FOR PANCHO VILLA

Pancho Villa may be one of the most recognizable names in both Mexican and American history. When he attacked Americans on U.S. soil on March 9, 1916, it was the equivalent of all-out war, reflecting that which was already taking place in Europe and other parts of the globe.

What would it take to catch Pancho Villa, the leader of the Mexican Revolution? After Villa crossed the border and raided Columbus, New Mexico, with about 400 of his men, an attack force under the command of General John "Black Jack" Pershing was sent off by President Woodrow Wilson to track down and bring Villa to justice and neutralize his army. It would be the first time ever that American military forces would use new technology that included staff cars, trucks, armored cars, motorcycles and airplanes, among other new inventions.

Pancho Villa was born Doroteo Arango in 1877; he changed his name to Francisco but was always known as Pancho Villa. He joined the Mexican Revolution against the

General John "Black Jack" Pershing sitting in the right rear of his 1916 Dodge Touring, nicknamed "Daisy." General Pershing admired the durability and reliability of Dodge cars and trucks, which would continue to be provided to the military for many years.

federal government to combat the oppressive rule of President Porfirio Diaz. Villa joined ideologist Francisco Madero to overthrow Diaz, and later fought against the new regime of President Venustiano Carranza and General Victoriano Huerta, who were officially recognized by President Woodrow Wilson in October of 1915 as being Mexico's legitimate leadership in the government. Villa felt betrayed by America.

Villa, along with his general Emiliano Zapata, had more than 40,000 men at one point, many of them expert equestrians. However, under Villa's reckless and frenzied command,

Top: Cadillac made a very significant contribution as a producer of vehicles which included the open touring staff car such as this 1916 model. *Bottom:* "Auto Truck" supply train about to leave from Camp Columbus, New Mexico, on a convoy into Mexico in 1916.

most were mowed down in the battle against General Alvaro Obregon in 1915. Major losses at Celaya, Leon and Agua Prieta forced Villa into desperation. After the defeats, Villa's men broke up into small armies of marauders, including the one that Villa led into Columbus.

General Pershing and Pancho Villa had met earlier in 1914 on friendly terms, but Villa wanted revenge. On January 10, 1916, Villa and his men had stopped a train in San Ysabel, Mexico, and murdered all the Americans on board, including nineteen engineers. International outrage ensued. After the raid on Columbus, which resulted in looting, arson and eighteen more American deaths, Pancho Villa was considered a vicious outlaw. He managed to get a solid 24-hour start ahead of organized American ground forces. Men of the 13th Cavalry from Camp Furlong at Columbus under Colonel Herbert Slocum did not have the resources to continue a prolonged chase, although they killed a few Villistas during the raid and pursued them some 15 miles across the border.

Once Brigadier General Pershing and the Quartermaster Corps got organized, the chase began. However, the Army was without any good knowledge or accurate maps of Chihuahua.

Pancho Villa and his men were excellent equestrians. It should be noted that Villa was not greatly interested in motor vehicles, but he wanted to have every advantage of the most modern equipment. He had bought several Indian Powerplus motorcycles in 1914, and, according to some eyewitnesses, had used them to attack Torreon during the Mexi-

Although Pancho Villa was known as an excellent horse rider, he also bought several Indian Powerplus motorcycles in 1914 and used them in a battle at Torreon against the Mexican government during the Revolution. Pancho Villa is shown here with one of them.

Top: Indian motorcycles at the beginning of World War I were very similar to those made by Harley-Davidson, but Indian was first in offering an electric starter and lights using a lead-acid storage battery. *Bottom:* Indian began producing its own machine gun sidecar units for the military in 1915 before Pancho Villa's attack on Columbus, New Mexico, in 1916.

can Revolution against the *Federales*. The U.S. Army first began buying Excelsior, Indian and Harley-Davidson motorcycles in 1913.

Although the landscape along the border with Mexico is a bleak, dry desert, the interior of Chihuahua features high, rugged, forested mountains, which Villa knew quite well. Being so familiar with the lay of the land allowed him to escape, hide and obtain help from the mostly cooperative, or coerced, locals. But when Villa had crossed the line, literally, the political and military leaders of the United States would not tolerate such a violation of the Mexican-American border, which had been established through the Treaty of Guadalupe Hidalgo in 1848 after the Mexican-American War. It was then revised in 1853 after the Gadsden Purchase.

The U.S. Army issued a "Special Application for Plans of the Quartermaster Department of Operations along the Border and Interior of Mexico." The "Table of Organization and Equipment" addressed the rapid procurement of trucks. Motorcycles had already been purchased starting in 1915 for patrol and messenger service in Texas along the border.

Even though General Pershing ordered Dodge staff cars, only a few were delivered. The first 1916 Dodge staff cars were easily recognizable with stock black paint, lack of mud guards at the rear and six-bolt wheels. Also, one of the earliest contractors with the military was Atterbury, which provided their Model R 1½-ton trucks in 1913, and these trucks were used on the Mexican border.

Then in June 15, 1916, the U.S. Army got bids for "officers cars," and Ford came in with the lowest bid at $450 for its touring model. Next came Dodge at $795, also guar-

Captain Daniel L. Porter, center, used a 1916 Reo as his staff car, leading a large convoy of supply trucks into Mexico during the Punitive Expedition.

Captain Daniel L. Porter, sitting on bumper at left, with his men mired on the trail in Mexico chasing Pancho Villa in 1916.

anteeing immediate shipment. General Pershing ordered more vehicles, of which a portion was delivered. Chief of Staff Hugh L. Scott ordered the initial 54 trucks used.

Other companies submitting bids included Elkhart, Hupmobile, Maxwell, Packard, Reo, Studebaker, Velie and Willys-Overland. By the end of 1916 the expedition had vehicles of a multitude of various makes, most of them Ford and Dodge, including General Pershing's Dodge "mobile headquarters" open touring staff car. A 1915 Reo served in the Punitive Expedition as the staff car for Captain Daniel L. Porter, who led a large convoy of supply trucks. Original personal photos, still extant, taken during the expedition show Captain Porter and men, with the Reo open car as well, negotiating steep unpaved trails and mired in mud to the axles with their trucks. At the time, the U.S. Marine Corps also bought Reo staff cars, which were called the Fifth Model and were sedans.

Eventually, over the next year, the Quartermaster Corps would test Cadillac, Dorris and Marmon cars as well under the supervision of Major John Madden, who was appointed chief quartermaster. Major B.F. Miller was appointed as the chief of the vehicle maintenance branch. At the end of the Punitive Expedition a testing station for motor transport was set up at Fort Russell in Marfa, Texas.

Of the new mechanical marvels available to the average person at the time, the motorcycle was one of the more popular ones. Whereas the modern pneumatic-tired pedal bicycle had gained wide popularity over the previous decade, bicycles with a gasoline motor (essentially the first motorcycles) were a whole new machine with countless applications, civilian and military.

The first specifically designed motorcycle for military use appeared in Canada in 1908 when Sergeant Northover of the Canadian Militia mounted a Maxim machine gun on a modified sidecar using a Harley-Davidson. Hiram Stevens Maxim, an American, had invented the machine gun in 1889 and patented it in England after losing a lawsuit to

One of Captain Porter's Quartermaster trucks attempting to negotiate rough terrain through Chihuahua, Mexico.

Henry Ford in the United States. The advantage of having a rapid-firing portable killing machine was soon lost as many armies on all sides adopted this design, and the motorcycle machine gun sidecar was used in various configurations in the ensuing years.

The Punitive Expedition forces obtained Harley-Davidson motorcycles, primarily for testing in off-road conditions. In 1916 Harley-Davidson offered an F-head 1000 cc (61 cid) 45-degree V-twin, which was just slightly less powerful than Indian's motor, yet both bikes were capable of 60 mph on a good day as long at it was on hard, flat ground. It was a different story in sand and soft soil.

Harley-Davidson motorcycles enjoyed using the marketing slogan "The Silent Gray Fellow" because the company stated "quiet pipes save lives," even though H-D had started racing their gray-paint machines. On the Harleys, lubrication was by pressurized feed pump plus auxiliary hand pump. Ignition was either magneto or generator battery type. The military opted for the magneto because the lead battery plates were prone to cracking as a result of off-road vibration.

All the large motorcycles at this time had spring-fork suspensions, and used kick starters, although Indian had briefly offered an electric starter just three years earlier. It

Pigeon lofts were mounted on sidecars, and pigeons were used often as message carriers in addition to telegraph, telephone and short-wave radio communication. Some pigeons were so reliable they were cited for meritorious service during World War I.

was not popular due to battery troubles. It was abandoned before the electric starter returned on motorcycles many years later. Chain drive was also adopted universally when increased horsepower precluded slippery belt drive long before the advent of gear belts. Transmissions were three-speed, although some of the smaller one-cylinder motorcycles the military had bought from Indian and Harley-Davidson used one speed. Harley-Davidson production was 8,527 in 1917 for the Model 17-F and 9,180 for the Model 17-J.

Half of all Harley-Davidson production, which was slightly less than that of Indian at that time, went to the U.S. Army. Harley-Davidson also began producing a combination motorcycle-sidecar for the military. Sidecars made by Flxible were the most prevalent during this period, but H-D switched to the Rogers Company in 1914, ordering 2,500 for that year alone. There was also the Model 16-GC, which was called a "gun car"; the Model 16-AC, an "ammunition car"; and the Model 16-SC, a "sidecar chassis and stretcher" for ambulance work.

Harleys equipped with machine guns were thoroughly tested in the desert after getting a workout in the forest near the Racine-Milwaukee area of Wisconsin, not far from where they were built. Photographs from the Milwaukee County Historical Society show both machine-gun-equipped sidecars and two-wheel bikes negotiating rugged desert terrain near the Mexican border. One version of the sidecar held a pigeon loft because pigeons were still used as messengers and were considered even more reliable than radio telegraph, especially where wires could be cut or were nonexistent. Some pigeons were even officially cited for meritorious service.

Besides field testing and training, motorcycles were used as courier vehicles, by and large. They were quite heavy and really not suited for the sandy/muddy off-road terrain. A few sensationalist pieces of journalism would try to create a different impression. One new release from 1916 read, "Early reports from Mexico ... extolled Private Gregg of the U.S. Seventh Cavalry, who rode his Harley-Davidson through a gang of banditos with his .45 Colt semi-automatic pistol blazing, killing one, wounding another, then delivering his dispatch case safely to headquarters." It is uncertain as to which "banditos" this reference was made, since those affiliated with Pancho Villa were already a hundred miles away. Harley-Davidson prided itself that it was the first American motorcycle to enter Germany after the Armistice on November 12, 1918.

Field testing proved that 90 percent of a motorcycle's efficiency depended on the rider and mechanic and 10 percent on the machine, unlike the JN-2 biplanes, in which those numbers would be reversed. Badly trained conscripts were prone to accidents, and poorly maintained machines were subject to breakdown. This moved the Milwaukee factory of Harley-Davidson to send out instructors for training rider soldiers and mechanics. Howard "Hap" Johnson was the first such instructor. This school for the armed services still exists as of this writing.

The U.S. Army still relied largely on horses and mules, and during the Punitive Expedition, which lasted a total of eleven months, over 9,300 horses were used in cavalry, as pack animals and to draw wagons and artillery. And the Army had finally bought motor trucks after the grueling test run in 1912. Pershing had under his command the 7th, 10th, 11th and 13th Cavalry Regiments as well as the 6th and 16th Infantry Regiments, a total of approximately 15,000 men.

A close-up of the 998 cc V-twin Indian motorcycle engine, which produced 16 hp, enough for 60 mph on a good day in 1915.

Indian had introduced the Powerplus in 1916, the company's first side-valve motor, which was considered more durable. It displaced 998 cc and produced 16 hp, using a three-speed transmission with single-chain drive. Both the Powerplus and Model J weighed just over 400 pounds. And both the civilian and military versions were nearly identical for 1916–1918. The overall appearance changed in 1917 when, because of diversion of materials due to the war effort, the wheels were painted black, making the two years easily distinguishable from others. Also, the Powerplus had a fully valanced (i.e., wrap-around) front fender, setting it apart from other makes at a distance.

As was the case with motorcycles of this vintage, most offered sidecars. Indian provided sidecars with seats but also with gun stowage platforms as well as gunner sidecars with Colt-

Advertising artwork from 1917 showed a motorcycle dispatch courier passing what appears to be one FWD truck following other trucks in a desert landscape.

Martin Rapid Fire Guns. George Hendee, founder of Indian, retired very comfortably in 1916, the year Indian sold 22,000 motorcycles. The following year profits were $540,000, a considerable sum for that era, outdone in 1918 with $733,000. Large contracts amounting to almost 20,000 motorcycles over three years shorted availability for civilian sales. Criticism was answered by an official company statement that read as follows: "There will be Indian Motorcycles, Sidecars and Delivery Cars for Civilian Buyers, But How Many and When Depends Entirely Upon the Requirements of Our Fighting Forces and Those of Our Allies Whose Orders Will Be Filled First."

Pancho Villa also used motorcycles in some of his escapades, although the repair and maintenance of gasoline engines was an arduous and labor-intensive activity at the time, and Villa was thoroughly familiar with horses. Competent mechanics were hard to find on either side of the border. General Pershing's soldiers used motorcycles in and around Columbus but did not get the chance to chase Pancho Villa into Mexico despite sensational press accounts. Motorcycles, especially with sidecars, were valuable for dispatch work, convoy control, military police, small parts supply, communication repair, medic duty and other auxiliary needs.

The success of Harley-Davidson motorcycles led to the selection of William S. Harley of Harley-Davidson as the head of the newly formed Society of Automotive Engineers committee, which later dealt with the standardization of motorcycles built for the military. When the idea of standardization was finally accepted, the Liberty Motorcycle was designed in the same vein as the Liberty Truck and Liberty Engine.

The Army bought a few Excelsior motorcycles, and in the final months a contract was made with Militaire motorcycles, which had a final version called the Militor. Excelsior motorcycles also used a 1000 cc air-cooled V2 motor as did Indian and Harley-David-

Top: White trucks were used in so-called truck trains to supply troops deep inside Mexico, with conditions changing from mud to dust depending on season. *Bottom:* Built in Clintonville, Wisconsin, FWD 4 × 4 trucks were diverted from shipment across the Atlantic, and some of them were sent to Columbus, New Mexico, along with numerous other makes in a fleet made up of whatever was available at the moment.

son. Excelsior motorcycles were founded by Ignez Schwinn, who became famous for his bicycles.

General Pershing would become an innovator in the U.S. Army when he asked not only for motor vehicles but also for aerial reconnaissance. Without being able to reconnoiter the landscape and follow the Villistas from a bird's-eye view, he knew the task of

Top: Two-wheel-drive trucks with smooth, hard rubber tires such as this 1916 White didn't stand much of a chance in the mud and sand in Mexico as Pancho Villa galloped away on horseback. *Bottom:* Captain Porter's "truck train" in 1916 relied on a few tanker trucks for fuel, which also had to cross the rough terrain.

catching the "banditos" would be extremely demanding, if not impossible. Although this discussion is focused on motor vehicles of the World War I period, the aircraft of these years are worth noting, since their early designs were essentially based on automotive engine technology.

The aircraft General Pershing employed for the job were the Curtiss JN-2 Jenny, basically prototypes of the later JN-3 and JN-4 Jennies. It is worth mentioning in brief a few accounts from the period of the Punitive Expedition, which paint a story of unbelievable courage and dedication when aviation was in its infancy, especially in the United States.

Top: Winthur trucks from one- to seven-ton capacity were used by the military during World War I, and were advertised as having been tested in the desert as in this ad of 1918. *Bottom:* Harley-Davidson motorcycles were thoroughly tested in the desert by 1916, with and without sidecars.

As a comparison, between 1908 and 1913, Germany spent the equivalent of $28,000,000 on aircraft, France approximately $26,000,000, and czarist Russia $11,500,000. The U.S. expenditure during this period was $460,000, ranking it behind feudal Japan. The responsibility was placed squarely on the shoulders of Congress, where every dollar had to be pulled like a tooth out of each eloquent orator's mouth arguing against the necessity and importance of something they simply didn't comprehend.

It had taken the Army a decade to buy motor vehicles—newfangled aeroplanes were even a harder sell. At that time, piloting heavier-than-air aircraft was still considered a type of aerial circus by people who grew up having never heard of or envisioned such flying machines, even though as a sport it had become quite popular with various shows and displays across the country. The Wright Brothers were already famous, indeed, but mired in various legal and patent issues.

The 1st Aero Squadron joined the Punitive Expedition on March 11, 1916, after Secretary of War Newton Baker ordered General Funston to attach the newly formed military branch to General Pershing's operation. The 1st Aero Squadron had been organized in 1914 at North Island near San Diego, California. At the time, it was composed of five pilots, thirty enlisted men and three Martin T biplanes under the command of Captain Benjamin D. Foulois, who had been initially trained by Orville Wright. During the period that Captain Foulois was trained, between 1909 and 1911, fatalities averaged one per every hundred hours spent in the air.

In 1915 Captain Foulois had been ordered to move the fledgling 1st Aero Squadron to Fort Sill, Oklahoma, from San Diego. In Europe, British, French and German aircraft were being used for reconnaissance, photography, mapping, artillery liaison and some bombardment. The airplanes now had machine guns with interrupter gears attached to the motors synchronizing with the propeller. They could reach over 100 mph and could climb over 15,000 feet. Captain Foulois was asked to see what he could do with the brand-new Curtiss JN-2 Jenny.

When the Jennies were uncrated fresh from the factory, the pilots at Fort Sill were less than impressed. The first JN-2 Jenny was an "underpowered, awkward looking machine," per evaluation of the time. The motor produced all of 90 hp. The tail surfaces were diminutive. The ailerons were actuated by shoulder harness wherein the pilot leaned to the left or right. This was imprecise and lacked a gradual, smooth movement, producing sudden attitude changes of the biplane and making it that much more difficult to control even if it were a stable machine, which it was not. Unfortunately, this was confirmed when the first trial of the plane took place. Lieutenant R.B. Sutton lifted off in calm weather and while at low altitude lost control, crashing to his death.

Overlooking the accident with nary an investigation, the Army planned to put the Jenny into operation along the Rio Grande to help in border control, which was increasingly becoming a problem (underscored after Pancho Villa's raid). Captain Foulois was instructed to move some of the JN-2s to Brownsville, Texas. The planes were partially disassembled, crated and sent by rail. Once reassembled in Brownsville they were tested again. According to their own accounts, Lieutenant J.C. Morrow and B.Q. Jones lifted off and climbed to 1,100 feet. Suddenly, the plane dropped in an inexplicable sideslip. They climbed up to 4,500 feet when the Jenny repeated its capricious bad manners.

Pilots continued to report the same problems. On several occasions missions were aborted when similar behavior was exhibited by a Jenny with "a mind of her own." On September 5, 1915, J.C. Morrow and an unnamed enlisted man took off for a sortie along the river. Before reaching more than a few hundred feet the plane went into a steep right spiral and both men were killed on impact.

At that point, artillery officers assigned as spotters to go up in the Jennies refused to fly, even risking court-martial. The original impression that the JN-2 was clumsy was proven out by two crashes and three fatalities, all in daylight, clear weather, without a

Top: As the JN-2 aircraft went down in Mexico, White trucks, such as this detail in 1916, were sent out carrying fuel and rations to look for the missing aviators. *Bottom:* General Pershing obtained ten Curtis JN-2 biplanes to use as scout and courier planes in the Punitive Expedition, six of which are seen here sitting side by side in the vast New Mexico desert near Columbus, which was attacked by Pancho Villa as World War I exploded in Europe.

shot being fired and with no apparent mechanical breakdown. The artillery officers signed a letter stating that they would fly only in time of war and in case of absolute necessity in the Curtiss JN-2.

These accidents finally got the attention of the Army brass. Back at the Massachusetts Institute of Technology (MIT), a model of the JN-2 was put through wind-tunnel tests. Since the airplane was already being built as a series, it should not have been a surprise, but the results were stunning. The JN-2 was unstable in any condition with the exception of level flight in calm air. Glenn Curtiss, once the "fastest man on Earth," was hauled in to Washington, D.C. There was little time to waste in drawing up plans for modifications to the idiosyncratic JN-2.

There were three basic problems: lack of horsepower, absence of ailerons on the lower wings, and inadequate surface area of the elevators and horizontal stabilizer. All three

Top: The JN-4 was a considerable improvement over the JN-2 and was used widely as a trainer. The star-in-circle insignia was adopted in May of 1917. *Bottom:* White trucks of the Third Aero Squadron, composed of ten Curtis JN-2 biplanes, stand at Fort Sam Houston. The airplanes were moved to Columbus, New Mexico, for the Punitive Expedition.

problems were rectified on the JN-3 and mass-produced JN-4. Glenn Curtiss wanted to make retrofits, which added a lot of weight. Engineers scrambled to reconcile recommended improvements that added heft with an aircraft that should have been lighter in the first place.

The V-8 motor did have aluminum pistons and crankcase, but the cylinders were of cast iron and the engine was water-cooled using a radiator. Additional horsepower of the later JN-3 and JN-4 iterations made all the difference. Pilots in the Punitive Expedition had to make do with the ten JN-2 Jennies that were already built and assigned to them. They were used only as observation planes and for some courier work. Additional crashes continued, with one setting one of the largest forest fires in Mexican history, although the two American pilots were not killed. Within a few months in 1916 the JN-2 flights were suspended when the Curtiss R-2 was introduced.

Even Pancho Villa tried to form his own air force at one point in 1915. He hired Edwin C. Parsons, a pilot from Holyoke, Massachusetts, to teach several of his men how to fly using five Wright "L" biplanes that Villa had bought that year. As Villa's men watched, Parsons crash-landed one of the planes. All the volunteers suddenly lost interest in flying and withdrew from participation. That was the end of Pancho Villa's air force.

Parsons survived and went on to distinguish himself with the LaFayette Escadrille in France in 1917. But the use of automotive engines in aircraft was soon abandoned, although those pilots in the Punitive Expedition risked their lives in some of the earliest primitive airplanes, powered by what were essentially car engines and other hardware and technology borrowed directly from the automobile.

It should be noted that telegraph lines ran straight up to El Paso along the rail lines in Chihuahua, and there were dozens of newspapermen as part of the entourage with the Army by 1916. They wrote about the latest hardship, incident and operation, which was then telegraphed for publication the next day. The soldiers used a radio telegraph communication system, simply called "wireless," mounted on trucks to relay messages among the various camps going into Mexico. White Motor Company photos show soldiers setting up thirty-foot antennae in the field.

In addition to his squadron of Curtiss Jenny JN-2 biplanes, General Pershing was using as many motor vehicles as he could possibly obtain. But buying up whatever was available at the moment would result in the eventual procurement of 128 different makes and models of various American-made motor vehicles during the Mexican campaign. In the end, about half of the trucks involved in the Punitive Expedition were built by either White or FWD. There was also the Jeffery Quad, renamed Nash Quad in 1917 when Charles Jeffery, son of founder Thomas Jeffery, sold the company after his father suddenly died, having himself survived the sinking of the *Lusitania* in 1915, as mentioned. In addition, General Pershing also bought Pierce-Arrow, Packard and Riker-Locomobile trucks.

Locomobile trucks, renamed Riker in 1916 for their designer, Andrew L. Riker, were also employed by the army against Villa. The standard Riker truck was a 3-ton open cab

The Army bought thirty Riker 3-ton trucks after they were fitted with special flanges allowing them to travel on railroad tracks in 1916.

Riker trucks were named after their design engineer and were built by Locomobile; this ad shows a speeding Army truck when in reality 10 mph was considered a good off-road clip at that time.

type, which had been introduced in 1912. Since the U.S. Army got stuck on the idea that only 1¹/₂-ton trucks were needed, Riker's representative, C.A. Wales, could not convince the military decision makers to purchase even one.

Then C.A. Wales came up with the idea of making the Riker truck into a type of transformable miniature locomotive in order to take advantage of the railroad lines crossing Texas and New Mexico and the tracks leading south into Mexico, which were off limits to the El Paso and Southwestern Railroad (EP and SWRR) companies, or any other American railroads, due to restrictions by the Mexican government. Andrew Riker and his engineers created flanges that were cast and machined in one piece, then sawed apart at the bolt lugs. The inside diameter fit over the hard rubber tires, while the outside diameter fit directly onto the rail track.

After an impressive run of 93 miles from Columbus to El Paso with twenty soldiers on board, the idea was proven out, especially with much fanfare by the press once the truck arrived in good order with cameras rolling. The army finally bought 30 Riker trucks, and they were used on occasion to bring supplies more rapidly than those trucks mired in the sand and mud.

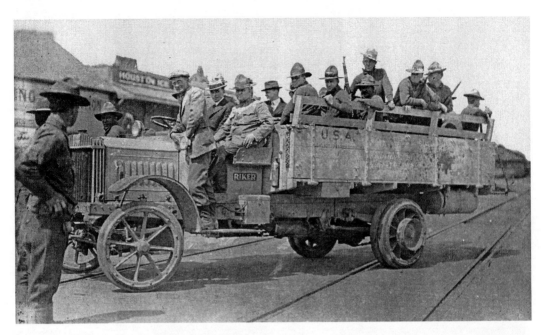

Top: Carrying a squad of soldiers, this 1916 Riker traveled 93 miles from El Paso to Columbus, New Mexico, and had its special wheel flanges removed to be driven into town with media cameras rolling. *Bottom:* Another demonstration of the Riker-Locomobile truck with special flanges for traveling on railroad tracks, developed by Andrew Riker.

Once the Riker trucks were purchased, Packard 3-ton trucks, powered by Packard's own 32 hp four-cylinder engine, also proved themselves in the Mexican desert, and 4,856 of these trucks were later shipped to Europe in 1917–1918.

It was during the conflict with Pancho Villa that the idea of a scout car was developed. In the vast open terrain in Texas, Arizona, New Mexico and Mexico, small, light, agile, durable open cars such as Ford and Dodge were used for reconnaissance. Their range and reliability would far outshine the horseman even if limited to at least a crude road. Quite soon, challenges in the field would bring out the creativity in those placed in charge of maintaining and repairing vehicles.

Modifications were gradually incorporated, such as the use of fatter tires with lower air pressure to keep from sinking into sand. Shorter fenders to avoid interference with rocks, logs and other obstacles low on the ground were now part of the design. Extra gasoline tanks and additional radiator cooling was needed. Machine guns were mounted in place of the rear seat for protection. Headlights were moved inward and higher up on the front of the car to avoid breakage, along with the advent of the brush guard.

Colonel Royal Davidson continued to experiment with this type of development at the Northwestern Academy. One example was a used 1912 Cadillac in which he installed a radio antenna, a cowl-mounted Colt .30 caliber machine-gun and extra spare tires. The vehicle was used in a transcontinental convoy in 1915 along with at least one other Cadillac armored car, ambulance, field kitchen and supply trucks.

Another experimental scout car was the Clark Observation Car developed by a designer named Oscar Marino. This one-off vehicle used nose-cone sheet metal for protecting the radiator and heavy steel disc wheels with headlights sitting atop thin, short fenders resembling a Pierce-Arrow. It was fitted with an 18-foot steel grid observation pyramid in the shape of a miniature Eiffel tower minus the arch.

Yet another experiment of the same period was a Saxon roadster fitted with a V-shape

This White armored car was built on a 1½-ton truck chassis and photographed at Fort Bliss, Texas, in 1916 during the Punitive Expedition.

White built several armored car prototypes, such as this one photographed in Mexico in 1916, before the company was sold to Nash.

armor over the radiator, pedestal floor-mounted machine gun on the passenger side and huge drum gas tank for long range.

Such experiments would lead to cars actually built and used in the field. Captain Arthur C. Crossman of the 33rd Michigan Infantry designed such a car based on the fast and light four-cylinder Model SF Studebaker. Five such vehicles were built, which featured a "bullet-resisting" body, gun stowage box, extra gas tank, water, tools and supplies. They were seen in a parade through El Paso in 1917 toward the end of the Punitive Expedition and did not see any real action, but a field army photo used the caption "Machine Gun Truck." As scout cars became increasingly well armed they also evolved into armored cars.

At the outset of the conflict, General Pershing used one hundred and sixty-two FWD and White trucks to ply back and forth from Columbus to the first field base at Colonia Dublan, nearly 200 miles into the interior of Mexico, coincidentally not far from where Randolph Hearst happened to have an enormous ranch. Press coverage included photos showing columns of White trucks with large canvas canopies headed south through a valley between bare, rock-strewn hills. The so-called "truck trains" could stay only on what might be called a roadway, at times breaking down or getting mired in sand and mud. But once the trains were in the "pipeline," there was a nearly constant flow of supplies, including food, feed for horses, ammunition and water. Boots were always needed as well as proper

Top: Chasing Pancho Villa into the Mexican interior required trucks to cross stream beds on crude dirt paths. *Bottom:* Bridges in Mexico were not strong enough to hold up to truck convoys, so stream beds, arroyos and ravines were crossed directly over the uncertain ground.

clothing, as few planners had anticipated bitter cold in higher elevations, with some stereotypical assumptions that "desert" was always translated to mean "heat."

Truck trains generally ran alongside actual train rail lines before entering the mountains. Starting in El Paso, the Mexican Northwestern Railroad consisted of two lines — one going directly south to the city of Chihuahua, the other traversing more westerly

Top: This view illustrates the size of one single truck convoy at the Mexican border in the Punitive Expedition against Pancho Villa and his men. *Bottom:* Captain Daniel Porter's truck convoy assembled near the Mexican border in 1916, showing tanker, Reo staff car and burro, which they used as their mascot.

through Colonia Dublan, then through Guerrero. Eventually Pershing used these rails, but through most of the campaign the Mexican government would not allow the Americans to use their rail lines.

Trucks were used to carry supplies and rarely to carry troops. They were either on horseback or on foot and were still expected to march and sleep on the ground. The entire gamut of advantages of motor transport had yet to be fully envisioned even by such great military leaders as General Pershing. However, Pershing was wise enough to purchase a number of Holt crawler tractors (being called Caterpillar—with the company also taking on the name). These tracked vehicles of various sizes, built first by Benjamin Holt in

Holt 75 Caterpillar tractors proved themselves in the desert, shown here towing horse feed and supply wagons at the Mexican border in 1916.

Stockton (and Best in Hayward), California, and then also in Peoria, Illinois, proved themselves convincingly at being able to cross all types of terrain and pull tremendous loads, but at very low speeds, large fuel consumption, high cost and substantial maintenance. Nevertheless, the Holt Caterpillar became a favorite of the U.S. Army in the desert, and later in the European theater of war. (Holt will be discussed further in Chapter IV.)

Another famous name to emerge out of the conflict was that of George S. Patton, who at the time was a lieutenant, later to become a famous World War II general. In the chase after Villa, Patton became an innovator when he turned three Dodge touring cars into armored cars by bolting steel plates to the bodies. They were used to rout some of Pancho Villa's rear guard out of an adobe bunker in a skirmish at San Miguelito. However, there is no evidence the improvised armored cars were used in actual combat. From all accounts, the minor battle involved infantry, and the Dodges remained parked far from the action.

Likewise it was to be for at least one armored car built on a Ford Model T chassis. A rare photo shows the improvised tall, narrow armored car amid Studebaker-Crossman machine gun cars in a large parade through El Paso in 1917.

Historians put the initial order for trucks by Pershing at six columns with each train having twenty-five trucks. Supplying spare parts was a tremendous challenge. Moreover, the Army did not have the drivers and mechanics to operate and repair vehicles. Civilians were hired and often arrived along with a new purchase of trucks. Meanwhile, the War Department hurriedly recruited qualified soldiers.

Although Ford trucks were also mentioned, the Ford Motor Company did not start manufacturing its own line of trucks until 1917. However, many converted passenger Model T cars were in existence already.

Holt Caterpillar used ads referring to General Pershing's raid into Mexico.

Pershing wrote that at one point he had 22 companies of 25 to 27 trucks each, "with complete repair shops and a large depot of spare parts at Columbus." The numbers vary depending at what point in the campaign the count was made and by whom. According to Army reports, toward the end of the Punitive Expedition there were 74 trains of 25 trucks each, hauling supplies back and forth as deep as 400 miles into the unforgiving Mexican terrain.

The deepest penetration by the U.S. Cavalry was approximately 500 miles to Parral, where an indecisive battle was fought with the Villistas, and perhaps ironically where Pancho Villa would eventually end up. The entire route was a dirt road, which was one long succession of mud, potholes, ruts, collapses, hairpin turns, stream and river crossings, sand pits and other challenges of scenic extremes. Some of the passes reached an altitude of 7,000 feet amid 12,000-foot peaks. The City of Chihuahua was eventually reached, but not by truck and only during final peace negotiations.

Prior to the treaty, the press divulged the location and size of the U.S. National Guard units that had been deployed all along the border. By the end of 1916 they numbered just over 10,000, in addition to the American Expeditionary Forces (AEF), which would soon leave Mexico for France. Motor truck and motorcycle units, along with their respective staff car deployments, were now part of the garrisons at Douglas, Arizona, and along the Texas border. There was talk of an all-out invasion of Mexico.

One lesson that was quickly learned by the American military from the Punitive Expedition out in the desert was the immense need for mobile repair and machine shops in order to maintain the new machine marvels based on the internal combustion engine, which, in addition to motor vehicles, would power ships, aircraft, generators, pumps and other newly developed mechanical devices. But the cost and complexity of maintaining so many types and makes of vehicles served to obfuscate their importance, and confused the military brass into thinking along traditional methods that relied on infantry, cavalry, navy and railroads.

The Punitive Expedition ended February 17, 1917, not long before Congress declared war on Germany on April 6. The lessons of standardization, training and organization were yet to be fully learned as the U.S. shipped a myriad of motor vehicles to Europe.

Reliance on modern self-propelled vehicles that did not require rails, horseshoes, boots or bodies of water would be the essence of the technological evolution that emerged from the Mexican campaign. Pancho Villa eventually "retired" in 1920, and to keep him satisfied and at bay, the established Mexican government under President Adolfo de la Huerta granted him and his wife a hacienda with 25,000 acres and 50 bodyguards. However, the owner of the property where Pancho Villa moved in took umbrage after he and his family were evicted. While being driven in his Dodge touring car, Pancho Villa was ambushed and killed in 1923 by his neighbors in Parral, Mexico, after a dispute over home furnishings. His cactus-roots revolution would result in an even more weakened and corrupt multi-ethnic nation in which a violent and destructive upheaval had done nothing for land reform or political equality despite sharing a long, broken U.S. border.

Chapter III

CLEVER MINDS AND MOTORS

As reluctant as many Americans were to send their men to the war in Europe, they were not so stingy with equipment and motor vehicles. Most people were keenly aware of the world conflict that was extending all across the continent and into the Middle East, China and Africa. Many civic groups organized humanitarian assistance by first sending money, food and ambulances to help the Allied cause.

For example, at this time the wealthy and patriotic citizens of New York had pooled their resources together, and by March of 1916 they had raised enough money to buy a fleet of vehicles for Battery A of the New York National Guard. The vehicles included 72 Harley-Davidson and Indian motorcycles, two trucks and a staff car, as well as three armored cars built by Mack, Locomobile and White. These had an open top where two Colt machine guns would be mounted, and adjustable shutters protected the front and sides of the vehicles.

Powered by a standard 221 cid, 45 hp four-cylinder engine, Mack used its 2-ton Model AB chassis with .20 inch plate on a 144-inch wheelbase. It had worm drive and dual rear wheels with solid rubber. The whole vehicle weighed 9,050 pounds with a Gray-Davis searchlight or two diagonally mounted machine guns with a curved shield. This type of plate, it should be noted, would only be effective against small arms fire and some shrapnel. A cannon shell as small as 37 mm would penetrate this type of shielding, leading to the concentrated effort of developing the armored tank.

The Locomobile and White armored cars were very similar to the Mack. A second, much lighter version (2^1/$_2$ tons) was built by White in 1917, again on an experimental basis. The first three armored cars mentioned were shipped to Columbus, New Mexico, although they did not see action. The Locomobile used the Model 48 chassis and a standard six-cylinder engine, which carried .20 inch steel plate on all sides but the top, which was open as with the other two armored cars.

The Jeffery-Quad Armored Car No. 1 built at the factory was also shipped to New Mexico but used only for training. Armor plating was .20-inch thick, and the car carried up to four Colt machine guns. It weighed over six tons empty and had solid rubber tires. There are no records of its actual use in fighting at that time, since Pancho Villa and his men were already far into Mexico's interior. Along with the three other armored cars mentioned above, these were used for training and in parades for recruiting and public relations. Armored cars were impressive-looking vehicles that perhaps, from a superficial point of view, reminded the public of riveted steel plates used on battleships. Journalists sometimes employed the term *landships* for tanks, stemming from Winston Churchill's Land-

1917 R-S

The World's Master Motorcycle

Up—up to still higher levels the Reading Standard now advances —time tested by many thousand exultant owners.

Fine has been *re-fined*—by an added year's development. And the 1917 Models are again without comparison.

A *transcendent* Reading Standard—unchanged in essentials and enriched in details. To better the best Reading Standard has been our aim—and the inspiration of the day's work.

In beauty, quality and luxury the 1917 R-S attains what seems to be the limit. Styles may change in a minor way, but we see no possible way of ever building a finer motorcycle.

Three Models for 1917

Model 17 T, 12 H. P. Twin Cylinder $275.00

Model 17 TE, 12 H. P. Twin Cylinder, equipped
      with Bosch Electric Lighting System 315.00

Model 17 S, 6 H. P. Single Cylinder 240.00

Let your distributor demonstrate the many features found on the R-S Machines only. Good territory still open.

Catalogue and information upon request

READING STANDARD COMPANY

511 WATER STREET   READING, PA.

Even though various U.S. military branches bought mostly Indian and Harley-Davidson motorcycles, they also tested a few other American makes such as Excelsior and Reading Standard.

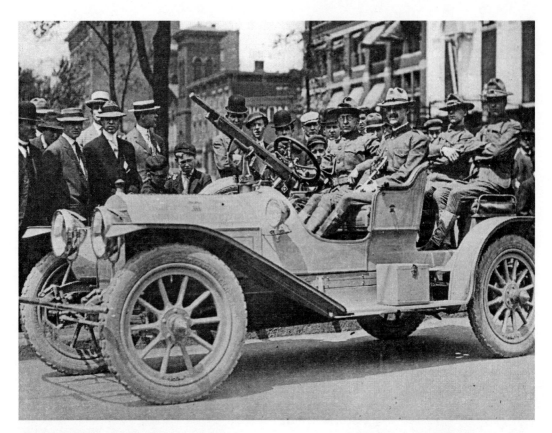

Top: This Cadillac machine gun car was built in 1915 on an earlier chassis. On the hood it reads "Military Academy Balloon Destroyer," making this one of Major Royal Davidson's designs. *Bottom:* Armored cars in action in Belgium. This artist's conception, published in *Leslie's Magazine* on January 7, 1915, illustrated a very rare sight in depicting this type of encounter, which was meant to excite the public's imagination.

Top: Mack used its AB truck chassis to build armored car prototypes, mostly used for recruiting, public relations and in parades such as this one in New York during 1916. Note soldiers standing up in the vehicles, which had open tops before complete enclosure became part of the design. *Bottom:* Another view of Mack and Locomobile armored cars of 1916, which were without gun turrets and still left soldiers vulnerable to grenades and ordnance of various kinds.

ship Committee. Nevertheless, the First Armored Motor Battery was disbanded late in 1917 and was not absorbed into the U.S. Army, which was yet to be convinced to use armored cars, because of their limited practicality without solid ground on which to travel.

Colonel Royal Davidson's next, but perhaps first, really successful vehicle was the Armored Machine Gun Car. It was based on a Cadillac open touring car and was completed in 1915. It was used in a convoy of military vehicles that traveled from Chicago on June 10 of that year and arrived in Los Angeles 40 days later. The Cadillac-based armored car had a lower profile, was more streamlined and was lighter than previous armored vehicles. Its effectiveness depended on a good road surface.

Top: This Mack armored car weighed 4½ tons and had two-wheel drive. It was tested at the Aberdeen Proving Ground by the Ordnance Department in 1916. *Bottom:* Mack continued to develop its armored car based on the AB chassis, shown here with a shutter over the radiator.

Top: Another view of the Mack AB armored car shows the open top where a machine gun would be mounted. This series from Mack was developed in 1916. *Bottom:* The framework of the Mack AB truck is clearly seen here, ready for its armor plate.

Top: Royal P. Davidson of the military academy at Lake Geneva used a 1915 Cadillac open touring car to build this "Armored Machine Gun Car." *Bottom:* Another view of the Military Naval Academy's "Armored Machine Gun Car" seen here with its forward-facing machine gun and room for one soldier in the rear.

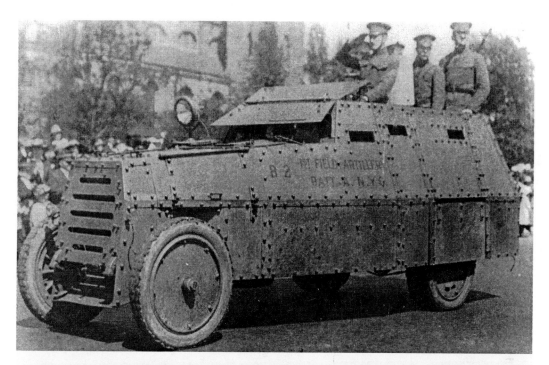

Top: One of the first armored car prototypes was built by Locomobile in 1916 for the 1st Field Artillery Battery of New York Garrison. It was never used in combat, because of its two-wheel drive and heavy weight in muddy fields without roads. *Bottom:* The Federal Motor Truck Company built its own version of an armored car, which included a rotating gun turret and dual rear solid-rubber tires with a crude tread pattern for slightly better two-wheel-drive traction.

Yet another company to try its hand at building an armored car was the Olympian Motor Company of Pontiac, Michigan. The vehicle design was rejected when it was shown in 1918, despite some improvements such as angled armor plate and protected rear wheels.

As named by the U.S. Ordnance Department, Armored Car No. 2 arrived from the White factory in 1915. It was based on a 1½-ton truck chassis with solid rubber tires. It was tested at Rock Island Arsenal, but again proved to be excessively top-heavy and weighed 9,000 pounds with only rear-wheel drive. The 36 hp White motor could build momentum up to 40 mph, but the basic problem of traction and maneuverability was not anywhere near being solved. The armor plating, inasmuch as being a shield for the crew, was also detrimental to access in that the personnel had to crawl through a small hatch in the right rear fender. In case of emergency, exiting this way would not be a strong suit of the design.

Three other armored cars that were built as prototypes were also used as public relations units rather than actual "war cars" used in combat. One was built on a Federal chassis and used by the New York National Guard in 1915. The second was an experimental vehicle from the Olympian Motors Company in Pontiac, Michigan, shown to the military in 1918 in hopes of getting a contract, but that did not materialize. The third was a boxlike contraption built by Detroit truck designer J.C. Wilson in 1918. His prototype was also rejected.

Besides supply trucks, staff cars became the most prevalent motor vehicles during World War I. General Pershing's staff car had been a 1916 Dodge Touring, which he nick-

This photograph of *Vole Sacrée* (Sacred Road) was taken in the spring of 1916 when the narrow gravel
path carried four-fifths of the supply line in the Battle of Verdun.

named "Daisy" in the Mexican campaign. Rumors turned to modern myth when stories were published that this car was shipped to France when the U.S. entered World War I. They may have been accurate, but General Pershing arrived in France, along with his Chief of Staff Major James Harbord on May 29, 1917, using enclosed Locomobile limousines in Europe. Daisy may have been there and used only temporarily. Nevertheless, with General Pershing's publicized enthusiasm for the durable, efficient cars, Dodge became an important and prolific manufacturer for the U.S. military beginning in 1916 and remained in that role for many decades.

The Punitive Expedition, although not directly related to the war in Europe, proved to be a very valuable experience for American political and military leaders who gradually realized the importance of motorized transportation and its standardization as policy rather than afterthought.

Before the United States entered the war, the first real large-scale test of motorized transport took place during the Battle of Verdun when the Douaumont and Vaux Forts were captured by the German army in 1916, near the city of Verdun. The strategic reason that convinced the German High Command to pick Verdun in February 1916 was Verdun's uncertain lines of supplies. The French railway lines were either interrupted by the frontlines or within range of German artillery.

By the spring of 1916 it was the now-famous *Vole Sacrée* (Sacred Road) that carried 78 percent of the traffic. (Originally, it was just called *La Route Departementale*—meaning county road—but it got its nickname from writer George Bernanos after the War). The other 22 percent of the traffic was moved by a metric gauge railway paralleling the *Vole Sacrée*.

White trucks traveling through the devastated town of Verdun in 1916 along with the cavalry, which was still a major part of any army in Europe.

Top: The road to Verdun known as *Vole Sacrée* had to be continuously maintained and rebuilt, 24 hours per day, with 750,000 tons of gravel eventually used along the route. *Bottom:* The French deployed 23 million artillery shells at Verdun between February and October 1916, some of which were transported by White trucks as seen in this photograph.

Under General Phillippe Petain, within four months, by June of 1916, a new standard gauge railway line was finished and the *Vole Sacrée* then carried light trucks, motorcycles and automobiles, as well as horsemen and horse-drawn traffic. Combining the road and the local railway lines, 221 French infantry divisions (about 2 million men) were brought in and out of the Verdun Salient during 1916 alone.

About 420,000 troops, 136,000 horses and 1,700 artillery were assigned to the Verdun Salient by the French General Staff. Nearly 10,000 military laborers were organized to widen the road to seven meters (22 feet), just enough for trucks to pass one another in each direction. The French grabbed every vehicle they could find on the streets of Paris and nearby towns, even vegetable trucks, and assembled more than 3,900 of them to ply back and forth to the defenses around Verdun. Of these, 3,000 were trucks, including 30 repair trucks, eight mobile tire and wheel shops and over 300 civilian buses. There were over 8,800 drivers and mechanics assigned to keep *Vole Sacrée* open at all times, even though top speed for the vehicles was around 15 mph.

From a statistical review of the entire operation, it has been closely estimated that 90,000 men per week were transported over the route. An average of 50,000 tons per week of materiel were moved. The mean distance logged by the entire motor vehicle operation was 600,000 miles per week.

Over 190,000 troops were assembled at the trenches using this dirt road where mud got 18 inches deep and gravel had to be shoveled almost continuously. With quarries running 24 hours a day, some 750,000 tons of gravel would eventually be used along this route. It should be noted that many of the thousands of miles of trenches in the entire region were dug using "ditchers" that were attached to the backs of trucks and were engine-driven, in addition to manual labor.

A total of 23,000,000 shells, of which 16,000,000 were 75 mm shells, were deployed by the French artillery at Verdun just between February and October of 1916. Transported first by truck or rail, these munitions were then taken to the battlefield by horse-drawn caissons in the last few miles. The smaller projectiles were packaged in wooden crates while the 75 mm shells were shipped unboxed with their powder charges separated away from the bodies.

About 2,000 tons of supplies were delivered daily by a continuous stream of trucks, day and night, week after week, using various makes and types, some imported from America. The 46-mile-long *Vole Sacrée* looked like "the folds of some gigantic and luminous serpent which never stopped and never ended," according to one soldier writing to his family back home.

By all accounts, the most prevalent American truck along this route was White, but there were actually only a few amid the French Berliet, Renault, Latil and Schneider vehicles. The White trucks were the Model TEBO 1-ton chassis, also used to build staff cars. Eventually, some 12,000 trucks altogether were used along the route.

Out of some 800 ambulances, the second most numerous vehicle was the Ford Model T ambulance. These hardy new vehicles plied the treacherous route, carrying wounded soldiers as German artillery continued to pummel the vulnerable roadway and those forced to travel upon it.

The gravel road was often under attack by German aircraft, which had to contend with fixed machine gun emplacements. Within a month of the salient several small airfields were improvised alongside *Vole Sacrée*, where seven Nieuport fighter squadrons were

Top: Only a dozen years after the Wright Brothers mastered heavier-than-air motor-propelled flight, the aircraft of World War I were quite primitive. This photograph from 1915 shows a French touring car towing a trailer with a wing assembly and landing gear section of an early biplane used by the military. *Bottom:* An American Gray Model 18-36 tractor used to smooth landing fields in France, May 1918.

The U.S. military used only a few Pierce-Arrow touring cars, such as this 1918 model, or enclosed limousines from this highly regarded company whose pricing was similar to other high-quality American automobiles such as Peerless, Packard, Cadillac and Locomobile.

assigned to the area, including *Escadrille Americaine* (to become the *Lafayette Escadrille*). It was based on its own airfield near Bar-le-Duc along the route.

Less than two months after the Pancho Villa campaign, on April 6, 1917, the United States Congress declared war in Europe. Largely due to the motorized effort against Villa, the U.S. Army had about 2,400 serviceable trucks by this time. After arriving in France in June of 1917, General Pershing wrote, "With our country by far the greatest producer in the world of automobiles and trucks, it was surprising that we were so poorly equipped with them." In part, General Pershing was also reacting to the purchasing spree by the War Department as America entered the war. What he found around Calles and Paris were hundreds of warehouses containing such items as bathtubs, lawn mowers, bookcases, stepladders, office desks, drums of floor wax and even spittoons. He immediately notified the War Department to discontinue shipments of such items.

It was in May of 1917, a month after the declaration of war, that the U.S. War Department asked for bids for a total of 74,400 motor vehicles. Somehow, this number was determined to be the final quantity required for the war effort. Fifty-nine companies responded with quotes from $420 for the Saxon to $4,500 for the Locomobile, and double that for a Locomobile limousine. The various military departments bought what they thought would best suit their particular needs. Of the total number, 1,000 units would be touring cars and 3,000 would be runabouts.

A relatively small peacetime American army would swell more than twenty-fold to 4,000,000, with half shipped overseas in one year. The American Expeditionary Force (AEF) was organized by May, and General Pershing arrived in France at the beginning of June. Motor vehicles were borrowed from local governments, but this supply was quickly exhausted, and the French government expected the Americans to supply their own vehi-

Top: Studebaker exported various models to Great Britain with right-hand steering, of which the touring model was common, shown here being driven by a corporal in England circa 1917. *Bottom:* Overland was also involved in exporting right-hand-steer touring cars, which were used by the British. The car is shown here with an officer, his wife, dog and driver.

Top: A British female soldier at the right-side steering wheel of a Studebaker circa 1917. *Bottom:* The standard Locomobile limousine with solid steel wheels was popular among the generals, such as this one photographed in France in 1918.

cles. But the availability of new vehicles back in the States was also limited, so that the used car market was soon plumbed. Major James Castleman was appointed purchasing agent in Paris. He first found cars for sale at Young, Corley and Dolan, a New York machinery export company. By the end of 1917, this company supplied 33 cars to the Quartermaster Department. But the scarcity of available officers' cars forced the purchase of whatever was available at the time. For example, 150 Studebaker four-cylinder motorcars were bought in England to fill the gap at the time. The Studebaker Model Four, which cost around $1,000 each at the time, was altered with right-hand steering for British roads, as were the Overland and Ford Model T.

European and British automakers were also prevailed upon to supply Allied staff cars. The makes included Austin, Daimler, De Dion Boutons, Delaunay-Bellevilles, Fiat, Panhard-Levassor, Singer, Sunbeam, Renault, Rolls-Royce, Vauxhall and Wolseley.

The difficulty of finding and purchasing adequate motor transport for Allied officers is exemplified by a report for the inspector general from Major James Castleman, Quartermaster Corps, of August 7, 1918:

> General Pershing called me on this date and directed me to get him some suitable cars for his use. I called on Gaston, Williams & Wigmore and asked if they could furnish ten Locomobiles in a rush order.... They quoted $9,750.00 each and stated they had no tonnage, that they would have to be brought over on Army transports or some U.S. Army tonnage. That killed their proposition even at that enormous price. I asked Young, Corley & Dolan if they could get me the ten Locomobiles and bring them over on their ships. Mr. Ely said he would try on the same terms, list price $7,000.00 plus freight and insurance. Mr. Ely reported that he had made the effort but had been blocked by Gaston, Williams & Wigmore on the grounds that they were the foreign agents of the Locomobile. As Locomobiles seemed out of the question I asked Mr. Ely if he could get special Marmons and ordered them for the General. They were not available and the order fell down. A few days later the Sales Manager of the Locomobile Company arrived in Paris and I went after him to get them. He made a special factory price and tried to bring them over by express but was blocked and that source fell down. I finally succeeded in landing them four months later through the War Department.

For his efforts Major Castleman was later investigated for irregularities in his transactions, including failure to submit to AEF regulations, overcharging for shipping, and other regulation violations. Despite recommendations from Chief Quartermaster General Rogers, Major Castleman was relieved of duty and his reserve commission was suspended. The firm of Young, Corley and Dolan was banned from doing business with the AEF.

At the same time, on the back cover of the September 1917 *National Geographic*, a full-page ad proclaimed, "The Locomobile is the car built in limited quantities and with such extreme carefulness. A production of only Four Cars a Day—for the exclusive class accustomed to the best and not content with compromise."

General orders were announced September 11, 1917, starting with a classification of all vehicles and directing that they all be painted olive drab with 4-inch ID numbers preceded with the letters US. French shipping crate stencils were adopted for this procedure, which were used only for vehicles of the AEF. But there were so many makes and models on hand by the beginning of 1918 that the Quartermaster Corps, given the situation's alacrity, gave notice to the adjunct general in April of 1918 that only certain vehicle makes would be repaired on a continuing basis. This list was separated into the vehicles stateside (Cadillac, Dodge, Ford and Studebaker) and in Europe (Cadillac, Dodge, Ford and Hudson). Individual agencies and departments would have to repair all other makes themselves.

American motorcars had been exported almost as soon as the war began, and initial assistance for the Allies had been organized through the Red Cross. A statement in the March 1917 issue of *National Geographic* said, "It is a most satisfactory fact that the Red Cross was able to call into the field and send to Europe the first actual help that we have extended to our allies ... (to) relieve the overworked staffs who have been struggling with their problem of caring for the wounded for nearly the last three years."

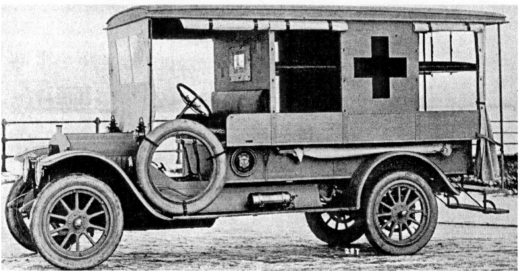

Top: Numerous organizations donated ambulances for shipment to Europe such as this 1916 White with open-slat sides funded by the Mercantile Club of Philadelphia. *Bottom:* This White ambulance, built with lots of fresh air in mind as were many other medical emergency vehicles, was donated to France by the state of Rhode Island.

As stated above, many light trucks and modified passenger cars were shipped as ambulances to Europe beginning in 1915, as with Kissel panel trucks, for example. Following the general pattern, there were many different makes, mostly converted from passenger cars and light trucks. Nearly all the ambulances shipped to Europe before America declared war were donated by civic groups, city governments, companies and other institutions such as the YMCA and American Field Service in addition to the Red Cross. Public subscriptions in Kansas City, the state of Rhode Island and the Mercantile Club of Philadelphia are three examples of the type of non-military humanitarian effort that was organized to help the Allies.

At the time it was somehow determined that fresh air was essential for the wounded soldiers' well-being, so many of the light ambulances of World War I had very basic box-type bodies built with slats, or they were left open-sided. Much of it had to do with the time and expense of building fully enclosed permanent bodies as those used by hospitals. The motorized ambulance became indispensable for transporting casualties back fast enough to make a soldier's recovery more than just a remote possibility. Autocar, Buick, Cadillac, Cunningham, Dodge, Ford, Garford, GMC, Hudson, IHC, King, Oldsmobile, Locomobile, Reo, Service, Stewart, Willys-Overland and White were some of the makes used to build ambulances, even if the companies themselves did not build them in their own factories. For example, a small number of Dodge light trucks were transformed into ambulances and sent to France even though there is no record of the Dodge factory producing such a vehicle on it own, although it did offer the factory screen-side body.

Ambulances were needed in such numbers that ammunition trucks were often used to carry materiel into battle and casualties in the other direction. Mechanical specifications were almost always identical to the civilian and commercial cars and trucks on which the bodies were built. A number of companies in America produced ambulances for shipment to Europe and elsewhere, such as Babcock Company, also a builder of screen-side bodies for Dodge, in addition to their factory screen-side models. Ironically, some of the first British "lorries" used as ambulances were intended to carry two injured horses.

One company that produced purpose-built ambulances was International Harvester (also known as IHC). In 1917 the Model H ambulance was built in limited numbers, but only a few were shipped to France. The exact number shipped overseas is not known, although the total number of Model H's produced has been cited at 2,204 for 1917 and 2,200 for 1918. Existing photographs show an enclosed body with windshield and pneumatic tires being used by the Red Cross. The Model H was powered by a 19.60 hp four-cylinder engine using a three-speed transmission. There was also the 1-ton Model F, which used the same motor.

As with many other makes, the U.S. Army used International (IHC) trucks such as this 1918 model, which appears to be in a military prison yard.

Top: IHC built several traction-engine type tractors such as this 1917 Model 15-30, shown here being used by the Engineer Corps in Vosges, France, photographed in December of 1918. *Bottom:* Another tow tractor manufactured by the IHC was this Titan Model 10-20, photographed at Love Field, Dallas, Texas, in 1918.

Opposite, top: Twin City was also a manufacturer of traction engines used for towing. Here the Model 40 is shown with a portable saw mill used by the 20th Engineer Corps. *Bottom:* Avery Company of Peoria, Illinois, built traction engines for towing, such as this 40–80 hp model used by the U.S. military.

The year 1916 was the last year for highwheelers from IHC, so called for their use of large horse-drawn wagon wheels. The ³/₄-ton Model H was joined by heavier models such as the 1¹/₂-ton Model K and 2-ton Model G. All the IHC trucks were built in Ohio. Each model used the same 201 cid engine but varied in chassis, transmission and wheel configurations. IHC provided large tractors (10–20 and 15–30) for towing, as used by the Engineer Corps. A few Avery, Gray and Twin Cities tractors were also in the mix.

Ernest Hemingway was the most famous casualty of World War I. He drove an ambulance, during which time his legs were severely injured. This plagued him for the rest of his well-known productive life as a writer. According to Hemingway, Gertrude Stein's famous comment about the "lost generation" came out of an incident when Stein herself worked as a volunteer nurse in France and couldn't get a young mechanic to properly fix her Ford Model T ambulance. The quip may have been related to a specific incident, but as is sometimes the case, it found a vastly larger meaning out of context through the medium of the published word.

On the other side, Lance Corporal Adolf Hitler had his own experience slogging through the trenches of World War I, which undoubtedly influenced his thinking in later decades. At Marcoing on September 28, 1918, Private Henry Tandey spared Hitler's life when he noticed Adolf Hitler was slightly wounded, and Tandey, knowing the rules of the Geneva Convention and his own conscience, could not force himself to shoot an at-the-time anonymous injured man. Hitler walked away without further harm and without being taken prisoner.

Cadillac, better known for its luxury automobiles, made a large contribution to the production of vehicles and equipment during World War I. The company was founded in 1902 by Henry Leland, one of the very few American engineers who started more than one large, successful auto company during the previous century. Cadillac and Lincoln were Henry Leland's creations. (Ransom Eli Olds was another such entrepreneur who started both Oldsmobile and Reo. These were only two among many brilliant American automotive engineers whose names are now buried deep in the annals of history.) More to the point, when Cadillac began manufacturing automobiles, no one in the company actually planned to build war materiel or military vehicles.

Founding Cadillac had been a very successful endeavor for Henry Leland and son Wilfred. After years of building precision gears and steam engines, Henry Leland was already fifty-eight years old when he was commissioned by Ransom Eli Olds to build an engine for the curved dash Oldsmobile. Leland had been in business with wealthy lumber magnate Robert C. Faulconer and tool designer Charles H. Norton who left the company earlier. Leland and Faulconer also built marine gasoline engines, so they were hired by Olds for their experience and know-how.

Even though Leland's engine for Olds was over 22 percent more powerful than the existing Oldsmobile engine, it was not accepted due to delays as a result of the disastrous fire at the Olds factory. In 1902 Leland showed the rejected engine to William Murphy and Lemuel W. Bowen, reluctant backers of Henry Ford's racing aspirations, and Cadillac was born, at first as a builder of engines (one-cylinder, copper-jacketed with 10 hp), and also transmissions and steering gears. Cadillac was named after sieur de Antoine de la Mothe Cadillac, the French explorer associated with the founding of Detroit.

The very first Cadillac was a prototype built at the end of 1902 before the company went into production, and it is generally accepted that as a manufacturer, Cadillac's com-

This armored car was built using a 1915 Cadillac chassis and was employed in Calcutta, India, during civil unrest, mostly as a personnel transporter, but it also bristled with light arms weapons.

mencement was in 1903. When salesman William Metzger took the prototype Model A Cadillac to the New York Automobile Show in January of 1903, he took orders for an astounding 2,286 cars before declaring they were "sold out." Of course, they had not even been built yet, but he was fully aware of the manufacturing capacity of the new company. The cars were successfully delivered and the enterprise thrived, using essentially the same one-cylinder motor for three more years. Cadillac was purchased by William Durant of General Motors fame in 1909.

General Motors was now composed of Buick and Cadillac as well as numerous smaller companies that Durant was gobbling up for his automotive empire. Original Cadillac factory archive materials from 1919 show precisely what the company produced between 1915 and 1918.

In addition to high-quality passenger cars, Cadillac's chassis, usually extended and modified, were used to build ambulances, limousines, fire trucks, armored vehicles, police cars and hearses. The fact that Cadillac made an important contribution to the war effort in World War I was proven by the young company's own production of staff cars, light military trucks, as well as tractor power trains, Liberty Engines and other motors, machinery, precision gauges and vital equipment.

The first Cadillac to see action in combat was a passenger car converted into an armored vehicle on a standard chassis. This took place in India after the outbreak of war there in 1914. Intended to quell civil unrest in Calcutta, one of the first armored cars was a modified Cadillac. The vehicle was customized by the local English constabulary.

The Cadillac armored car had two Maxim machine guns and could carry several sol-

Above: This Cadillac open touring appears to be right-hand steer intended for use by a British ser-geant, who gives an idea of the proportions of the vehicle by standing next to it. *Below:* Under license Cadillac built the V-12 Liberty engine for aircraft. At the end of the war this engine was also briefly adopted for the Liberty Mark VIII tank prototype built in the U.S.

The Liberty Engine

diers who also used slit openings for rifle fire. The armor was 5 mm, which added enough weight to keep the vehicle limited to only the hardest of road surfaces available at a time and place where such conditions were unusual. This type of armored vehicle spent most of its life as an armored personnel carrier rather than as a combat assault vehicle.

The Cadillac Company employed approximately 7,000 men and women during 1915–1918 in what Cadillac Company literature referred to as the "Gasoline War," an appropriate nom de guerre among others. The largest contribution in terms of production was Cadillac's output of staff cars for the Allied commanders. All these vehicles were basically Model 57 seven-passenger cars, powered by Cadillac's own V-8 engine, which had been designed by Henry Leland. Cadillac first offered the mass-produced 70 bhp V-8 motor in its cars in 1915, although the V-8 motor was already in existence, such as the one built by Scripps-Booth in 1912 in America, or the Rolls V-8 of 1904 in England.

With very minor modifications from the civilian version, the U.S. military used more than 300 Model 57 Cadillac limousines powered by the Cadillac V-8 designed by Henry Leland, who also founded Lincoln with his son.

Cadillacs outnumbered other automobile makes in military motor pools among the doughboys of the First World War serving on all fronts in France. The company's own literature states "2,095 cars were shipped overseas and 199 to various military posts in the U.S. Two hundred twenty-one were delivered to the Canadian Government." (It is a wonder that the etymology of the term *doughboy*, so often used only in reference to the infantry of World War I, as was the same jargon used in World War II with the term *G.I.*, has never been established. Experts cite everything from the Spanish word *adobe* to *doughnut* so this detail may, and deservedly so, be unsolved.)

Cadillac continues:

War conditions gave rise to many requirements for motor equipment of a nature hitherto unheard of. Although Cadillac seven-passenger cars met the major needs of the army for rapid, dependable passenger car service, a demand was created also for a special type of enclosed car for the use of the officers. The Cadillac Company met this requirement with a limousine body, of standard Cadillac construction and equipped to army specifications, mounted on a standard 125-inch wheelbase Cadillac chassis.

In exterior appearance this limousine, except for its olive-drab finish, resembled the standard car, but the interior was especially adapted to the rough and ready uses of war. It was upholstered in leather instead of mohair velvet, the curtains were canvas instead of taffeta silk, the floor was covered with cocoa mat and the passenger compartment was provided with a desk intended for the use of officers in referring to their maps and charts while traveling from one part of the war zone to another. More than 300 of these special types of enclosed cars were furnished the Government for overseas service.

One was presented as a special gift to General John Pershing at the end of the war. Each part on it was imprinted with a tiny American flag. The car was painted suburban blue with the interior a blue mohair antique to "match the body artistically set off by a gold background; fixtures are of gold; a ladies' vanity case, a gentlemen's smoking set and electric lighter are among the conveniences; five cord tires are part of the equipment."

In France a general's Cadillac limousine was denoted by one or more stars in the windshield depending on rank.

Although the ladies' vanity case was an elegant touch, designers may have forgotten that General Pershing's wife, and all his children but one, died in an accidental house fire at the Army Presidio in San Francisco a few years earlier. (Although *presidio* in Spanish means "prison," as it may have originally been used, the San Francisco Presidio was an entire military camp complete with forts, hospital, housing, warehouses, landing field and other associated facilities at the tip of the Golden Gate peninsula where the bridge by this name was built much later.)

The actual Western Union cablegram (per Cadillac documents) sent from General Pershing to the Cadillac president, Richard H. Collins, reads as follows: "Profoundly touched by delicate sentiment that prompted action. Your employees will advise later regarding disposition of car." Erroneous variations of this telegram have been published. This motor vehicle military gem, in the true sense of the word, has never been found.

It was during World War I that Henry Leland and his son left the company. According to William C. Durant, they were fired due to their differences of personality and overlaps in ambitions. According to the Lelands, they resigned because Durant refused to build the Liberty aero engine. But eventually, Cadillac proceeded into Liberty motor assembly. Meanwhile, the Lelands got a $10,000,000 advance to build the Liberty aero engine and hired some 6,000 employees, but the war ended. The Lincoln Motor Company began building exceptional passenger cars; later in 1922, this large, well-organized firm was acquired by Henry Ford for $8 million after the company went into receivership.

During World War I, the Cadillac Company was one of several to produce the Liberty Aircraft (or aero) engine. According to company literature of the time, "The Liberty Engine was a standardized engine. The complete interchangeability of its parts not only

The 2½-ton military tractor was powered by a Cadillac V-8 motor using dual oil sump so the vehicle could be used in steep terrain, and a magneto was used to withstand a lot of vibration when fairly primitive lead-acid batteries would crumble internally.

facilitated quantity production, but quick repair and overhauling. It was known among the craft as an 'apple tree repair job.' Old 'file to fit' methods of construction gave way to the greater ease and accuracy of the gauge system."

Cadillac also provided V-8 water-cooled engines, transmissions and clutches for the 2½-ton Artillery Tractor. The standard Cadillac V-8 motor was a ninety-degree L-head design with a cast-iron block and an aluminum crankcase with three main bearings and removable cylinder heads. Displacement was 314.5 ci producing SAE 31.25 hp. Company literature of 1919 reads, "The only deviation from the standard Cadillac V-type engine were: a slightly different oil pan and two oil sumps to facilitate lubrication, no matter what position the tractor might get into while under operation; the magneto system was substituted for the battery-generator to withstand the intense vibration caused by rough travel." The engine had under a quarter-inch of armor plating, but other components and the driver were left unprotected.

Searchlight trucks were also built by Cadillac during World War I. The longer 145-inch Cadillac chassis was used along with a specially built General Electric generator, which was mounted between the frame bars and in front of the rear axle. Otherwise, the light truck's power train was standard, except that the modified selective sliding gear transmission could engage the generator. The vehicle had a canvas-covered open cab and a large canvas canopy where the searchlight was carried.

A ramp was used to roll out the searchlight, which was connected by a cable to the

Cadillac built searchlight trucks with an auxiliary chassis on board that held a 60-inch light which could be rolled down a ramp and attached by an electrical umbilical cord. The truck was capable of an outstanding 50 mph for fast escape.

generator. Therefore, the Cadillac served as a light truck used to carry the entire searchlight unit instead of pulling a trailer, giving the vehicle more versatility, especially around airfields. The small four-wheel auxiliary chassis, also built by Cadillac, carried a 60-inch searchlight, which was capable of throwing light for fifteen miles. Most importantly, the searchlight "wagon" could be placed at a distance away from the truck using the long umbilical cord cable, so that, in case of destruction by enemy fire, the motor truck itself and crew could remain intact. The truck and all equipment weighed 8,000 pounds (compared to 4,425 for a standard Model 57 seven-passenger), yet was capable of over 50 mph on good surface.

Cadillac V-8 engines were also used in Britain as the motive power for observation balloon winches. The entire piece of equipment was built as a unit on a flat platform that could be mounted on a truck. Company literature points out,

> In addition to the more important tasks of producing Army motor cars, Liberty Engines and tractor power plants, Cadillac was called upon to produce the following: Three hundred and fifty thousand cartridges for Three Inch Trench Mortar Shells for the Jackson, Church, Wilcox Company of Saginaw, Michigan. Three hundred sixty-three thousand seven hundred ninety-six miscellaneous screws, turn-buckles, and other small parts used in airplane construction for the Aircraft Division of the Fisher Body Corporation, Detroit, Michigan. Three thousand beveled drive gears for use on the Ford Tractor, for the Fordson Company, Dearborn, Michigan.

Many Cadillac employees were sent off for military duty in World War I. Out of a total of 2,693 that were enlisted from Cadillac in the "Great War," 1,206 came from the Cadillac factory (of whom five were killed) and 1,487 from the retail organization across the nation (of whom 28 were killed), according to company documentation.

Company literature also addressed yet another personnel problem:

> One of the most exasperating problems which continually confronted American manufacturers during the war was the insidious work of the pro–German in the shops, and Cadillac naturally had to contend with its share of his evil practices. Men were found putting emery into the machines. One, when notified that his services were no longer needed, threatened to bring "his gang and blow up the factory at seven o'clock that evening." Others tried to influence their fellow employees to "Lay down on the job. There is no credit in it."
>
> There was too much loyalty in the make-up of the Cadillac employees, however, to allow such conditions to exist. Evil practices were discovered and dealt with in the early stages of the war.

Thus Cadillac succeeded in avoiding serious pro–German annoyances which were suffered by various other war industries.

Yet another challenge for the Cadillac Company of World War I was dealing with the Spanish influenza, which killed tens of thousands of people around the world at that time. Cadillac documents state,

When the Spanish Influenza was most prevalent, Cadillac was not without its share of trouble. As many as 130 cases a week developed, hindering production, at a time when efficiency should have been the highest. Early measures of precaution, rigidly enforced, were all that prevented very serious consequences. Men and women in the shops were watched closely, and the minute they showed the first symptoms of the disease were sent home and put under the care of a Cadillac physician, or where it was preferred, the family physician. With the exercise of such extreme precautions, however, but six deaths developed out of approximately 1,700 cases.

In 1919 Cadillac's President and General Manager R. H. Collins wrote,

The Cadillac organization is glad that it was able to contribute something to the strength of the nation and its allies; proud if that contribution was even a step toward victory. It is an honor that Cadillac was called upon to manufacture machines of war, that there were in its employ so many competent, red-blooded loyal men and women able to contribute to industrial requirements of war.

These veterans of the shops were allotted the industrial chores of the war. They remained at home, faithfully performing the various tasks to which they were assigned. There were no fond good-byes, no mothers' blessings nor tears to soften their departure from the every-day pursuits. When the war was won, they wore no *croix de guerre* or other distinguished insignia of valor. They remained clad in the simple uniforms of their craft, content that they had done what they had been required to do.

By 1918 when this photograph was taken, the U.S. Post Office used numerous makes of postal vehicles, including motorcycles, as well as aircraft such as this De Havilland DH4, which took 80 hours to cross the country delivering mail along the way.

Top: Prior to his illustrious career as a racing driver and ace in World War I, Eddie Rickenbacker worked as a chauffeur, shown here driving William Jennings Bryant in 1909. *Bottom:* This photograph of Eddie Rickenbacker and various officers was taken in northern France in 1917 when he was chauffeur for General Pershing.

American industry has been called upon to transform and retool for war on several occasions. Not all companies have been able to return to civilian production in each of those situations, but Cadillac was able to prevail. Another such company was Dodge.

Dodge played a major role in motorizing the U.S. forces during World War I. Once Dodge proved itself in the Punitive Expedition, there was no doubt Dodge Brothers vehicles would be shipped to Europe, especially with the enthusiastic support of General Pershing, who was for a time chauffeured in France by Sgt. Eddie Rickenbacker.

Born Edward Vernon Rickenbacker in Columbus, Ohio, 1890, known as "Eddie," he was famous as a successful race car driver before World War I and proposed to form a flying squadron made up entirely of racing drivers. In May of 1917 he sailed to France as part of the American Expeditionary Forces (AEF). Despite a terrible problem with airsickness, he transferred in March 1918, joining the 94th Aero Pursuit Squadron, the famous "Hat in the Ring" squadron. Two months before the end of the war, Rickenbacker was named commanding officer of the 94th. He had achieved 26 victories, downing 22 aircraft and 4 balloons, and received the title "American Ace of Aces."

Aircraft of all types began to have a huge impact on the war's outcome. Rickenbacker's counterpart ace in the German air force was Baron Manfred von Richthofen, who was known as the "Red Baron." However, unlike Rickenbacker, who went on to a career in auto design and civilian aviation, Richthofen was shot down on April 21, 1918.

Rickenbacker's success before World War I began included racing for Maxwell as well as for Duesenberg. Both companies were to play significant roles as racing was suspended and war production began. Maxwell was involved in the manufacturing of M1917 tanks in the U.S. at the end of the war, discussed further on.

The brothers Fred and Augie Duesenberg, experimenting with internal combustion engine design just after the turn of the century, combined forces in 1913 as the Duesenberg Motor Company. At first their horizontal-valve rocker-arm (walking beam) four-cylinder engine was used in Mason racing cars, and then under the Duesenberg name, with Rickenbacker making a name for himself as well. The brothers incorporated in 1916 with $1,500,000 in venture capital, remaining employees in their own enterprise. Their huge factory in Elizabeth, New Jersey, produced aero engines and artillery tractors under license during the war. It was only after the war that they embarked on building their famous overhead-cam straight-eight that powered the most extravagant cars ever built in America—the Model J Duesenbergs fitted with dazzling custom coachwork on an individual basis.

Compared to many other makes, Dodge was a latecomer in automobile production when the two brothers first offered their own Dodge car in 1914 after having contracted for Henry Ford, producing essential components for the huge Ford company.

John and Horace Dodge, both born in Niles, Michigan, only a few years after the Civil War, followed their father into the machine shop industry. They went into business with an investor named Evans and produced a very modern-looking E&D bicycle at the turn of the century.

In 1901 the two brothers moved to Detroit where they opened their own business as master craftsmen in the machining industry. Auto components became their mainstay within two years, working for Ransom Eli Olds and Henry Leland. They met up with Henry Ford before he founded his company and became allied with him, entirely dropping their association with other auto builders. Their factory in Hamtramck, Michigan,

Prior to building some of the most extravagant cars in America, brothers Fred and Augie Duesenberg designed and built racing cars, some of which were driven by Eddie Rickenbacker, and their engines were used for different applications during World War I, as heralded in this 1918 ad.

Top: Most Dodges used in World War I were light trucks and Open Touring cars, but a few closed sedans such as this 1918 model were used by the American Expeditionary Forces in France. *Bottom:* This photograph taken in 1917 shows the Dodge Open Touring popular with the U.S. military, here being used for Army courier duty.

at that time located outside Detroit, became one of the largest automotive components operations in the world by 1910.

As part owners of the Ford Motor Company, they prospered tremendously, but fell out with Henry Ford by 1914 due to different business philosophies. It was then that they started their own company to produce motor vehicles. Dodge Brothers, Inc. was formed on July 17, 1914, capitalized with $5,000,000, and on November 14, 1914, the first Dodge rolled out of the factory. It was a touring car, which continued in production along with a roadster and sedan, all the models being eventually used by the U.S. military.

Reliability was the key ingredient in the design and production of Dodge vehicles. Early advertising modestly proclaimed, "It speaks for itself." Some records show that 250 Dodge cars were eventually used in the Punitive Expedition against Pancho Villa. The U.S. Army and Dodge formed an ongoing partnership almost from the start. The Dodge name remained prominent in the association of American industrial output and military world leadership by way of an equation in which durability and reliability were the common denominator, not extravagance and opulent stylization.

By the second year of manufacturing, Dodge production was up to 71,400 cars, fourth in line behind Ford, Willys, Overland and Buick. This also led to pressure from thousands of dealerships, and even more customers, wondering when Dodge would offer a light truck or commercial chassis. By February of 1917 the Hamtramck factory fabricated several delivery body light trucks without changing the overall design of the basic Dodge passenger vehicle. In November of 1917 the new Dodge commercial car was offered, and it would later become a series-produced ambulance for the AEF.

The civilian screen-side ¹/₂-ton capacity version, selling at first for $885, would become popular with many businesses, all the way from those delivering light packages to dog catchers. The U.S. government also wanted the new screen-side Dodge light truck and placed an order for 9,350 for the Ordnance Department, Quartermaster Corps and Signal Corps. Within one year, by November of 1918, a total of 2,644 Dodge light trucks were actually delivered to the military. Dodge also provided a closed-panel delivery truck the same size as the screen-side, one being called the Business Car (panel) and the other the Commercial Car. In 1919 the rest of the order was canceled.

At first the Dodge passenger car chassis was used to build light trucks, adopting the same reliable 24 hp four-cylinder motor capable of propelling the vehicle up to 60 mph at a time when trucks traveling at 25 mph were considered normal road speed. What was unusual in the first pilot run in production of the light trucks was that the gas tank was part of the dashboard. Without a body to hide the tank, this may have been a logical decision at first. Other truck builders used this design, but Dodge switched almost immediately, placing the tank behind the driver.

The fact that a leak-proof reservoir was necessary to hold enough energy-density fuel to give the internal combustion engine an adequate supply of hydrocarbons for long-range functioning presented an inconvenient design problem for engineers—how to find an elegant way of hiding the gasoline (petrol) tank somewhere on the vehicle. Other means of propulsion, such as the steam engine with its burner, coal box or fuel tank in addition to the water tank, or the electric vehicle, with its large lead-acid batteries, were equally challenging from an engineering point of view, as well as being a challenge in aesthetics and practicability.

The Dodge company built light repair trucks for the Ordnance Department. The

The U.S. Army used Dodge autos stateside, such as this Open Touring with its top up photographed in 1918 with Army driver and three members of the Women's Radio Corps.

Dodge light truck of 1916 to 1918 had a heavier suspension than that of the passenger car. A third version of the Light Repair Truck had acetylene lamps in addition to the center-mounted swivel spot light and a canvas over the open cab as well as tools and spares.

Bodies built by Budd were used by Dodge, and a "low silhouette" body was adopted for "contact trucks" sent to France as repair trucks, and 1,800 of these ½-ton vehicles were shipped in the first year of direct American involvement. The khaki-colored Dodge cars had assigned serial numbers painted in white using common crude stencils, which became a sort of military vehicle tradition for decades. In addition to vehicle mass production, the Dodge factory produced recoil mechanisms for France's 155 mm artillery. These were actually built at a special facility for the war effort without profit.

The first Dodge trucks were derived directly from passenger cars, including running gear, and after rigorous testing under strict security, production began on October 25, 1917. Within the following year, these trucks were built first in the form of ambulances for the American Expeditionary Forces in Europe, then as screen-side, light cargo, light repair and panel trucks.

The exact number has been disputed, but it is safe to say that at least 12,000 Dodge Brothers vehicles were involved in military use between 1916 and 1918. This includes 7,400 four-cylinder passenger cars with 175 roadsters used for training. Dodges were not completely knocked down (CKD), but rather had their windshields, wheels and fenders removed, and then the entire vehicle was crated for shipment. Photos show each crate then being carried by a separate truck to a central railway station in Michigan; the vehi-

In addition to Open Touring and Sedans, the military also used the Dodge Roadster, such as this example of 1917. Many Dodges remained standard factory black in color, but they could be identified by their seven-bolt Kelsey wheels.

cles would end up floating on a ship across the Atlantic Ocean, hopefully without any acquaintance of German submarine torpedoes.

Although very similar to the passenger car under the sheet metal, the Dodge Brothers truck had a light commercial chassis that was four inches longer than the first 110-inch automobile. The new 114-inch chassis was also standard for Dodge passenger cars by 1917. On the screen-side trucks the screens themselves were easily removable, and roll-down oil cloth was provided for the sides and cab. Some records show that 2,644 of these inline four-cylinder-engine-powered screen-side trucks were delivered. Small detail changes in 1917 at Dodge continued, such as a slight repositioning of the headlights and radiator, and a rear license plate bracket with electric lamp mounting on a crossbar within the spare tire assembly for the civilian market.

The venerable 212 cid Dodge motor produced 35 hp and was coupled through a dry-plate disc clutch to a three-speed selective sliding-gear transmission. Springs were heavier and wheels were larger, but otherwise the chassis was essentially the same, although longer than that of the passenger car. Dodge quickly gained a reputation for ruggedness. The Dodge Light Repair Truck was also built in considerable numbers, and at least 1,012 were known to be delivered. They carried machine shop tools for repairs to machinery, other vehicles and artillery.

For heavier mobile repair shops, specially designed trailers were used and towed by a variety of trucks that were powerful enough for the job. For example, the Second Mobile Ordnance Repair Shop on the Soissons Front repaired and placed into Allied service twenty-eight captured cannon ranging from 77 mm to 210 mm and turned them against the enemy that had left them behind during retreat along with a cache of projectiles.

Another detail of interest on the military iteration of the Dodge trucks was the gasoline tank mounted slightly above and behind the wooden bench seat (for gravity feed to the Stewart carburetor). It was built in two sections with a valve to switch from one side to the other in case the tank was ruptured by gunfire or shrapnel in an obviously fortuitous situation wherein the driver was not hit. The weather curtains were used as cushions on the seat when not in use. In addition to bodies built by Budd, there were also Military Police trucks, and these bodies were built by Hoover of York, Pennsylvania. These had a combination wood frame body with screen sides and were taller with a rounded roof and canopy covering the driver's seat.

Although the civilian and military versions were nearly identical, a few details differentiated the two. One of the visible changes was the use of seven-rim-bolt Kelsey wheels beginning in January of 1917. Any Dodge with the six-bolt Stanweld rim could definitely be dated prior to that. Olive drab paint was used on many vehicles, but, as mentioned, many were first shipped to Europe in standard black from the factory, which was the common civilian color of the day used by Dodge Brothers, Ford and other manufacturers. Special-use vehicles from Dodge Brothers included balloon winch trucks, fire engines, lab trucks and disinfectors. Dodge cars and trucks roared through major battles at Château-Thierry, St. Mihiel, Belleau Wood, Marne, Meuse-Argonne and others.

Dodge produced a total of slightly over 101,000 vehicles in the calendar year 1917 (of which 90,000 were passenger cars) and a total of just over 82,000 for the calendar year 1918. (Also reported as an official year production number was 90,000 for 1917 and 62,000 for 1918. Judging from the "rounded-off" nature of all these quantities, they have been used as "guestimates." In 1917 serial numbers started at 116339 and ended at 217925 without skipping, and in 1918 started at 217926 and ended at 300000 without skipping.)

By the end of the war at least many thousands of Dodges of all types had been delivered to the military, although accurate numbers have never been established and estimates

This 1918 Dodge panel truck had numerous uses. Its seven-bolt Kelsey wheels were once again an indication of a vehicle used by the military.

have gone up as high as 20,000. Numbers vary wildly because there were different military departments in different countries, privately shipped vehicles and vehicles that never left the United States, vehicles lost at sea and vehicles that never left the factory prior to the Treaty of Versailles.

At the end of the war tracked vehicles became the focus of American military engineers, as the strategic effects of tank warfare and the use of Caterpillar tractors proved to be superior in the field over all other methods of off-road mobility. Dodge engaged in an experiment at Aberdeen Proving Ground in 1918 using a six-wheel truck with an extra pair of wheels (also called bogie wheels) that were mounted on a spring-suspended, non-driving axle. This axle was held by radius rods attached to the rear axle housing. Several different flexible tracks were then attached to the two pairs of in-line wheels, creating what has been called a "half-track." The military evaluators stated, "This machine can not be considered in any sense of the word as replacing a tractor; it is merely a means of leaving the road for short distances."

The experiment brought to light the idea of developing new motor vehicle designs as an outcome of World War I. Nearly every form of military vehicle that was invented by 1918 would continue to be used and improved in the "crucible" of this war. During the sudden upsurge in production in 1917 and 1918, a number of variations were incorporated into Dodge touring, roadsters and sedans and $1/2$-ton and $3/4$-ton trucks; ignition systems were from Delco as well as North East, black-painted and nickel-plated headlight rims were both used depending on shortages, and speedometer manufacturers were interchanged and some had kilometers marked on them for European roads. Both Eisenmann and Simms magnetos were used, depending on availability. On March 28, 1918, the factory began using a "duck" type of material for the tops, which differed from the lighter canvas, but by the end of the year Dodge returned to the smoother original material. Mud guards differed or were absent. There were slight variations in upholstery. Optional equipment such as Motometers and spotlights added even more to the variations.

All these minor changes usually overlapped in time. In the final analysis by the Military Vehicle Preservation Association (MVPA), because of the rush to fill orders for the military and civilian population simultaneously, precise production numbers for various makes, let alone variations in details, may never have an exact accounting, as long as the overall picture is clear in the context of history.

Chapter IV

SLOGGING THOUGH
MUD AND SMOKE

American motor vehicles had never been used in military operations in any large numbers (except in the Punitive Expedition of 1916–1917), and the industry was in its infancy with thousands of companies (counting parts suppliers) vying for a portion of the new, lucrative market. No standard procurement policy had been adopted by the United States War Department before the chase of Pancho Villa. The recommendations of the Quartermaster Corps from the experience of the Mexican campaign had little influence if any at all. The Ordnance Corps, Signal Corps, Engineer Corps and Medical Department, among others, proceeded with purchases of motor vehicles from an available long list of companies that were building a finished product at the time, and there were hundreds.

With numerous vehicle builders to chose from, each department selected and purchased vehicles for their staff cars as they wished. The Signal Corps, with the inception of the Air Service, had a preference for Hudson and Paige. The largest Hudson was the 7PS, which was based on the Super-Six in-line motor providing 29.4 hp. These were specially built as staff cars, ambulances and personnel carriers.

Ford was popular with the Medical department and provided light ambulances and touring cars, discussed further on. Elsewhere in the military, there were numerous specialized trucks in the form of motorized kitchens, laundries, dental labs, shoemakers' and horse-shoers' shops, generator plants and various types of machine shops. Whatever it would take to keep hundreds of thousand of soldiers mobilized began gradually to be associated with motorized vehicles as they intermixed with horse-drawn conveyances.

The following list from the Society of Automotive Historians (SAH) gives an idea of the complexity of motorizing the American Expeditionary Force (AEF) and other Allied armies in Europe. This is a partial list of makes of American motorcars used by the U.S.: Briscoe, Buick, Cadillac, Chalmers, Chandler, Cole, Dodge, Dorris, Dort, Ford, Hudson, Hupmobile, Lexington, Locomobile, Marmon, McFarlan, National, Packard, Paige, Pierce-Arrow, Reo, Studebaker, White and Winton. The military was buying anything that fit the bill when it came to cars for officers, for couriers, and other personnel and for handling the administration of a huge military force.

For example, a handful of National limousines were used in France. These were exotic cars powered by a V-12 engine in 1918, but not the only make to have such an engine. Another example was the rare Cole Model 860G powered by a V-8 motor similar to that of Cadillac. Packard advertised its Twin-Six, which was a V-12, and there were many other

Top: Although many historians have played down the role of armored cars used in combat during the Great War, they were involved in heavy action, as this photograph attests from Chavonne in April of 1917. *Bottom:* Hudson Open Touring cars were also used as staff cars in Europe and were popular with several branches of the military.

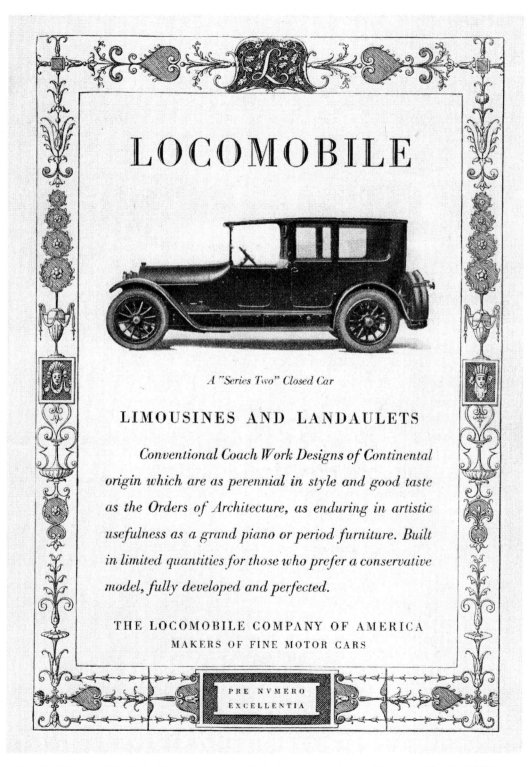

Standard Locomobile limousines were some of the most expensive staff cars used by the AEF in France, bringing charges of extravagance by the French Parliament.

Top: Locomobile open touring cars were also used in Europe as staff cars by the high-ranking officers of the AEF. *Bottom:* During the World War I era there were a number of expensive automobiles, some of which were used as staff cars, such as this 1918 Marmon open touring Model 34.

examples of engines of larger size at the time: the Briscoe Ferro V-8, the 45 bhp Buick ohv six, the Chalmers in-line six, the Dorris 80 hp six, the Hudson 76 hp Super-Six, the Lexington Thoroughbred Six, the powerful T-head Locomobile in-line six, the advanced Model 48 Marmon ohv six of 1916, the Teetor-Hartley six for McFarlan of 1916, the six-cylinder Paige whose advertising boasted "The Most Beautiful Car in America," the ultra-quiet Dual Valve Six from Pierce-Arrow, the new 45 hp six at Reo in 1916, the durable

Top: National was one of only a few companies that built a V-12 during World War I, and this ad shows both civilians and an officer in context of the year 1918. *Bottom:* One of the longest surviving makes of the best American manufacturers was Packard. This 1918 limousine was used in very small numbers by the AEF, and Packard eventually succumbed to market stresses after other high-quality American manufacturers were devastated during the Great Depression.

"The Most Beautiful Car in America" was an extravagant claim in 1917, and the AEF used only one such Open Touring Paige in France.

Studebaker 54 hp L-head six, the 16-valve four-cylinder at White, and the Winton six. At the Winton Company, much production was shifted over to military equipment in 1917, which helped the company financially but was not always the case for other automakers. This brief listing of motors illustrates the increasing popularity of larger, more powerful engines, which marketing departments eagerly presented to the public among the average four-cylinder motor. Very few motor vehicle manufacturers still used two-cylinder or three-cylinder motors (cyclecars were one exception, two-cycle three-cylinder motors at Chase for the latter), and the ostentation of the V-16 was not to arrive for nearly another two decades (such as the Cadillac of 1934).

At the time, the multitude of automobile and truck manufacturers competed for the attention of the buyers in a variety of ways. Prices ranged at a ratio of 10 to 1. By 1914 there was the reliable although plebeian Ford Model T for $500, up to $5,000 for a standard Pierce-Arrow. A special limousine could reach $10,000. Other more moderately priced cars such as the Chalmers included the latest factory gadgetry, such as the dynamometer. Rather than simply using test drivers on a track, whose driving techniques and approach to evaluation could vary considerably from person to person, the electric dynamometer provided a scientific approach. Company advertising explained to the average motorist whose budget was around $2,000, "Great chains are fastened to the rear wheels and to giant dynamos. Running under their own power, the motors work against electrical resistance. Accurate instruments measure the horsepower developed by the

As with other auto manufacturers during World War I, Paige advertising tried to create a subtle mix of civilian and military images, such as in this ad in 1918.

motors. Expert mechanics judge the fitness of every working part for long road service." Eventually, the use of dynamometers became an industry standard.

One-third of the marques used by the AEF officers were represented by fewer than four individual vehicles each, but they were a cross-section of what was available on the American market. Postwar records show that out of about 9,500 passenger cars used by the AEF (makes specifically cited above), 722 of these were limousines, bringing accusations of extravagance from the French Parliament. For example, General Pershing rode in a Locomobile Model 48 in France and eventually ordered nineteen Locomobiles at $7,000–$9,000 each. A special Locomobile limousine was also built for him.

A few Packard limousines were also purchased at similar prices. Such opulence was justified as a need for military prestige and show of leadership. It was pointed out that the large vehicles were less susceptible to gunfire, explosives and disrepair. Even Lawrence of

Major General Andre Brewster used this Series 48 Winton Limousine, which cost half the price of a Locomobile Limousine. This photograph of Brewster was taken in France in 1918.

Arabia arrived in distant Damascus chauffeured in a Rolls-Royce while Ford Model T's brought in Allied soldiers. Model T Patrol Cars were used quite extensively not only in France but also in Mesopotamia, Egypt and Libya.

Army Chief of Staff General Peyton March rode in a Locomobile, as did other generals with two stars or more. Major General Andre Brewster used a Series 48 Winton limousine according to photographs. The elegant Winton cost half as much as the Locomobile. At the time, individual reputation among officers was intertwined with the complexity of opposites in modesty and flamboyance, while reinforcing the discretion of individual choice.

In response to a directive from General Pershing, these officers' cars were fitted with steel disc wheels in lieu of the standard wood spoke type. The Locomobile Special Overseas Limousine, a later development at the end of 1918, also had steel disc wheels, but its entire custom body was narrower for "better aerodynamics" along with a V-shape windshield. It was powered by a T-head six-cylinder motor producing 48.6 hp and rode on a 142-inch wheelbase. General Pershing traveled frequently between his headquarters at Chaumont, various field commands and government offices in Paris using two limousines in case of tire or mechanical failure, and perhaps to thwart an attack.

Major James Castleman, who was placed in charge of purchasing vehicles, ordered 129 sedans and limousines on September 27, 1917. Within the next month an additional

Top: Using some of General Pershing's own design suggestions, Locomobile built this "Overseas Limousine" using solid metal wheels and simpler, heavier sheet metal. *Bottom:* General Pershing with driver and an officer are seen here with one of his Locomobile "Overseas Limousines," which used a narrower body and V-windshield for better aerodynamics and protection. Accusations of opulence were dismissed by the claim for a need of military prestige and show of leadership.

369 such cars were ordered. The first cars were Winton, Dorris, National and Cole sedans and limousines.

On the other hand, Ford supplied large quantities of smaller vehicles for the war effort. Prior to the Punitive Expedition in 1916, twenty-six out of the seventy-three passenger staff cars owned by the U.S. Army were Ford Model T's, the first five being purchased by the Army in 1913. Three years later the Army owned 26 Model T's, primarily because of their low price. They were also easy to drive due to the simplicity of operating the two-speed planetary transmission, which was shifted by pedal, as opposed to other cars that had unsynchronized three-speed (and a few four-speed) selective sliding-gear transmissions. Those required more instruction and training for a new driver at a time when operating a motor vehicle was entirely foreign to most people and quite complicated for everyone on the best of days. Both Model T and 1-ton Model T Fords at this time were powered by a 20 hp 176.7 cid L-head four-cylinder motor using a thermo-syphoning cooling system. Simplicity was the main theme.

Irrespective of Henry Ford's Peace Commission, Peace Ship, and reluctance to send materiel, before the Armistice in 1918 Ford had delivered 5,379 touring cars, 175 roadsters and 16 closed cars to the U.S. Army, according to company records. This should be contrasted to the number of Ford cars actually ordered, which totaled over 20,650 before the Armistice was signed. A fifteen percent discount was given to the military by the Ford Motor Company, which resulted in a "break-even" policy per vehicle. The French government also bought 8,000 touring staff cars and 500 ambulances from Ford. Numerous Ford Model T Patrol Cars armed with Lewis guns were used across the Middle East and in North Africa.

It should be noted that various sources cited varying numbers of vehicles by the end of the war, differing in that many of the cars and trucks were scrapped or sold as surplus before the Treaty of Versailles was signed in 1919. Also, procurement orders were kept secret until February 1918 when they were mandated to be published by the Secretary of War.

Beginning in 1919 when an official accounting was made, passenger cars in the use of the AEF totaled 8,947 American-built open and closed units by April of that year. Another ten percent of this number was represented by European makes. Cadillac, Dodge and Ford topped the list with a combined number of 5,948 in the European theater of war alone.

As the war became increasingly international in scope, Ford Model T's were used as light patrol cars in the North African desert by the Duke of Westminster Armored Car Squadron against the German-backed Senussi, who were moving toward Egypt from Libya. The light Model T's equipped with machine guns were often more effective in the desert sand than heavier autos and armored cars and became a celebrated component in rescuing captured British seamen 120 miles behind enemy lines at the beginning of 1917.

In the Gaza battles of February 1917, Model T Fords were again used in combat. In certain types of terrain and off-road conditions "light and quick" was by far the superior motor vehicle to have, and this was reflected ever afterwards in light military vehicle development.

Opposite, top: **This photograph taken in Jebel Hamrin, Mesopotamia, in 1917 shows the effectiveness of the Ford Model T in the desert. This column of Model T's carrying British forces could maneuver across soft sand without getting mired as heavier vehicles often did.** *Bottom:* **As Arab soldiers ride horses in the opposite direction, British forces enter Damascus with Ford Model T cars in 1918.**

Top: World War I spanned the globe, as illustrated by this photograph of a White truck bringing vital supplies into Jerusalem in 1918. *Bottom:* The war reached as far away as French Indo-China. This photograph shows Chinese drivers of a column of American White trucks under the command of French officers in 1918.

Six Ford Model T's with Lewis machine guns were involved in battles of the Arab Revolt pitting Lawrence of Arabia's men against the Turks. The successful use in desert conditions led to the Ford Model T to be used again, and 300 of these were brought in to support two partial battalions of infantry with 32 Lewis gun cars and 150 soldiers transported in 50 Model T's. When Damascus fell to the Allies, the British were driving mostly Ford Model T's, among other makes.

In addition, Ford also provided 5,745 ambulances and 5,492 light trucks, the latter of which were based on the Model T but were expanded and reinforced and were first factory-produced in 1917 (as opposed to numerous after-market conversions from various manufacturers available in previous years). A factory Ford TT truck had a much stronger chassis than the other T models, with 24-inch longer wheelbase, stiffer suspension and artillery-type wheels with solid rubber tires. Similar to some of the after-market conversions sold up until then, it used a rugged worm-gear rear axle. Ford also donated 943 vehicles to the Red Cross along with $500,000, as mentioned previously.

Henry Ford and Son incorporated on July 27, 1917, the same day as production of the first 1-ton truck began, just six weeks before Henry Ford II was born. This was the first time Ford began producing trucks, not just chassis for after-market bodies or for conversions. Ford cars and trucks of 1917 could be easily distinguished by their painted radiators due to a wartime brass shortage and corresponding frugality in later years.

The Ford tractor project had begun in 1907 as the Automobile Plow, and at least a dozen prototypes were finished by 1915. Ford spent his own money in 1916 developing the Fordson tractor to avoid interference from the company stockholders. The first Fordson mass-produced tractor rolled off the assembly line on October 8, 1917.

Although originally intended for American farmers, the first series were shipped to England with the plan to help alleviate food shortages resulting from major losses in shipping due to very effective German submarine warfare. Henry Ford wanted to ensure a steady supply of tractors and acquired land at Cork County in Ireland, his ancestral home region. However, before the factory was completed, the war ended. A little over 7,000 Fordson tractors were brought to Great Britain by ship during the war. A few were converted experimentally for towing artillery, for which they were not intended or well suited. In 1918, 34,167 Fordsons were assembled and 41,725 one-ton trucks were built.

Ford also built Eagle Boats for chasing submarines as well as howitzers, helmets, field kitchens, caissons, gas masks and listening devices, the latter being used in tunneling work

Of the hundreds of motor vehicles donated to the Red Cross, the most prevalent was the ambulance built on the new 1-ton Ford chassis introduced in 1917.

In Great Britain, the American Red Cross used Harley-Davidson motorcycles with sidecars, which were mounted on the left side for left-hand road traffic. Shown here are the "Flying Squadron" in 1918, priding themselves on being able to get "under way" within three minutes of the time a call for help is received.

among the endless trenches. In 1916 more than 500,000 Ford motor vehicles were built, and in April of 1917 the 2-millionth Ford Model T rolled off the line. Ford would end up providing 39,000 vehicles from American, Canadian and British factories for the war effort. September 4, 1917, was the day of the birth of Edsel Ford, who, as a brilliant designer, would develop much of the finest styling, especially in Lincoln motorcars of the 1930s. It may be said he was perhaps overshadowed by his father, but Edsel's own name would later be on an automobile, albeit not one with which he may have wanted to be associated.

During World War I Ford was also developing two small tanks. One was a two-man 3-ton tank powered by two Model T engines, each with its own electric starter. Both tank designs used Ford planetary transmissions. The two-motor tank was steered by using different gear ratios in the two transmissions for the two motors and varying foot brake pres-

Top: The first production Fordson tractor was built on July 12, 1917; two weeks later, Henry Ford and Son was incorporated after a decade of development. *Bottom:* Henry Ford, at lower far right, and his engineering team, in front of the first Fordson tractor shipped to England in October of 1917, addressed to the Ministry of Munitions as opposed to farmers to whom Ford originally wanted to send his new machines.

The Ford Model T was so common and versatile that several light armored cars were built using its chassis. This later version was fabricated for the Royal Air Services.

sure. Both motors produced 45 hp, and by disengaging one of them, an about-face 360-degree turn was made, but driving this vehicle required much training. Capable of 10 mph, it had a very cramped design with the only view for the gunner being through the muzzle of the gun. The other tank was a 3-man version powered by the Ford tractor engine, and only one prototype was ever built. The 3-ton tank carried a 75 mm howitzer or a machine gun. Out of 15,000 ordered by General Headquarters in France after testing there, only 15 were delivered before the Armistice.

In regard to driver training, not only were fresh-faced soldiers expected to be able to operate a variety of planetary as well as sliding-gear transmissions, which were yet to be known for many years as "synchronized or unsynchronized gearboxes," but vehicles, especially trucks, were still built as left-hand and right-hand drive, whether or not they were of English or European/American build. Consequently, drivers had to be "ambidextrous" in addition to knowing much about hand-cranking to start a vehicle; controlling the spark advance, hand and foot fuel control, and manual chokes; and handling the steering of autos, trucks and armored cars with solid or pneumatic tires. Drivers also had to learn various aspects of maintaining and keeping a primitive motor vehicle running. These skills, perhaps lost even to today's professional driver, required much stamina to perform.

Top: In 1918 Ford built a two-man tank powered by two Model T engines that were electrically started. *Bottom:* The military ordered 15,000 two-man tanks, but only 15 were delivered before the order was canceled by the time of the Armistice.

Top: Another version of the truly American-made Ford two-man tank with different armament. By controlling the two 45 hp Model T motors separately, the tank was capable of a 360-degree turn and top speed was 8 to 10 mph, twice that of the Renault FT-17. *Bottom:* A prototype of the Ford 3-ton tank had a fixed armored machine gun tube and could be used as a light tow tractor or radio and reconnaissance vehicle.

Chevrolet as a make (as famous as it is today) was fairly insignificant in World War I, because for the calendar year 1918, the first year of manufacture for Chevrolet trucks, production only amounted to 879 units. GMC trucks, having evolved from the acquisition of the Rapid and Reliance companies before World War I, produced the Model 15 and Model 16 (1/2-ton and 3/4-ton, respectively), the latter as an ambulance beginning in 1917.

Over 5,000 GMC ambulances were used by the U.S. Army. The Model 15 was powered by a 19.6 hp four-cylinder L-head Continental engine using a three-speed sliding gear transmission, shaft drive and bevel gear rear axle. The Model 16 had a slightly larger motor with 22.50 hp. Also in 1917, GMC built the 1-ton Model 21 and 2-ton Model 23 with the same motor, but production was fewer than 500 of each. With the GMC nameplate first appearing in 1912, the make went through a major transition in 1915 when it abandoned its electric trucks of which there had been seven models.

It would be negligent to overlook the spectacular and soaring development of General Motors, considering its production capacities by World War I, as well as the founder's "larger than life" career and rather tragic biography. Unlike the names of other famous American automotive companies such as Buick, Chrysler, Ford, Dodge, Mack and numerous others, named after their founders, the name William Crapo Durant is rather obscure if not totally unknown to many people today. Yet he organized the largest (at one time) vehicle-manufacturing company in the world (along with other products and goods production), also started Chevrolet and later created Durant Motors, which built automobiles under his own name, as well as the Star, the Flint and light trucks named Rugby, the latter mostly for export.

Durant was a born salesman and dealmaker known for his wild gambles, especially in business ventures. As with other gentlemen gamblers, he won big-time, but his losses were also huge, including bets in the stock market.

Born in 1861 in Boston, just two years before Henry Ford, Billy Durant, as he was known, dropped out of high school and began working at a lumberyard near Flint, Michigan. Besides being located propitiously, Durant had a grandfather who had been a state senator and governor of Michigan. Perhaps it was this background that gave Durant the type of self-confidence all salesmen require or wish they had. Billy Durant tried his hand at selling groceries, lumber, cigars, real estate, insurance and even patent medicine (or "snake oil" as it was called).

One day in 1886 he accepted a ride in a horse and buggy and was very impressed with its unusual features. In the following days he and his friend, J. Dallas Dort, bought the Flint Road Cart Company along with its patented spring suspension for the total sum of $2,000. The name was soon changed to the Durant-Dort Carriage Company, and it became one of the largest horse-drawn-wagon companies in America. The Durant-Dort Company was built up from a relatively small investment into a $2,000,000 company by 1906.

Remarkably, Durant at first detested motor vehicles, but when presented with a good business opportunity he did not hesitate to buy into the ailing Buick Motor Company in David Dunbar Buick, having made a fortune as an inventor of the method of applying porcelain to iron, primarily for bathroom fixtures and bathtubs, sold his successful plumbing enterprise and began building gasoline engines using an innovative valve-in-head design. Despite its superior design and performance, the engine did not make Buick money. When Durant showed a Buick motorcar prototype at the New York Automobile Show in 1905, he received 1,108 orders. Within several months the two-cylinder 22 hp Buick Model C was delivered to each of its new customers, and by 1906 production was up to 1,400 cars. The company also began building light trucks and buses in Flint, Michigan. By 1907 production had more than tripled to 4,641 vehicles for the year.

Durant's dizzying success was accompanied by his taking new risks. He acquired various companies to expand his empire while making it more self-sufficient instead of rely-

Three years after the company was started by David Dunlap Buick, jitney buses were built in small numbers such as this one photographed in 1906 in Jackson, Michigan.

ing on independent suppliers. He bought companies that produced axles, wheels, sheet metal, paint and other components, allowing each firm to stay semi-autonomous.

Durant envisioned a "consolidation" in which he would have control of a multitude of associated companies. He was a restless bargainer who was driven by the power of acquisition. In 1908 without any fanfare, he had articles of incorporation drawn up using the name General Motors. Capital stock was listed at only $2,000, and the names of the incorporators were unfamiliar so as not to draw attention. Twelve days later, with a minimum of public announcements and working behind his puppet group of company leaders, the capital was increased to $1,250,000.

According to Durant, General Motors was a holding company, which immediately bought out Buick for $3,750,000 using a variety of deal options. Durant was in control of both Buick and GM, so the transaction was entirely in his hands. He soon bought Olds Motor Works and Cadillac Motor Company. All three of these companies built both passenger and commercial vehicles at the beginning, but the preponderance of GM vehicles that were shipped to Europe for the war effort were GM and Buick ambulances and Cadillac staff cars.

It has been noted that Durant wanted to be at the top of the motor-vehicle industry, but in reality he did not know the market or about the design and inner workings of cars and trucks. What he did was to gamble on various companies, knowing that some of them would become important pieces of the puzzle he was arranging.

Opposite, top: **Until this previously unpublished photograph proved it a century later, it was uncertain that Buick produced trucks as early as 1906, such as this flatbed.** *Bottom:* **The 1906 Cadillac Osceola, named after a Wisconsin Indian tribe, proved the idea of a fully enclosed motor car.**

Even though the Buick motor was an excellent design, the company was failing in 1904 when Billy Durant bought it as part of his empire called General Motors. This C-cab van was from 1906.

For some journalists of the era it would appear that GM functioned on pure magic. In reality, a number of people held the giant enterprise together, as scattered as it was. Durant was very adept at delegating authority, and he surrounded himself with very capable, experienced people. It was men such as Meyer Prentis, treasurer of GM in the early years, who kept a wise rein on Durant's penchant for new acquisitions and who could consolidate the monthly operation statements of the various divisions and subsidiaries.

By the end of 1909 Durant had purchased or obtained controlling interest in such companies as Buick, Olds, Cadillac, W.F. Stewart Factory, Cartercar, Seagar Motor Works, Oakland Motor Company (which became Pontiac), Michigan Motor Castings Company, and Randolph Truck Company, plus smaller machine shops and component producers around Flint with whom he was familiar from the days of carriage-making. Durant's risk-taking investments were based on the clever intuition with which he was well endowed, and investing heavily in the automotive industry at this early stage has been called a stroke of genius.

Enticing young men to join the military sometimes included popularizing songs, such as "Come On Papa." In part, the lyrics went, "Sweet Marie, in gay Paree, Had a motor car, It filled her heart with joy, To drive a Yankee boy; On the sly, she'd wink her eye, If one came her way, she'd stop her motor car, and then she'd say, Come on Papa, hop in ze motor car."

General Motors produced many vehicles for the war effort, but this crawler was only a one-off tank prototype, designed by Walter Marr.

At one point Billy Durant negotiated to buy out Henry Ford, but Ford was simply asking for too much cash, considering that his challenge to the Selden patent legal case was still brewing in court and bubbling in the press, and the Ford Model T was only then beginning to roll from the factory floor.

As a business negotiator, Durant made swift decisions involving enormous amounts of cash. Even though this approach would eventually make GM a powerhouse, Durant was making deals that were considered brash and reckless, and the cash to continue day-to-day operations dwindled. Suddenly, GM was on the verge of collapse, nearing the point that employees and vendors would not be paid. In September of 1910 New York bank moguls took over GM, and Durant was moved aside from direct financial control.

Durant saw the importance of expanding into the commercial vehicle and truck market, and he had already set up purchases by 1911 of Rapid Motor Vehicle Company (formed by the Grabowsky family, a pioneering truck builder located in Detroit) as well as the Reliance Motor Car Company of Owosso, Michigan. Both companies had been building reliable trucks for several years, and for a brief period after these two acquisitions, the Rapid, Reliance and GMC nameplates were used interchangeably on the trucks that were sold, with GMC eventually eclipsing the other names altogether, as may be surmised.

It was at this point that Durant, although remaining as vice president of GM, lost financial and strategic control of the company. It was stated in the press that Durant's gambling "methodology" had so shaken up the loan institutions that he was forced to be pulled away from the automotive "roulette table" for the company's own good and the stability of the banks themselves. At the same time, GM began building a series of battery-pow-

Trucks for Every Haulage Purpose

Electric powered between 1912 and 1915, GMC trucks were switched to gasoline power when Billy Durant's Chevrolet Company acquired GM. The press likened this acquisition to "Jonah swallowing the whale."

ered electric trucks through the end of 1915, but there is no evidence that these short-range, slow vehicles were used in the war in Europe. Many were used highly effectively as city maintenance vehicles, especially on the East Coast.

Nevertheless, Durant would not be dissuaded from resorting to his old habits and business formulas. He surreptitiously hired the famous, then retired, race car driver Louis Chevrolet to build a prototype using the Chevrolet name. The Chevrolet Company was quietly incorporated in 1911, with Durant holding all the cards, but once again installing himself as vice president even though he had complete control of the company, including ownership of the Chevrolet name.

At the same time, still skulking in the shadows at GM, Durant began taking over new companies such as the Little Motor Company and the Mason Motor Company, both in Flint, and the Republic Motor Company, which took up an entire block in New York City as an auxiliary factory.

Meanwhile, the creation of the Chevrolet "French-type" car, which was to be light and inexpensive, with help from French engineers including the renown Etienne Planche, was not progressing in the direction that Durant had envisioned. Louis Chevrolet had created a large prototype, called "ungainly" by more than one automotive journalist of the day, and Durant quickly parted ways with the famous racer. The press inserted a few personal jousts, such as Louis Chevrolet's perpetual cigarette addiction, which Durant apparently detested, but the bottom line was that Durant now owned the Chevrolet name, which continued without the man himself and along with considerable bitterness over the matter.

Using the Chevrolet Company to buy out important small companies, Durant soon had control of Imperial Wheel and formed Sterling Motor in 1912. Secretly, with the help of his colleague Pierre du Pont, Durant bought out GM stock. By this stealth business manner through the Chevrolet Company he quietly and gradually acquired General Motors by September of 1915. Using bluffing tactics and playing "close to the vest," Durant became the owner of General Motors. Charles Nash resigned as president of GM in June of 1916 (going on to buy the Jeffery Company), and Durant installed himself as president of General Motors. The press called it "Jonah swallowing the whale."

Walter Chrysler became president of Buick, with David Dunbar Buick long gone and truly struggling even after being a successful inventor and designer. GM moved forward with more risk-taking acquisitions. As might be predicted, not all gambles paid off in such a new, competitive and perhaps cut-throat industry. Durant gambled on the Sieve-Grip Tractor Company in Stockton, California. His plan was to get GM into the farm tractor manufacturing business to give Ford (Fordson) a run for his money. Even though the "sieve-grip" wheel idea was entirely functional and rather a clever idea, GM could not produce a tractor at a profit. The Iron Horse, a tractor steered with leather reins, was a disaster, both as an engineering concept and as a financial venture. Yet the purchase of the Fisher Body Company, which eventually became the preeminent mass producer of motor-car bodies, was a lucky deal indeed. Fisher remained GM's subsidiary responsible for all GM sheet metal for decades.

Chevrolet's light truck production expanded rapidly, but the anticipation of the war's end was miscalculated dramatically, as so many wars' durations are, even within the best circles and minds of military and industrial leaders. In 1919 Chevrolet truck production output shot up to 7,300 for that year alone. It was too late for the war effort.

The aggressive "take-all-or-nothing" approach Billy Durant was possessed by, in a manner of speaking, worked on a wild thermometer-type scale that left little stability for the company, its employees or stockholders. According to Alfred P. Sloan, president of GM just a few years later and a man who was perhaps notorious for his steady hand and even keel in business practices, sales had gone from $58,000,000 in 1915 to $452,000,000 by the end of the war. But the war was over.

Walter Chrysler left GM to start his own company, not able to cope with Durant's business schemes, and in the major post-war recession of 1920 Durant lost $90,000,000 in stock investments, $12,000,000 of his personal money, which represented his own financial aggressiveness and acumen that had been based on stock market gambles. The banks that held together GM's immense industrial complex were not sympathetic and ousted Durant entirely. The great William Crapo Durant was simply shown out the door.

Although this part of Durant's biography follows World War I quite far past the timeline of the history being discussed here, it must be noted that Durant founded yet another automotive empire under his own name, with factories in Lansing, Michigan; Long Island, New York; Muncie, Indiana; and Oakland, California. But he was spending much time in Europe vacationing with his young, second wife, and did not watch closely enough to see that Durant Motors was continuing to plummet financially.

The stock-market crash of 1929 took Durant and Durant Motors down like a house in a mudslide. He lost $40,000,000 within three years. In 1933 Durant Motors was liq-

Top: The Chevrolet Tourer of 1917 was powered by a V-8, but the company stuck with an overhead-valve four-cylinder motor for the next decade as Billy Durant started another company using his own name. *Bottom:* General Motors built several thousand 1-ton ambulances, such as this one shown in what appears to be a posed photograph.

uidated. He was forced to sell everything, even his personal belongings, including his wife's company stock, jewelry, furs, et cetera. He filed for bankruptcy in 1936, stating he had $914,000 in debts and $250 in assets. For the next ten years when he was in his seventies and eighties, without any retirement funds, he worked at a bowling alley renting shoes and flipping hamburgers, talking of starting a bowling empire. He died the same year as Henry Ford, in 1947.

Durant's loyal friend, who had remained in the carriage business for another decade, Josiah Dallas Dort, eventually started his own auto manufacturing enterprise called the Dort Motor Car Company, which produced its first vehicle in the form of a touring model designed largely by Etienne Planche. He was the engineer who had helped Louis Chevrolet build his first car, deemed unacceptable by Billy Durant. The first obstacle the new

After Henry Ford teamed up with Josiah Dallas Dort, the two parted ways and Dort started his own company. Here, soldiers assemble a Dort vehicle circa 1917 as part of their training to become Army mechanics.

Dort company faced was a lawsuit from the Dart Motor Truck Company, which claimed name infringement, the names being obviously similar but easily distinguishable to the average literate pedestrian. The case was thrown out of court in 1917, in part upon the basis that Dort did not manufacture trucks (until 1921).

In terms of Dort's involvement in World War I it must be mentioned that the U.S. Army as well as automotive mechanic schools sometimes used Dort cars for training purposes, and existing photos show such activity. One of the biggest challenges at the time was to find enough competent mechanics, and schools for the trade opened across the Midwest, East Coast and elsewhere. Even as far as Kansas City, Missouri, "The Million Dollar" Sweeney Automobile & Tractor School offered numerous classes and training programs. Their elaborate 72-page booklet of 1918 listed the available training in automotive departments, including: "parts assembly, forging and tool making, vulcanizing, oxy-acetylene welding, brazing, machine shop, piston ring fitting, valve grinding, soldering, babbitting, valve timing, motor block, experimental room, electric starting, lighting, battery, magneto, bodywork model repair, heavy trucks, farm lighting, stationary engines, heating and power plant department and gasoline tractors." There was also a description of an employment department, salesmanship department, business management studies, student social life activity, dormitories and alumni interaction. This particular list from the brochure printed by Charles E. Brown well intimates the complexity of the motor vehicle and the need for numerous specialists, both in the United States and abroad.

By the second decade of the 20th century, the motorcar was already a machine of considerable assembly requiring numerous skills, many not even listed in the Sweeney School prospectus. As a result, the one overwhelming social change in many countries, not just in the United States, was the rather sudden need and introduction of women into the workforce at factories of all types. This also prompted the training of many female auto mechanics, as men went off to war.

One good example of this type of traditional role switching took place at FWD in Clintonville, Wisconsin. Clintonville, which was not a large city in the first decades of the 20th century, was in great need of new employees to fulfill the giant contracts once the military realized the potential superiority of the four-wheel-drive vehicles the company had created. Local women were employed as test drivers, and at the age of 18 in 1918, Ms. Mildred Sawyer was one of 21 women hired to do this type of work, which required considerable strength and agility. (Even today there are not many men who can drive an FWD Model B, with its steering as cooperative as the horns of a bull, no synchromesh in any gear, stiff clutch, manual spark advance, suspension calling for a kidney belt, hand crank starter, gasoline tank a few inches from the back of the neck, and so forth.)

In an interview for the American Truck Historical Society (ATHS) in 1989, at which time Ms. Sawyer was curator of the FWD museum, she stated, "We were respected and never harassed. We were all treated equally." She also noted that the male employees at FWD included mostly married farmers, who were accustomed to working women. But such equality was not evenly recognized among all communities throughout the entire

As men went off to war, factories needed women to take over as assemblers and mechanics, changing the social fabric in many countries.

Munitions factories hired women by the thousands in the U.S. and in Europe, such as this brave driver of an electric vehicle that carried artillery shells through the factory.

United States of that era, as women had yet to obtain the right to vote nationally, although in nineteen western states they were granted that right in 1912.

Women's suffrage, the movement to bring equality in voting rights, began after the Civil War. Susan B. Anthony was president of the National American Woman Suffrage Association from 1892 to 1900. Another suffragist was Alice Paul, who started the more militant, direct-action National Woman's Party. Both groups' activities led to the granting of the ballot to American women across all America only after World War I, in 1920, when the 19th Amendment to the Constitution was adopted. This was also the era of Pro-

The National League for Woman's Service, among several women's organizations, had its own motor corps, shown here hand-cranking a Ford in 1918.

hibition, which was pioneered by the Woman's Christian Temperance Union (WCTU), the Anti-Saloon League of America, and the National Prohibition Party, which pressed for a constitutional amendment in 1913. The 18th Amendment was ratified in January 1919 as World War I ended, and the Volstead Act, passed nine months later, gave the government the authority to enforce the law, resulting in smuggling and much gangster activity in regard to illegal alcohol distribution and consumption.

During World War I women did not serve directly in the military but were active in such organizations as the Red Cross, Daughters of the American Revolution Hospital Corps, Navy Nurse Corps, Motor Corps of America and the National League for Woman's Service (NLWS), which had its own motor corps. The latter organization was founded in January of 1917 by a group of patriotic women and was sanctioned by Secretary of State James W. Wilson. The NLWS was set up for "constructive patriotism" and cooperated with the Red Cross and the YWCA.

Among the largest motor vehicle manufacturers involved in the First World War was White. White had provided some steam cars for the Signal Corps even before World War I. According to the *White Service Record*, published by White in 1919, 18,000 White trucks served in Europe during World War I. Production of the White 1½-ton would reach such a demand that they were assembled at the factories of Peerless and Winton.

White was founded by Thomas H. White and his four sons in 1900. The company was reorganized in 1916, and $25 million in capital was added in 1917. White built 1-ton, 1½-ton, 3-ton and 5-ton trucks in addition to over 400 staff cars. White also began developing a series of armored cars using its heaviest truck chassis.

Top: White used its 1-ton truck chassis to build the Observation Car, which was essentially the same as the White staff car, here shown next to a Harley-Davidson with sidecar. *Bottom:* One of the most useful trucks in the terrain built by White was the portable machine shop, such as this one with the Canadian Expeditionary Forces. A lathe is visible through the open side door.

Having provided most of the trucks for the Punitive Expedition, White was already cooperating with the Quartermaster Corps when the U.S. entered the war in Europe. White also built ambulances, field wireless (radio) trucks, fire engines, mobile machine shops, aircraft tenders, anti-aircraft gun mountings, trench scavengers (coroners' trucks), water purifiers, reconnaissance cars and range-finding cars.

Top: This White truck of 1917 was fitted with a rudimentary Gallagher troop transport body and was driven between Camp Gordon and Camp Oglethorpe in Georgia. *Bottom:* White built this armored car in 1916, which was similar to the Mack and Locomobile prototypes. This one has an experimental rotating shutter on its radiator shell.

The standard White AA truck was developed but not manufactured in quantity for the Quartermaster Corps. White also produced buses for the Quartermaster Corps for use as personnel carriers. Engineers and designers at White were versatile and quite comfortable working with the military, a phenomenon more likely to be fostered among large companies that could afford to "roll with the punches" as designs were modified, restarted

Top: White called this "Armored Car No. 2," which was photographed at the Aberdeen Proving Ground in June of 1916. *Bottom:* As with a number of armored car prototypes, this 1917 White was used in parades for public relations and for recruiting purposes.

Top: Another view of the 1917 White armored car shows the vehicle in parade guise promoting patriotism and camaraderie with its display of both the American and British flags. Note license plate. *Bottom:* As aircraft became increasingly important in World War I, anti-aircraft guns were developed, such as the one here that is mounted on a White truck in 1918.

or contracts entirely and suddenly dropped, often representing the type of business pummeling that a small company could rarely withstand.

White's cooperation, for example, was exemplified by the alterations to their open touring staff car, based on the 1-ton truck chassis, which was difficult to put to use in inclement weather. A bolt-on winter top was quickly developed using isinglass panels for

Top: Shipbuilding was crucial in the war effort, and here a White truck delivers components at a merchant marine shipyard on the Great Lakes. *Bottom:* A White truck on the Somme Front in a French convoy, with horse-drawn artillery yielding right of way on the dirt road.

windows. This was an early form of "plastic" but not as clearly transparent as more standard silicon-based glass.

When the AEF took inventory in France during its first year in Europe in 1917, there were 294 different makes/body types of trucks, of which 213 were manufactured in the U.S. In order to maintain these vehicles, mechanics had to cope with tens of thousands

Top: A 1918 White combination pumping fire-engine, chemical, hose-and-ladder truck at Fort Funston on the Pacific Coast in San Francisco. *Bottom:* A White truck tows a biplane in a parade for recruiting purposes. Note proximity of man sitting on the two-wheel trailer and the rotating propeller just behind him.

of non-interchangeable parts, plus both English and metric hardware. Overall, Fiat was the largest provider of vehicles for the Allies with 45,000 at the end of the war, compared to Ford, White and Dodge, which provided the largest numbers from the United States. White began to provide its Model TBC trucks in 1912, long before the troubles with Pancho Villa. There was also an American FIAT truck company, which was independent of the Italian company.

The U.S. Navy purchased Winther trucks, such as this 6-ton 1917 model carrying logs in California.

The lack of a centralized procurement policy allowed each military branch to buy vehicles as its officers chose. For example, the 33rd Michigan Infantry bought five Studebaker-Crossman machine gun cars that were "bullet resisting" by having a heavier steel body. The U.S. Marine Corps used one 15 hp Saxon to build a scout car that also had a pedestal-mounted machine gun. The Army also evaluated one Clark Observation Car, named after the designer, which was based on a Pierce-Arrow and had an eighteen-foot tower on which to climb for reconnaissance.

The Navy bought 2-ton Winther and Winther-Marwin trucks, albeit in very small numbers. Although the Winther Company was contracted to build the standardized Liberty B truck, the war ended just as they had begun to tool up for production. Winther was always a 4 × 2 vehicle whereas its 4 × 4 was always called Winther-Marwin, the latter name derived from that of Martin Winther, the engineer who designed the four-wheel-drive system. The Winther Model 48 used by the Navy had a 25.6 hp Wisconsin engine. Most of the Winthers had solid rubber tires, but pneumatic tires were also fitted even on the 4 × 4 Winther-Marwin. The company was defunct a decade after the end of World War I.

Commerce, Federal, Kelly-Springfield, Selden, Standard, Velie and Wilson also provided trucks to the Quartermaster Corps. Mobile kitchens, usually on horse-drawn trailers, were eventually mounted on 3-ton Walter cab-over-engine (COE) trucks toward the end of the war.

Peerless, Packard and Pierce-Arrow, all known for their luxury cars (as the three great "P" marques of the era), built rugged, utilitarian trucks for both the British and American forces in Europe. Packard had gotten involved with the U.S. Army in 1909 when a 3-ton truck, along with a very similar Frayer-Miller, was tested in Massachusetts carrying three-pounder Driggs-Schroeder "pom-pom" guns. These guns were derived from naval weapons, weighed 500 pounds each and were capable of 100 rounds per minute. Because the guns lacked the normal field artillery range of the day, the U.S. War Department was not impressed at that time even after a successful demonstration during field maneuvers.

However, the performance of the Packard trucks was noted, and several were purchased before World War I. These were used as troop and provision carriers. Packard's 24 hp motor was cast in cylinder pairs and the three-speed transmission was built as a unit with the differential, although final drive was still by chain in the early iterations. Wheelbase was 144 inches and top speed was a governed 12 mph. The Packard 3-ton Army Truck remained without any basic changes through 1918, with the exception that worm drive had superseded the chain drive of 1914–1915.

Pierce-Arrow, known for their luxury cars, also built reliable trucks up to 5-ton capacity. There was also the lighter 2-ton model, which was used by the Quartermaster Corps Machine Gun Battalion at Camp Merritt, among other places. All Pierce-Arrow trucks had fully floating enclosed gear rear axles at a time when many of the larger trucks used chain drive, and Packard advertising often referred to "chainless drive." The 2-ton Pierce-Arrow was powered by a 279 cid four-cylinder engine that produced 28 hp.

Looking back at the historical picture, armored vehicles were first developed in the form of partially armored steam traction engines. The Burrell-Boydell Traction Engine appeared in England during 1847. The first one known in the United States was built and designed by Charles S. Dickinson who supported the Confederate side. His machine consisted of a cannon mounted on a partially armored steam traction engine. It was captured by the Union Army before it could be deployed in 1861.

Most of the development of the earliest armored cars took place in Europe (Simms, S.G.V. Austro-Daimler, Charron-Giradot-Voigt, Ehrhardt, 1902–1906). The name of Major Davidson in the United States comes up frequently as mentioned before, and he is

A Packard truck and four soldiers on a postcard of 1917 promoted camaraderie for recruitment.

The stalemate in Europe by 1917 was broken once the United States entered the war. Large shipments of food and supplies also arrived from America, illustrated here with a Packard truck being loaded with corned beef at Calles in 1918.

credited with building three armored cars based on Cadillac chassis in 1909. These were intended for use against giant zeppelins, which would later be utilized by the German army for observation, strafing and bombing during World War I. (Zeppelins were named after the German aviation pioneer, Ferdinand von Zeppelin, who designed the first rigid dirigible in 1900 and whose airships went into series production in 1906. He died in 1917.) Along with using spotlight trucks, Davidson realized that a fast machine-gun–equipped

Packard built numerous trucks used by the military in World War I, such as this 1918 1½-ton model.

vehicle could eliminate intruders from the sky, and these vehicles were dubbed Balloon Destroyers.

The three vehicles were entered in the Glidden Tour of 1910, a grueling run from Cleveland to Chicago via Mississippi and Texas, and among only nine out of 38 vehicles that finished, two were the Balloon Destroyers manned by Davidson's cadets. In 1911 two more Cadillac cars were outfitted with wireless radio-antenna units and powerful searchlights for use at night, when dirigibles were tested for reconnaissance.

Cadillac built four such vehicles for the government of Guatemala in 1913. All had armor shields for the machine guns but were not covered entirely with steel plates until a new design of 1915 by Davidson. This new design was fully armored and carried a Colt machine gun in an opening just behind the armored cover over the driver. Again, the U.S. military gave only a lukewarm response to this type of vehicle, which was considered experimental, and did not order more units.

Some of the earliest American-built armored cars specifically fabricated for the war effort in Europe came from Autocar. The first sector of the Canadian Expeditionary Force (CEF) which arrived in England on October 16, 1914, included a Motor Machine Gun Corps consisting of twenty armored cars built on standard commercial chassis with solid tires.

The man behind this project was Raymond Brutinel, who had served in the French Army prior to World War I and was living in Canada in 1914. He cooperated with Sir Clifford Sifton in creating a motorized machine gun outfit. Bethlehem Steel Corporation provided the $^3/_4$-inch plate. However, the driver still had to look above the front plate and had no head protection. This was because the vehicles were intended to carry two machine guns up to the front lines, at first air-cooled Colts, then .303 Vickers water-cooled units. Even though the British military leaders thought very little of these vehicles, King George V praised their value upon inspection, and they proved their worth in an offensive against the Germans in March of 1918.

The second contingent of the Canadian Expeditionary Force (CEF) was equipped with armored cars built on 38 hp Packard passenger car chassis, which had wire-spoke wheels and pneumatic tires. These had a driver's observation port across the entire front as well as side ports, and the engine and radiator were fully protected. A set of flaps covering the radiator could be opened and closed from the driver's position. A round turret held an air-cooled Colt machine gun and a bicycle seat for the gunner. It is believed there were eight such vehicles built in Detroit at the time. In England, Wolseley, subsidiary of Vickers at the time, used a 3-ton chain-drive Packard truck chassis to build an armored car, which was shipped to the eastern front in Russia.

The King Motor Car Company of Detroit, Michigan, known for its passenger cars, built an armored car for the U.S. Ordnance Department based on its Model 8 chassis. It was designed by Captain W.A. Ross, who incorporated a beveled-edge machine gun turret mounted with a .30 caliber Benet-Mercier machine gun, similar to that of armored cars built for the British Royal Naval Air Service. One version of the King armored car, built for the Army, had wire-spoke wheels fitted with pneumatic tires, dual on the rear,

Autocar still used its 2-cylinder motor in its truck chassis when this armored car was built for the Canadian Expeditionary Forces in 1918.

and spares hung on each side. It was protected by $^1/_4$-inch riveted steel plate at a time when large structural welding was yet to become common practice. It had a crew of three, weighed 5,280 pounds and also carried 12-inch-wide planks for crossing ditches. This vehicle and a second version were both tested by the U.S. Marine Corps in 1916–1917 without further orders for production.

The idea of fitting an armored car with pneumatic tires might not seem logical, since many trucks used solid rubber tires, but traction was of greater importance and early solid rubber tires were without tread due to the complexity and cost of molds. This armored car was illustrated in an advertisement for passenger cars in which the Secretary of War was shown reviewing cavalry, along with the slogan "The Car of No Regrets." The Marine Corps version had solid rubber tires with chains, a different turret and a rear door of different design. The vehicle carried $^3/_{16}$-inch armor. It was actually used in operations in the United States and in the Caribbean.

Yet another armored car of World War I was built on a Reo Model F chassis in 1916. It had an elaborately shaped armored body but no turret and was powered by the standard Reo 35 hp four-cylinder engine. It also had pneumatic tires and was used by the Michigan National Guard but only for training and demonstration. Ransom Eli Olds continued to make a name for himself even after selling it along with his company to the new owners of Oldsmobile who accused him of trademark infringement. He simply switched to using his initials and continued in the motor vehicle industry, making a brief incursion into the field of armored car fabrication, with which so many companies were at least briefly infatuated.

When the AEF landed in Europe, the French military wanted to buy 150 armored cars for security use. General Pershing nixed the requisition, but not before one wooden prototype by King was built. It featured twin turrets, one fore and one aft.

King Motor Car Company built several open touring staff cars and advertised them as "The Car of No Regrets" using a military theme. These cars are not listed in Army records.

The cover of *Leslie's Magazine* from January 7, 1915, showed an unusual if not improbable encounter with German infantry.

White built a few armored cars, but as with many such vehicles, it became clear early on during the Punitive Expedition against Pancho Villa that very heavy, wheeled vehicles such as armored cars would be fairly useless in areas where roads were sand pits or muddy bogs. A heavy armored vehicle on the narrow solid-rubber wheels of the day would become mired almost immediately.

Built in cooperation with the Carnegie Steel Corporation, White used its 2-ton truck chassis for a prototype, and a second one with a lower profile was built on an experimental basis a year later in 1917. Because of off-road limitations, these were used for recruit-

Opposite, top: The King Motor Car Company of Detroit, Michigan, built this armored car with a turret, pneumatic tires with duals at the rear as well as complete spare wheel-and-tire assemblies carried on each side. *Bottom:* The King Armored Car could maneuver off-road better than other such vehicles because it was lighter and used dual pneumatic tires. This front view shows unusual octagonal headlights and radiator with doors open.

Top: In 1916 Reo used its Model F chassis to build an armored car that was used by the Michigan National Guard for training. *Bottom:* A second version of the Reo armored car of 1916 shows a more complex radiator shell, single top barbed wire cutter and artillery wheels.

ment, promoting patriotism, showing off the latest military engineering and as parade vehicles. Photos of the Armored Battery National Guard of New York show that these particular armored cars spent more time on the well-paved streets of the city than in any combat situation. The lighter White armored car was built on a $1^1/2$-ton chassis but still weighed 7,400 pounds following the philosophy of "heavier is better" despite all associated disadvantages. This vehicle was fabricated by the Van Dorn Iron Works of Cleveland, Ohio, using $^1/_4$-inch steel plate and was powered by a standard 45 hp four-cylinder motor allowing a top speed of 40 mph. Once again, it was used as a promotional and recruitment tool rather than a combat vehicle, though it may have looked like a formidable one to onlookers.

For any large operation or institution, a fire department is a necessity, and during World War I it was American La France that was closely involved with the military. During this time, American La France provided two basic fire engines for the military: a four-cylinder model and a six-cylinder model. Both engines were of very large displacement. The four was 564 cid and the six 846 cid. These were known as triple combination pumpers, which meant they carried a rotary gear pump, chemical tank and hoses. There were also ladder trucks and other variations of the fire engine.

Other companies of the era, including Ahrens-Fox and Seagrave, also played an important role in furnishing fire engines and fire apparatus during World War I. There were also much more diminutive efforts in the form of a motorcycle with sidecar carrying Pyrene fire extinguishers, hoses and a stretcher for emergency work, such as those developed by the Indian Company.

As with many wars and conflicts, the need to dominate the enemy would bring out the inventiveness of human nature, and the idea of an amphibious vehicle was put into actuality. It was not the first time people had thought of a wheeled vehicle that could also float and be propelled in water.

Before World War I ended, a company named the Hydro Motor Car Company in Canton, Ohio, built its first Amphibian Car. It was apparently offered to the Quartermaster Corps for evaluation, but one photo that survives shows a much more recreational utilization of the boat-with-wheels type of vehicle. From some indicators, Ford Model T components were used. There was not much use for an amphibious car during World War I, but the innovation of a land-and-water vehicle (as with aircraft that could land on both water or solid ground) got designers and engineers to develop new ideas over the following years.

As with many auto manufacturers, the Franklin Company was diverted away from passenger car production, in this case to design a heavy-duty transmission for tanks. Known for developing air-cooled-engine luxury cars, the Franklin engineering team, under the capable John Wilkinson, was given a three-week deadline, and they delivered the blueprints to Bridgeport, Connecticut, on time.

Franklin was then engaged to manufacture major components for aircraft engines, small castings such as gun sights, lighting stations and other parts and assemblies for the war effort. One million dollars' worth of new machinery was installed by 1918 at the South Geddes Street factory in Syracuse, New York, after the Federal War Industries Board demanded the company concentrate on the war effort. The well-known Franklin cars ceased to be produced by October of 1918. Production of the Series 9 was resumed, and Franklin continued manufacturing until the company succumbed to the Great Depression in 1934.

The Republic Motor Truck Company of Michigan manufactured trucks but also tractors for towing, such as this 1918 model with specially designed positive traction rear wheels.

Because of the great need for trucks of all types, any make was welcome before spare parts and repair work boggled the efforts of mechanics in Europe. Standardization was the answer, but before it became policy, aside from the larger companies, dozens of lesser known makes were used by the U.S. Army. Military documents list several truck builders, including Atterbury, Autocar, Commerce, Dart, Denby, Federal, Gramm-Bernstein, Hudson, Kelly-Springfield, Lippard-Stewart, Overland, Paige, Reo, Republic, Selden, Service, Velie, Vim, Wilson, and Winther. Some companies such as Republic also built tractors for the military. In the final accounting by the assistant secretary of war, director of munitions in 1919, American companies that provided significant (at least 2000) of various factory-built trucks and ambulances for the war effort consisted of Dodge, Ford, FWD, GMC, Mack, Nash Quad, Packard, Pierce-Arrow and White.

Chapter V

ACCELERATED PROGRESS IN THE INDUSTRIAL REVOLUTION

The volatility of European politics that would arouse and ultimately destroy so many millions of vulnerable human beings across the globe, plunging them headlong into devastating world cataclysm, was incited by an unprecedented acceleration of technological progress during the Industrial Revolution.

Once our planet had been discovered to be covered largely by oceans and vast unexplored areas of terra firma only a few centuries prior to World War I, the larger and more aggressive societies in Europe quickly mapped out a plan of dominance over the lands, waterways and resources they considered theirs for the taking. Native populations' rights were barely taken into account, if at all in many instances.

In Europe, astounding progress was taking place in the fields of engineering and science that would propel warfare far beyond the ancient measures of equestrian superiority, excellence in swordsmanship, power of number of marching spear- and sword-bearing legions, or mastery of the winds among canvas sails under the familiar glimmer of distant stars.

The spoils of victory would belong to those who possessed better technology, still following the processes and ancient traditions of self-aggrandizement, but ultimately through the complexity of mechanisms that relied on metallurgy, new fuels and energy derived from petroleum, electricity and powerful explosives. It would be necessary to take advantage of significant progress in metallurgy and the science of chemistry, the precision of accurate metal forming and machining, and the knowledge of electrical power. Human populations numbering in the millions could organize entire communities and societies for the single purpose of domination over their rivals through large-scale and well-synchronized manufacturing. The strategies of war and military aggression remained much the same, still left mostly to old men in decorated uniforms and young officers with uncontrolled hormonal fluctuations, some who had survived earlier conflicts but who could not see beyond the trappings of conquest and exploitation. It was as if technology and industry had finally and permanently outpaced the realms of ethics, morality and diplomacy.

By World War I the backbone of the Industrial Revolution was bubbling in the cauldron of metallurgical sciences. Without the discoveries and progress in the science of alloying metal there would be little if any evolution in the development of railroads, motor vehicles, aircraft, steel ships, road and bridge construction, ordnance design as well as other industries intended in large part for conquest of a world then considered so vast and

Casting 30 tons of molten steel in one operation had become a reality at the beginning of the 1900s.

BLAST FURNACE

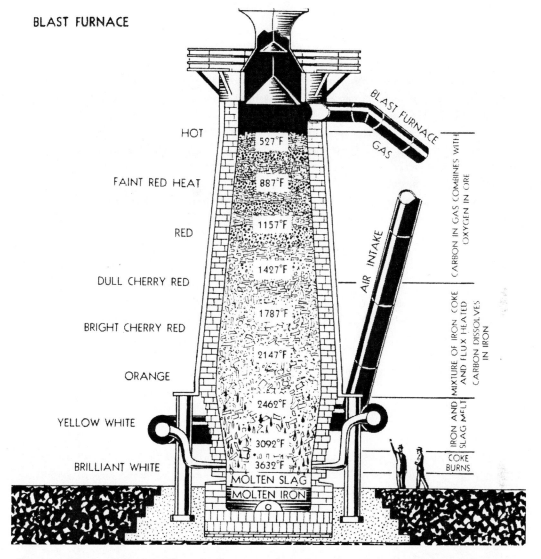

HOT 527°F

FAINT RED HEAT 887°F

RED 1157°F

DULL CHERRY RED 1427°F

BRIGHT CHERRY RED 1787°F

ORANGE 2147°F

YELLOW WHITE 2462°F

BRILLIANT WHITE 3092°F
3632°F

MOLTEN SLAG
MOLTEN IRON

BLAST FURNACE GAS

AIR INTAKE

CARBON IN GAS COMBINES WITH OXYGEN IN ORE

MIXTURE OF IRON COKE AND FLUX HEATED
CARBON DISSOLVES IN IRON

IRON AND SLAG MELT

COKE BURNS

The blast furnace of the 1800s allowed industry to make high-grade steel throughout western Europe and the U.S.

seemingly unclaimed by those mesmerized by their own vanity and nationalism. Advances in engines, transmissions, axles, wheels, chassis and other components relied entirely on the development of combining and hardening (annealing, coating, lubricating, et cetera) different metals for increased strength and durability. Without the scientific knowledge of steel making, as well as the alloying of other metals, most weapons used in World War I would have been impossible to manufacture, no matter what clever craftsmanship or assembly line practices might have been employed in prior decades.

During the 1800s, the metal used the most in constructing railroads, ships, bridges and consequently motor vehicles was iron, the fourth most abundant element on the surface of the planet. The Assyrians, Babylonians, Chaldeans, Egyptians, Hebrews and other ancient peoples called iron "the metal of heaven" in their languages because this amazing, strong, yet malleable substance fell out of the sky in the form of meteors that were composed mostly of iron and nickel. It was yet to be discovered that nickel and iron were also present in the ground over which people had trudged for countless millennia.

The initial utilization of iron by the Egyptians has been traced back to 4000 B.C., and the Hindus were smelting iron from earthen ore as early as 2000 B.C. The Iron Age, as it is now called, was characterized by a period in human activity of smelting iron in a number of areas of the world around 1000 B.C. It overlapped and followed the Bronze Age and Stone Age. Copper had been smelted as early as 10,000 B.C. Aside from the "metal of heaven" notion, it was a great and mysterious puzzle as to where metals, namely iron, actually originated. Even men as learned as Aristotle surmised that metals grew from some type of seeds underground.

With the use of leather bellows by 1000 B.C., the temperature of iron could be doubled, turning it into a red malleable substance that would glow to a bright red and could be hammered into many tools and weapons. Very early methods of smelting iron ore involved building a furnace on high ground where there was adequate air draft. The iron ore was stacked over charcoal on top of clay and surrounded by stone. This type of primitive method was employed for nearly two thousand years before the Catlan Forge was developed at Catalonia in northern Spain in the early 1600s.

One very important contribution to the craft of obtaining iron from ore was made by D. Dudley in 1620. He substituted coal for wood charcoal in smelting, which simultaneously improved the quality of the iron and greatly slowed the destruction of forests, which were being wiped out to produce the enormous quantities of charcoal needed for this process.

Almost exactly a century later, Abraham Darby introduced coke, burning at an even higher temperature and more evenly than coal, and the practice of smelting was quickly improved. Charcoal was still used to make certain types of iron, but this amounted to a small fraction of total output. Crude steel was still pounded out by blacksmiths until Henry Cort invented the rolling mill in England in 1783.

The next biggest and one of the most significant breakthroughs was accomplished by Henry Bessemer in 1855–1856. There were several different methods of making steel, but all of them were too expensive and none of the methods allowed for large-quantity production. Cast iron, also called pig iron, was relatively simple to produce, but getting rid of the extra carbon was quite difficult. Controlling precisely the amount of carbon was the secret behind making good steel.

Henry Bessemer developed a type of converter that used air blown through the pig iron. Until then everyone assumed that a blast of cold air would cool the iron. Instead, the air raised the temperature, in the process burning away and vaporizing the carbon and impurities.

Bessemer announced his discovery in 1856 in a paper titled "The Manufacture of Malleable Iron and Steel Without Fuel." Over the next few years, Bessemer's patented method was so successful that he became a millionaire and was knighted in England where he resided. (Bessemer Trucks were later built in Grove City, Pennsylvania, near the heart of the American steel industry of the era. The company had almost nothing to do with Henry Bessemer except that it was named after his invention.)

While Henry Bessemer was working on his discoveries in England, a man by the name of William Kelly of Eddyville, Kentucky, had also developed a similar process in America. Kelly realized that Bessemer was getting the credit for this type of smelting, and so he obtained a patent of his own in 1857. Rather than fight one another over legal rights, companies used these two almost identical methods under both patents after 1866, avoiding years of litigation at a time when steel production was imperative.

The Bessemer converter could hold up to 20 tons of cast iron. The process involved pouring 2,200-degree-Fahrenheit molten iron into the converter as it received a blast of air for fifteen minutes. Pig iron usually contained 3.7 percent carbon, 1.3 percent silicon, 0.05 percent sulfur and 0.75 percent manganese. Various impurities are burned away by the time the iron attains 3,500 degrees Fahrenheit and it turns brilliant white. The correct amounts of carbon and manganese need to be added before the iron can be poured into ingots.

By World War I giant sheet metal presses could stamp out entire tops for automobiles, trucks and other motor vehicles, as well as components for large machinery.

Sir William Siemens developed a new "Open Hearth" furnace, which was first used to distill zinc. By 1863 this type of furnace was used by the Martin Company in France to make steel. The Open Hearth method has been called the Siemens-Martin process, and it eventually became the predominant method for making steel, mainly due to the fact that each hearth could hold up to 260 tons of steel, and this method eliminated the sulfur and phosphorus present in steel. (Today, much steel is produced in electric furnaces.)

While metallurgical advances were used throughout Europe and the United States for industrial development in various categories of nation building, Germany also concentrated on the invention and manufacturing of new and more awesome firepower in the form of gargantuan artillery. Building the monstrous weapons required not only great knowledge of metallurgy, but also huge factories, machine shops and other industrial might, which was of particular interest to "Cannon King" Alfred Krupp, who inherited the Krupp works in Essen, Germany.

Alfred Krupp's ancestors had been in the armament business since the 1500s. In Essen, Friedrich Krupp, Alfred's father, had built a large forge in 1818 for the production of steel. His son Alfred, who was a metallurgist, developed methods of producing cast steel in huge masses equal to that of the English furnaces. He became known for his enormous siege guns used in the Franco-Prussian War of 1870.

Continuing in the family tradition, ever larger artillery pieces were built for planned military domination over France and other European neighbors, culminating in the 420 mm "Big Bertha," named after Krupp's granddaughter. It has been considered the largest-caliber road model artillery piece ever used in any war. (There were larger artillery pieces in World War II, but these required railroad cars for transport.) Five such howitzers were built before World War I and nine in total.

In order to attack France through Belgium and northern France, the Belgian forts at Liège would first have to be destroyed, then forts around Namur, subsequently the French fortress at Maubeuge, and others along the way to Paris. Once the M-type road model was developed, the entire "Big Bertha" weapon weighed 47 tons and was transported in five sections, which were towed by tractors. This weapon should not be confused with the "Paris Gun" mentioned further on.

The M-type road model 420 mm Krupp could launch a 16.5-inch diameter shell that weighed 1,764 pounds with a range of just over 10,500 yards. (There was a heavier shell for a version of the 420 mm Gama-Gerat for rail transport.) It took 200 men to service each battery.

Although the German Army had already entered the city of Liège on August 8, 1914, they were unable to overcome any of the 12 surrounding forts that had been built under General Brailmont in the 1890s. Two "Big Berthas" were summoned and brought on August 12, assembled and trained on Fort Pontisse. The giant steel-nose projectiles crashed through the 8-foot-thick concrete of the fort with delayed fuses triggering high explosives. Within 24 hours the fort was reduced to rubble and those inside shredded to bits.

With the additional Skoda 305 mm and 210 mm howitzers, the Germans methodically attacked the remaining forts. On August 15 an ammunition magazine was hit by a 420 mm projectile at Fort Loncin, and in the huge explosion 350 men were buried in the resulting crater. The last of the Belgian Liège forts surrendered, but this gave time for the Allies to mobilize and move in defense of Paris, where the Germans were stalled at the

By 1906, six open-hearth blast furnaces were producing 400,000 tons of steel per year in the U.S., with enormous capacities such as at this plant in Ensley, Alabama, photographed that year.

First Battle of the Marne as the famous "taxi-corps" outran the invaders. It then became a lesson of strategy: enormous artillery moving at a snail's pace across bad roads could be thwarted by fast, large-scale maneuvering using motor transport.

Even the so-called Paris Gun, which was first used on March 23, 1918, could not intimidate an entire city or an entire nation by the random bombardment of heavy, distant, and occasional artillery fire. A feat of technology involving metallurgy and metal fabrication, the Paris Gun could launch a projectile over a distance of 74 miles. The 232 mm *Parisgeshultz*, which was developed from a 380 mm naval gun, used a 78-foot extension (50-feet of which was rifled) to achieve a muzzle velocity of 5,407 feet per second. The gun fired at an elevation of 55 degrees used a shell weighing 275 pounds.

The high pressure that developed from the muzzle velocity wore out the bore of the gun within fifty shots, so shells were ringed with bands before the original tube was rebored up to 260 mm in diameter. One can imagine the size of the metal lathes involved. Krupp built six and Skoda built three such guns, pushing the achievement of metallurgical science and construction in artillery to its maximum, but it was strategically almost without consequence, despite 256 deaths from the explosions around the city where the Parisians scoffed at the attacks, according to the press of the day.

It is most significant to note that the development of steel in the 1800s and early 1900s meant there was rapid development in metallurgical science, which had been based on trial and error. The development of modern alloy steels for at least a century involved optimizing the properties of metals from which many weapons and specialized motor vehicle components were fabricated from the start to the end of the Great War.

Nickel has been a very common metal used to make alloy steel. With about 5 percent nickel, the alloy has increased strength and is called "meteor steel" because that is the composition of extraterrestrial projectiles of which about 100,000,000 fall to Earth every year. Nickel steel has been used for steering gear parts, pistons, axles and transmission gears.

Chromium, tungsten, molybdenum and vanadium are all metals used to make alloy steel. When all four are present, "high speed steel" is formed for use in cutting tools. Tungsten has a very high melting point of about 6,000 degrees Fahrenheit and is used in lightbulb filaments. Chrome steel is very hard and is used to make files, as well as high-luster surface finishes. Vanadium is the hardest of all the metals, and when combined with chrome it has been used to fabricate gears, axles and springs.

Ever since the advent of automobile manufacturing, there have been many types of presses, forging machines and cutting machines to create the appropriate shapes for use in the manufacturing of motor vehicle components. In the days of World War I, there were few electric welders due to the limited availability of high electrical current (amperage). However, acetylene torches were in existence by World War I and brazing and soldering were common practice. Nevertheless, at that time vehicles were most often fastened together by rivets, screws, bolts and pins. It should not be underestimated how significant was the quality of such small components in holding large parts and sections together. Even the monumental disaster of the *Titanic* just two years before World War I began has now been partly blamed on substandard rivets holding the hull plates together, as they sheered and popped apart once the "unsinkable" ship hit the iceberg.

One of the first significant metallurgical laboratories for microscopic studies of steel and other alloys was organized by Karl Zimmerschied at General Motors. Zimmerschied later became president of Chevrolet. Under the microscope, steel's "fingerprint" can show whether it has been properly alloyed, hardened and annealed.

As World War I started in Europe, the United States auto industry alone used 20 percent of the steel and 57 percent of the malleable iron produced in America, eventually totaling about 7,000,000 tons annually by the time of the Great Depression. Because of the increasing use of aluminum (quantities of which were shipped in the form of bauxite—hydrated aluminum oxides—from Jamaica, Brazil, Australia and Guinea, among the few countries with this natural resource in practical quantities), the percentage of steel in a motor vehicle produced after World War I has notably diminished. Although aluminum did exist and was used in small amounts in World War I, a power plant of high capacity was required to raise the powdered and purified bauxite to 470 Fahrenheit, create a molten state and then conduct a very high electric current through the liquid material to extract the aluminum. This precluded the production of aluminum at low cost until such facilities and equipment were more conveniently and adequately available. When aluminum was first discovered and used in the mid–1800s, it was more expensive than gold. The major advantages of aluminum over ferrous alloys are its light weight, electrical conductivity and rapid surface oxidation, which creates a thin "skin" resistant to tarnishing and deeper disintegration. (Aluminum is the third most abundant element on the earth's crust and the most abundant metal overall.)

Besides the need to protect all ferrous metals from oxidation (in addition to alloys not containing iron), engineers and designers also needed to take into account that steels, depending on their chemical makeup, can expand and contract due to major temperature

GRAIN IN TREE

GRAIN IN CRANKSHAFT

FORGING A CRANKSHAFT

Factory literature from General Motors illustrated the task of forging an engine's crankshaft, which involved much manual handling at the time.

changes. Radical fluctuations of dimensional tolerances and hardness (brittleness, elasticity, so forth) may well weaken the structural integrity of any mechanism's components. Compared to steel, aluminum is subject to even greater expansion and contraction and other changes of composition due to high temperatures alone, especially in the inner workings of vehicles and weapons.

Alloy steel was in great demand during World War I for manufacturing war machinery and vehicles. *Automotive Industries* explained in July of 1917:

Normally, it would require 75 tons of alloy steel per 1000 cars produced. Cars of almost equal quality can be produced with 23 tons or less of alloy steel per 1000 cars. The three main parts of the car where alloys are practically indispensable are the clashing gears in the gearbox, torsional members in the rear axle and the balls used in ball bearings. The other transmission gears could be made of high carbon steel and, if the heat treatments were carefully worked and held to close limits, the gears would be just as good and last nearly as long as the chrome nickel gears now employed. The gears which have to endure shock, however, should be made of chrome steel, although even these can be produced satisfactorily by metallurgists from carbon steel. Every automobile company threatened by shortage of alloy steel has been busy on the question of the possibility of dispensing with alloy steel. The Cadillac company, if it had to, could reduce the alloy steels to 75 or 100 lbs. to a chassis. This is true with Buick and the other companies in the General Motors group, where the metallurgical matters are handled through a central staff.... The

Ford company uses 300,000 tons of alloy steel a year in its present product, or about 30 lbs. to a car. A large percentage of the steel used in the Ford car is vanadium, yet the amount of ferrovanadium used in a car by chemical analysis is .15 of one percent.... The transmission manufacturers are not so fortunate, for they can hardly manage without from 20 to 50 gross pounds of nickel steel per gearset, though they need not have chrome. Much the same applies to axle makers, who need something more than a plain case-hardening steel for bevel pinions and differentials as well as for the driveshafts.

It was often stated that "high-grade" cars suffered greater loss in quality and business during World War I, as their product was cheapened through quotas, limits and material shortages. By and large, the American automotive industry was forced to learn the lesson that it could still build sufficiently durable motor vehicles without the need for the highest quality of metal components as when before the war began.

The discussion of iron and steel metallurgy in relation to the advances of the Industrial Revolution must take into account the development of steam power. In the 1600s, various experiments in Europe culminated in what is now considered the first practical steam engine built by Thomas Savery in 1698 and subsequently by Thomas Newcomen in 1705, but these primitive engines were used almost exclusively to pump water out of mines and were not suitable for propulsion.

After meeting physicist Joseph Black, who was studying the thermodynamic properties of steam in 1755 in London, Scottish engineer James Watt patented in 1769 a more advanced steam engine that was primarily improved by the use of a separate steam condenser. In 1769–1771, Nicolas-Joseph Cugnot, living in France, ran the first steam-powered road machine with some degree of success in an attempt to create a military vehicle. His second steam machine accidentally broke through a wall in Paris, landing him in prison.

But elsewhere, especially in England, inventors for a time met with more acceptance of the industrial pioneering spirit. Oliver Evans in the U.S. was granted a patent on his first steam-powered land vehicle in 1789. Between 1774 and 1800 James Watt formed a partnership with Matthew Boulton, whose production shop built more efficient steam engines than the Newcomen type. In England, Watt also developed the twin-action piston engine, which obtained steam on both sides of the piston; he later adapted the engine to transform the reciprocating motion into rotary motion along with a centrifugal governor to keep the steam engine moving at a constant speed. Watt was not the inventor of the steam engine itself, but his complex improvements allowed the steam engine to become a source of motive power. The steam engine was soon mounted in the first locomotive by Richard Trevithick in 1804 at the Penydarren Iron Works in Wales. Railways, as they were called in Great Britain, were already in use for horse-drawn public transportation, by which the harnessed animals merely pulled the passenger cars along a solid, fixed, predesignated set of iron bars, preventing undesirable lapses in course direction and unintended destinations.

Although the first steam locomotive was too heavy for the rail tracks of the time, this development prompted George Stephenson to build the steam engine named Locomotion, which became the first locomotive in 1825 at the Stockton and Darlington Railway in England. Within four years, a design competition was organized by the Liverpool and

Opposite, top: **This rare photograph from 1866 shows Richard Dudgeon's second steam vehicle plying the streets of New York City at a time when most steam power was limited to railroad tracks and ships.** *Bottom:* **Stanley Steamer was the most prolific of the steam vehicle builders, producing commercial vehicles such as this delivery express wagon of 1908.**

Manchester Railway; George Stephenson's son Robert won the competition for his locomotive, the Rocket, which was specifically designed for passenger service by 1829. English
manufacturing of locomotives developed so rapidly that between 1829 and 1841 the United
States imported approximately one hundred British locomotives.

American ingenuity prompted its own pioneers to develop locomotives, such as Peter
Cooper's Tom Thumb of 1830. The same year, a locomotive named Best Friend of
Charleston, along with passenger cars, was the first train built for sale in the United States.
It made its debut on Christmas Day of that year. Much further development of the steam
locomotive took place over the next century, both here and in other parts of the world.
However, it is the focus of this discussion to address the vehicles designed for use on roads
and open ground, and especially for military use.

Per patent of 1789 mentioned above, the amphibious four-wheel steam-powered vehicle of 1803–1805 built by Oliver Evans in Philadelphia has always been cited as the earliest self-propelled vehicle built in America. In the following years, a few boiler explosions
resulting in death and injury, notably in London, kept the road steam vehicle from becoming a popular mode of passenger road transportation during the 1800s, with additional
opposition of the Road Trusts in England. Perhaps the worst accident involved the John
Scott Russell coach near Paisley, England, of July 29, 1834, in which five passengers died
from a boiler explosion with others injured. The Red Flag Act then severely curtailed
development of steam carriages in England by forcing a man to walk in front of all steam-
propelled conveyances warning of the vehicle's approach. This helped tremendously to
advance the British railway system.

Yet numerous steam carriages such as the Trevithick London Road Carriage of 1803
(predating his locomotive by a year), Walter Hancock's of 1826, Sir Goldsworthy Gur-
ney's of 1830, Colonel Maceroni's of 1833, Yarrow & Hilditch of 1862 and R.W. Thomson's of 1867, among others, were quite successful in England, as was Charles Dietz's
steam-powered tractor, which pulled passengers over the roads around Paris and Bordeaux
up to 1850.

In the United States Dr. J. Carhart, a professor of physics at Wisconsin State University, in conjunction with the J.W. Case Company, built a steam tractor that won a 200-
mile race in 1871.

The Rocket was a Stanley Steamer that set a world speed record of 121.57 mph in 1906 at Ormond
Beach, convincing many people that steam propulsion was the superior method of powering a vehicle. This photograph also serves as a contrast to the stodgy square trucks and cars of the era that
would finally get streamlining two decades later.

The Breeding Steam Truck of 1915 was a rare breed but at least one example remains extant. The complexity of the boiler system and time it took for start-up precluded steam vehicles from much military use at the front in Europe when minutes and even seconds counted and could mean life or death. At the same time, vast reserves of petroleum were being discovered.

Amédée Bollée-Pere in France built fully functional steam cars for a decade beginning in 1873. One of his most advanced was the La Mancelle built in 1878, which featured a front-mounted steam engine, shaft drive to a differential (invented by Frenchman Onésiphore Pecqueur a half century earlier), steering wheel and boiler safely tucked away behind the passenger compartment.

In the United States, Apollo Kinsley of Hartford, Connecticut, Nathan Read of Salem, Massachusetts, and Richard Dudgeon of New York City all built functional steam road

12

Abner Doble, sitting at the wheel of his Old Antelope in 1917, built a few dozen sophisticated steam vehicles, including luxury cars, at his factory in San Francisco.

carriages before the Civil War and before the invention of the internal combustion engine. Other steam carriage builders and operators in the U.S. at the time have also been given credit, such as Joseph Dixon, Harrison Dyer, Rufus Porter and William T. James.

Throughout the 1800s, steam traction engines were built for work in the field, primarily for threshing and plowing. There were about 200 successful makes, from Advance and Avery to Westinghouse and Wood Brothers, many built in England, but some in America and on the European continent.

However, steam power, with its combined weight of the boiler, cylinders, firebox, coal, frame, axles, wheels and other components, was better suited for use on rails that could hold the massive machines. Steam locomotive trains spanned the American continent by 1869. The Golden Spike in Utah honored the moment when the rails met from east and west crossing the entire continent.

The rather complex shut-down and start-up of steam engines prevented their practical and prompt use. They were not destined to become a convenient mode of road transportation, especially after the electric starter motor was invented by Charles Kettering at General Motors in 1912. The streamlining and miniaturization of steam components would eventually be accomplished, but not before the technology and infrastructure of the internal combustion engine got a remarkable head start in the modern world at the beginning of the 20th century.

Left: By World War I Abner Doble's company produced a flash boiler that was capable of producing steam two minutes from start-up, but these were hand-tooled one at a time and very expensive. *Right:* The Doble steam engine was coupled directly to the rear axle without the need for a transmission or a differential, the advantage of most steam-powered vehicles. *Below:* The Doble compound steam engine was one of the most sophisticated of its kind, but the cost and complexity of the Doble automobile, truck and bus precluded their mass production.

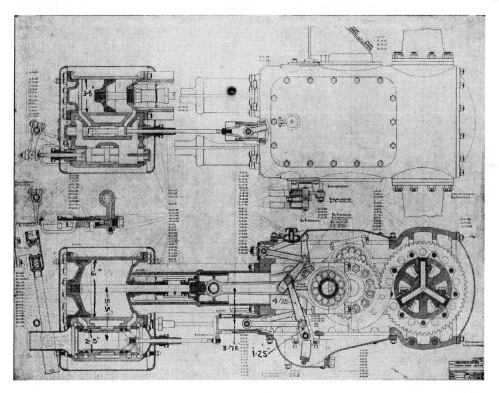

Inventors who understood the problem of heating water into steam pondered a method of creating the expansion of gas and air without the use of steam. The first such challenge to steam power was from Éttienne Lenoir in France, who patented "an engine dilated by the combustion of gas" in 1860.

It would be two German inventors who built the first internal combustion vehicles

The Steamobile of 1918–1919 was built by the Winslow Boiler and Engineering Company of Chicago, which designed its Uni-flow V-4 engine that resembled an internal combustion engine at a time when few people were convinced of the future of steam power for road vehicles.

in the world, working nearly simultaneously and only a few kilometers apart from each other, unbeknownst to one another. Karl Benz completed his vehicle in 1885 and patented it a year later as the Benz Patent Motorwagen. Gottlieb Daimler attached an engine to a motorcycle in 1885, fitted a motor to a carriage in 1886 and in 1889 built the Steelwheeler with his assistant Wilhelm Maybach. This vehicle was shown at the 1889 Paris World Exhibition.

    Karl Benz had little financial backing and built his first set of motorcars in his own small shop. He had begun at the Mannheim Gas Motor Works in 1877, developing the two-cycle gasoline engine. The four-cycle engine had already been invented in 1872 by Nicholas August Otto. Daimler patented his own design of the four-cycle motor in 1883.

Karl Benz built his Patent Motorwagen in 1885–1886 in Germany at the same time Gottlieb Daimler created his own first horseless carriage in another city not far away, unbeknownst to each other. Each inventor also built his first internal combustion engine, and both have been honored as inventors of the gasoline-powered automobile.

While Daimler was building his first "motorcycle," Benz completed his Motorwagen in his shop as a three-wheeler, and from the beginning it was conceived as a complete motorcar rather than a motorized horse buggy. Instead of using a hot-tube ignition as Daimler did, the Benz vehicle had electric ignition using a battery, and also included a throttle control, mechanical valves and horizontal flywheel (to overcome centrifugal force).

The Benz Motorwagen also used a differential, which had been invented in France in 1827. This combination of elements and components in the design has placed this vehicle on the pedestal of being considered the first automobile in the world. However, Karl Benz, Daimler and Maybach are all cited as the inventors of the motorcar or automobile (along with all the other names used to describe the self-propelled conveyance that would change the world).

However, it would be quite an oversight to ignore the utmost importance of the discovery and development of petroleum, as part and parcel of the Industrial Revolution, and especially as the propulsion fuel for motor vehicles, as well as for ships, aircraft, stationary engines and other machinery based on the internal combustion engine. In fact, World War I was sometimes referred to as the "gasoline war" as mentioned previously.

Oil was known in ancient times as it oozed to the surface in various parts of the world. In this gooey form known as bitumen, it was best known in Mesopotamia in what is now Baghdad. It was used as mortar and sealant and later in warfare. The gases that escaped among the pits at Hit along the Euphrates near Baghdad would ignite and could

explain the Babylonians' worship of fire. Also, according to the Roman historian Pliny, it was used for medicinal purposes to stop bleeding, treat cataracts and gout, cure aching teeth, soothe a cough, stop diarrhea, relieve fever and rheumatism and to cure other ailments. Many folk medicine uses of "raw" petroleum came down through the ages.

Rock oil, as it was known, was also found in parts of Europe, especially in Galicia and Rumania where a simple illuminating lamp, called the Vienna Lamp, was invented in the mid–1800s. In the United States, oil seeped to the surface in rural northern Pennsylvania at Oil Creek, which was also known as Seneca Creek, named after the local Indians. But in North America no use had been found for the goo except to make medicinal products. Only a few gallons a day could be collected from Oil Creek by using rags to soak up the substance as it floated on the water. The La Brea Tar Pits in southern California were yet to be recognized as having much importance except for the fact that Indians and animals had drowned in the giant sludgy puddles over the millennia. A museum located on Wilshire Boulevard in Los Angeles is now dedicated to this history.

In the 19th century, illumination was accomplished using various forms and iterations of the European Vienna Lamp (later called the kerosene lamp). The fuel for these lamps came from either camphene, which was distilled from turpentine; town-gas, which was derived from coal; or from sperm whale oil. Camphene and town-gas were very expensive, and the sperm whale population had been nearly wiped out by the mid–1800s.

Along came Dr. Abraham Gesner, a Canadian, who patented a method to extract illuminating oil from asphalt or crude oil. In his 1854 U.S. patent he called the hydrocarbon liquid "Kerosene" after the combination of Greek words *keros* and *elaion*, meaning "wax" and "oil." This process was also being accomplished in Europe to a small degree, but there was insufficient availability of crude oil (rock oil) in North America to make abundant amounts of Kerosene (which became a generic word). The use of crude petroleum oil remained only as a folk medicine. Dr. Gesner had yet to license his patent.

The potential of using rock oil for illumination was a great inspiration to a New York lawyer named George Bissell. After seeing a vial of petroleum folk medicine at Dartmouth College, he realized it was flammable and dreamed of finding enough of it to create a profitable venture in the illuminant industry, which was enormous. Along with James Townsend, president of the Bank of New Haven, he formed the Pennsylvania Rock Oil Company. They hired a famous chemist named Dr. Benjamin Silliman. The professor of chemistry made a careful evaluation of the potential uses of rock oil in its various distillate forms, and after publishing his very favorable report, Bissell and Townsend gathered investors for their new venture.

But the problem was that so little oil could be gathered off Oil Creek in Pennsylvania. One day, Bissell saw an ad in a pharmacy window that showed salt drilling derricks, which had been used for centuries. With the help of E.L. Drake, a jack-of-all-trades, and experienced salt driller William Smith, they set out to try and drill for oil near Titusville, Pennsylvania. Using the name of Seneca Oil Company on some purchased farm land about two miles from this backwoods town, population 125, they began their task using a steam engine in 1858.

With Bissell, Townsend and investors back in New York wringing their hands in

Opposite: **This photograph from 1859 shows Edwin Drake and his drilling rig in Titusville, Pennsylvania, where oil drilling first began.**

In the drilling process, when underground gas pressure was very high, a "gusher" was the result, which was completely unexpected by the first petroleum pioneers. Here, Captain Anthony Lucas's oil well at Spindletop erupts on January 10, 1901, marking the beginning of the Texas oil industry.

anticipation, the drillers persevered but without any success. A year passed and many derided the whole concept, believing that oil was a form of "drippings" from coal beds and could exist only in small quantities. Just as money literally ran out, oil came to the surface where a broken drill had left an open hole. On August 27, 1859, Drake and Smith filled several barrels with a simple hand pump. They notified Bissell and Townsend.

News of the discovery spread quickly, and within one year there were seventy-five oil rigs pumping oil at Titusville. Propelled by underground gases, the first "gusher" astonished everyone in 1861. Whereas production for 1860 was 450,000 barrels, by 1862 it was 3 million. Rock oil was dubbed "black gold."

Because railroad cars had to carry crude oil to refineries, yet another industry immediately expanded and had to keep up with production. Refineries were essential to "cracking," or refining, crude oil. The story of oil would not be complete without the name of John D. Rockefeller. By 1865 he was owner of the largest refinery in Cleveland and along with his partner, Henry Flagler, would soon dominate the oil industry. The company also controlled production of petroleum by-products such

For the first few decades of the motor industry, oil was distributed in large canisters resembling milk cans, which most often carried five gallons and had a narrower sealed top to make pouring more easy.

as petroleum jelly (Vaseline), paraffin, as well as gasoline, which was used only as a solvent then.

In a joint stock arrangement, the Standard Oil Company was created in January of Under the meticulous and thorough leadership of Rockefeller and through very aggressive growth and acquisition (with accusations of unscrupulous business practices), nine years later Standard Oil refined 90 percent of the kerosene in America. Effectively, Rockefeller had created a stranglehold on the oil producers, of which there were thousands, depending on how they were counted, because anyone could build an oil well in his field and be called a producer.

Even before the invention of the internal combustion engine, Rockefeller controlled refining and the transport of oil. In order to wrest some control from him, the oil producers united in an effort to build a huge pipeline, which would be called the Tidewater Pipeline. The project seemed technically impossible at a time when standard pipelines were simply wooden tubes. The Tidewater Pipeline was to travel 110 miles from the Oil Regions, as they were called in northern Pennsylvania, to a connection point with the Pennsylvania and Reading Railroad.

In order to throw off Rockefeller and his men, who resorted to sabotage, construction began in secrecy with deceptions as to the exact route and magnitude of the project. But by May of 1879 oil was flowing at the other end of the line. Tidewater, with the Producers' and Refiners' Oil Company of the 1890s reorganized as Pure Oil, was to be one of the few entities that Standard Oil would not control for decades.

Large five-ton tankers, such as this Mack Type Two, could carry 1,200 gallons in 1909 at a time when distribution was essential to the infrastructure of gasoline-powered vehicles.

In the 1890s, the so-called "oil wars" could be described as acts of intrigue and surreptitious manipulation by four main players: Standard Oil, the Rothschilds, the Nobels and a group of multiple Russian oil producers. Underselling and deceitful acquisition were two primary strategies, while on the surface polite discussion about mergers and cooperation were promulgated at opportune interludes filled with friendly overtures.

Meanwhile, Aeilko Jans Zijlker, a manager of tobacco plantations in East Sumatra, discovered that the locals were using kerosene torches and found that petroleum was oozing out of the ground there. An oil well was drilled in 1885, beginning a grand new venture called Royal Dutch when King William III lent his name to the new enterprise.

The boom in and around Los Angeles had fizzled out rather rapidly as reserves were soon exhausted in this particular area. Professor Silliman, who had made extravagant claims as to the inexhaustible supply of underground oil, was temporarily proven wrong and forced to resign his professorship at Yale. However, some of his predictions later came true as new oil reserves were discovered in Ventura County, San Fernando Valley and off-shore in southern California as well as elsewhere in America, Mexico and other areas where the professor surmised there might be underground reserves.

In Texas, a one-armed mechanic named Patillo Higgins, who refused to give up his dream, teamed up with Captain Anthony Lucas, and they discovered oil in Beaumont at Spindletop, which caused a mad dash for oil well claims and an effort by Shell Oil to buy into the entire production. The company contracted to buy half the production of crude oil from the area at 25 cents per barrel for the following twenty years. But oil continued to be discovered in Texas, Kansas, Oklahoma and Colorado, and when the Spindletop wells began to dry up, the price went up to 35 cents per barrel. Demand was skyrocketing as the gasoline-powered motor vehicle became increasingly popular and widespread in its various uses.

After President William McKinley's assassination in 1901, Theodore Roosevelt became president and was reelected in 1904. Immediately, he launched an investigation into Standard Oil and the petroleum industry. The Roosevelt Administration brought suit in Federal Circuit Court during November of 1906 against Standard Oil, charging it with "conspiracy to restrain trade" under the Sherman Antitrust Act of 1890. Fanned by public outrage, the court fined John Rockefeller and Standard Oil $29,000,000, at which the oil mogul scoffed. However, in 1909 the court also ordered a dissolution of Standard Oil, which was appealed, but upheld, by May of 1911, and the monopoly was given six months to dissolve itself. The new largest separate entity was Standard Oil of New Jersey, half of the total net value, which became Exxon. Standard of California became

In the early days of motoring, oil was hand-pumped one quart at a time into a specially designed spouted pitcher for filling an engine to its proper capacity.

Chevron, Standard Oil of New York, Mobil. The Indiana branch became Amoco, Continental then became Conoco, and Atlantic became part of ARCO and subsequently Sun.

One of the major beneficial results of the break-up was the introduction of new, unrestrained research and development, which, under the leadership of a Ph.D. chemist, William Burton at Indiana Standard Oil, improved the yield of gasoline from crude oil more than two-fold, from 20 percent to 45 percent.

Meanwhile, French geologists had published numerous reports on the presence of petroleum in Persia, what became Iran after 1935. As a result of Persian General Antoine Kitabgi's efforts in negotiating with British millionaire William Knox D'Arcy, the Shah Muzaffar al Din signed a historic agreement on May 28, 1901, that allowed the new English company to obtain oil from three-fourths of Persian territory, despite unsuccessful protestation by the Russians. After wasteful fits and starts, oil was finally found in October of 1903. But D'Arcy had spent so much of his investment in development that he was forced to turn to Thomas Boverton Redwood, an English chemist, consultant and expert on petroleum who had advised the Royal Navy to adopt fuel oil instead of using coal. Near-

When Touring, Look for This Sign

John Rockefeller's Oil Trust monopoly was broken up into several smaller companies by the Roosevelt Administration and companies such as Texaco became enormous giants in and of themselves.

ing bankruptcy, D'Arcy finally got the cooperation of the Royal Admiralty, and a small company called Burmah Oil headquartered in Scotland developed the Persian oil venture in 1905, dubbed the Concession Syndicate.

Oil exploration was then shifted from around Baghdad by this outfit to southwestern Persia. However, in 1906, fired up by local mullahs against the despotic Shah in an atmosphere of xenophobia, Tehran erupted in violent riots. An armed military guard was placed to protect the oil drilling rigs. The Shah was removed, a parliament was created, and Persia was to be partitioned. The first wells dried up and a new site called Masjid-I-Suleiman in the middle of the desert would become the next chance at finding large oil fields in what was described as an act of desperation by Burmah Oil and George Reynolds, who oversaw the actual operations. But no oil was found and the management at Burmah Oil sent notice for all operations to be discontinued. With that letter in transit, on May 25, 1908, after extreme hardship in unbearable conditions, oil was finally hit with a "gusher," helping to make the Anglo-Persian Oil Company, as it was called, a success.

The interest in petroleum by the British government was headed by Admiral John Fisher and Winston Churchill, who inherited a British Navy that was already in the midst of building 56 oil-burning destroyers and 74 such submarines. Winston Churchill's political career began in Parliament in 1901 at age 26, and he was president of the Board of Trade and Home Secretary by 1910. By this time he was convinced that oil would allow British warships to attain top speeds of 25 knots, a 20 percent improvement over coal power, and these speeds could be accomplished with fewer men, eliminating half the stok-

The irony was lost in this *National Geographic* ad for petroleum products showing oil flowing down a page and Yosemite in the background. Automobiles were already crowding the picturesque valley in this early ad.

In what was then called Constantinople, Turkey, this 1910 air-cooled-engine Franklin was an excellent choice to transform into a partially-armored machine-gun patrol car.

ers and coal engineers on a ship. It allowed a greater range and much easier refueling at sea. In a battle men would not have to be diverted to shovel coal from various bunkers and bins within the ship.

The enormous British naval programs of 1912, 1913 and 1914, in reaction to German naval expansion, included the construction of ships all powered by oil and none by coal. Oil and the internal combustion engines installed in ships, motor vehicles and aircraft, as well as many stationary machines, would change the entire character of transportation and therefore of war.

By 1916, 20 percent of the British Navy's oil needs were provided by the Anglo-Persian Oil Company. What came as a surprise to the British was that British Petroleum, which was a name used only by the actual owners of the company entirely controlled by

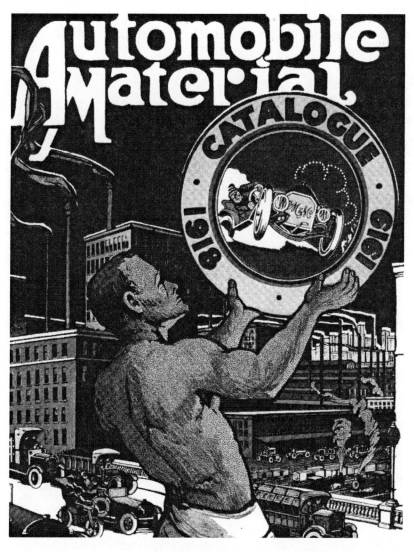

Fueled by new petroleum discoveries around the globe, the motor vehicle industry grew at a tremendous pace in America and Europe. This American "catalogue" from M&M advertised countless parts and accessories for the civilian market.

Deutsche Bank, had been set up to distribute Rumanian oil, where the only oil fields in Europe existed. As the war began, the British took over British Petroleum and integrated it with the Anglo-Persian Company. At the same time, Turkish Petroleum, also controlled by the Deutsche Bank, was reorganized so that 50 percent of it was owned by Anglo-Persian, and Shell and Deutsche Bank owned 25 percent each. To the benefit of the Allies, this particular agreement had been drawn up on March 19, 1914, just before World War I fragmented so many nations.

In England there was much public agitation against Royal Dutch and Shell. However, after repeated rejections by the British Admiralty, a refinery was built in Rotterdam for the production of toluol, a key ingredient in making TNT explosives. It was known that the quite advanced German chemical industry was buying the toluol for their own production of explosives. In January of 1915, a clandestine operation took place in which the entire toluol laboratory was disassembled in the middle of the night and shipped to Somerset, England, where it was reassembled. By November of 1917, Prime Minister Georges Clemenceau warned President Woodrow Wilson that France would run out of oil and gasoline by March of 1918. On December 15, 1917, Clemenceau sent President Wilson a message stating, "Gasoline was as vital as blood in the coming battles." Wilson responded accordingly and adequate supplies of fuel and oil were quickly shipped to Europe.

The United States was producing 65 percent of world output of petroleum in 1914 with a total of 266 million barrels per year, which increased to 355 million barrels and 67 percent of total world production by 1917. With such enormous output and needs to match, in order to control and coordinate the country's allocations of petroleum products, President Wilson created the Fuel Administration. It was headed by a California petroleum engineer named Mark Requa, who became the first energy czar in America.

In Germany the need for oil became so vital that Germany attacked Rumania in order to take over its Wallachian Plain oil fields. On November 17, 1917, German forces finally broke through mountain passes and entered the country. After much negotiation with a reluctant Rumanian government, British Colonel John Norton-Griffiths, sometimes wielding a sledgehammer himself, was placed in charge of destroying the Rumanian oil production plants beginning on November 26, 1917. Within days he had destroyed 70 refineries and 800,000 tons of crude oil reserves. When the German army finally did reach the oil production facilities, Colonel Norton-Griffiths had escaped, earning a medal of honor, and it would take six months before repairs could be made, crippling the German military and its gasoline-based infrastructure.

Another goal of the German army was to capture the refineries at Baku on the Caspian Sea. A British force was sent through Persia, which fended off the German army for a month. However, upon their departure, Turkish fighters entered Baku and amid the chaotic fighting, the Armenian workers were killed and the oil facilities were sabotaged by the local Muslims, thereby again denying Germany the vital petroleum and gasoline they desperately needed for their war machine.

After the Armistice was signed on November 11, 1918, Senator Berenger, who was the director of France's *Comite General du Petrole*, stated, "Oil—the blood of the earth—was the blood of victory.... As oil had been the blood of war, so it would be the blood of the peace."

Britain's earlier colonization of India and the poorly disguised attempt to dominate Mesopotamia and the Middle East in order to obtain oil helped fuel regional, tribal and sectarian conflict in the entire region, whether it was directly related to the war in Europe or not. With new nations drawn rather arbitrarily on the map and notwithstanding the military successes of the most famous Allied hero of World War I in this part of the world, Lawrence of Arabia (British born T.E. Lawrence), the territorial turmoil and subdivision led to continuing wars and social and political unrest.

Petroleum's by-product named "gasoline" or "petrol," and elsewhere "benzene" (often nicknamed "gas" in America), which was of little use to anyone in 1890, suddenly became one of the most important substances and commodities on Earth, as the internal combustion engine became ubiquitous, and The Great War (to be reminded again here as the Gasoline War) had exploded in Europe.

In the 1890s when electric- and gasoline-powered vehicles appeared, steam power

There was something prophetic about the name "Globe—the Universal Gasoline" as internal combustion transportation became ubiquitous around the world, introduced and spread even more rapidly by the events of World War I.

seemed refined enough for on-road applications after nearly a century of the existence of the steam traction engine and the occasional steam bus in addition to all the maritime applications. After steam power had been successful in railroad and marine use for a century, it would appear to be the logical motive power for road vehicles, especially for large commercial trucks.

Before World War I there was still much controversy surrounding which method of propulsion would be best for motor vehicles. There were numerous companies building all three forms of vehicles. Steam cars and trucks were being manufactured by several firms in America: Breeding, Grout, Herschmann, Locomobile, Mobile, Morgan, Stanley and White. To prove a point, some of these makes participated in the first commercial vehicle competition in 1903, sponsored by the fledgling Automobile Club of America.

The very first truck show and truck competition in the United States took place on May 20 and 21, 1903. The event was a test of and tribute to the variety of fuel and technology still considered viable at the time: coke, coal, kerosene, gasoline or lead-acid batteries.

The contest took place around Central Park and across the Harlem River in New York City. Fourteen vehicles were entered, of which one was withdrawn. *The Horseless Age* at the time mused: "The motor must end its purely butterfly existence and be made to assume its share of the world's work, if it is to survive."

Starting from the Automobile Club of America headquarters at Fifth and 58th Street, the trucks were each required to make a 20-mile run to 230th Street and back. They left in three-minute intervals. On the first day only the Blaisdell did not finish when a hand pump broke and the gasoline supply, used to heat the steam boiler, caught fire. Temporarily out of order but not eliminated was the large Herschmann, which was delayed by a leaky boiler. This truck carried a 10,000-pound block of granite, undoubtedly for visual effect since five tons of gravel would not have the same dramatic look to it.

The following day, a flat tire resulted in one of the Union trucks overturning, injuring the driver. Further details were not given, but none of the vehicles had even the most basic safety features. At the time, trucks were not built with enclosed cabs or even lights. The driver was lucky to have a padded seat cushion.

The winner was the light Knox, which was referred to in the press as the Waterless Knox in that its engine was air-cooled. This particularly unusual design had one cylinder and used the "Old Porcupine" cooling system, so called because instead of ribs or fins it had many steel dowels pressed into the cylinder block. The truck carried 1,250 pounds of lead and was driven by Harry A. Knox himself. It was a tiller-steered vehicle with a two-speed epicyclic transmission that had no reverse gear.

Harry A. Knox was a graduate of the Springfield Technical Institute in Massachusetts. As an engineer he designed elevators in the late 1890s. His neighbor was Frank Duryea, the automotive pioneer, who encouraged Knox to enter the new field, which Knox did in 1900, building three-wheelers. Advertising of the day stated, "Knox—the car that never drinks." Harry Knox resigned abruptly in 1904 and went on to build Atlas vehicles. Knox became Knox-Martin, building three-wheel tractors for pulling trailers. The company also built four-wheel four-cylinder trucks and buses, some of which were exported as far away as Japan.

During the truck competition of 1903 the lighter trucks were required to make an additional 20-mile run along the streets of Manhattan, and the winning Knox covered this route in three hours and 35 minutes, having consumed four gallons of gasoline. That was an average of 11.3 mph. Over the two-day run, the Knox used ten and a half gallons of gasoline, which included simulated delivery stops on the second day. That means it averaged about eight miles per gallon.

By comparison the largest truck, which was the Coulthard, used 1,335 pounds of coke and 869 gallons of water to cover 60 miles during the two days. The Waverly Electric used $2.50 worth of electricity to have its batteries charged for its required 80-mile route.

The following year, a more extensive commercial vehicle test included three Knox trucks. Among the top six of the 1904 competition, three were electric vehicles from Columbia and Cantono. Out of eighteen entries, the class winner was a truck built by the Consolidated Motor Company headquartered in New York City. Carrying one-and-a-half

The 1903 Knox, with its light weight and one-cylinder "porcupine" gasoline engine, was the winner of the first American truck competition in New York City, beating steam- and electric-powered commercial vehicles.

tons of cargo it covered 239$\frac{1}{2}$ miles in 25.39 hours. There was also a gasoline/electric hybrid truck built by the Fischer Company.

The press and the public observed the truck trials with utmost skepticism. Motor vehicles were an entirely new technology, unknown and unproven. Those in the commercial transportation business scoffed at the notion that horses would be supplanted by machines. Yet men of vision who promoted progress knew the days of the horse-drawn wagon were numbered. But criticism resounded even from some of the boosters. The *Horseless Age* commented on the lack of safety of the trucks:

> A well-trained horse will often prevent a collision with an intersecting vehicle through its instinct of self preservation, but with the motor vehicle there is no such safeguard, and all safety depends upon the alertness of the driver and his facilities for watching the road in all directions.

As stated, it was not clear at the beginning of the 20th century which motive power would be the ideal choice for self-propelled vehicles. Progressive thinkers lampooned the horse, as did journalist Sylvestor Baxter in 1899:

> It is peculiarly appropriate that some cold facts about the horse be laid before the public at the present time. These will substantiate that the horse is an animal of extraordinary little sense— using the word as synonymous with judgment. He has a remarkably delicate perception, coupled with a very slight power of correlation. He is, therefore, subject to seizure at any moment with fits of the most violent insanity, induced at the slightest provocation. This, together with the enor-

mous reserve strength of the animal, makes him an exceedingly dangerous engine to be practically given the freedom of the road in our populous communities.... He is the chief maker of the vast and overwhelming din that envelopes the modern city.... Then at the end of the day every frequented street that meanwhile has not been constantly cleaned is literally carpeted with a warm, brown matting of comminuted horse-dropping, smelling to high heaven and destined in no inconsiderable part to be scattered as fine dust in all directions, laden with countless millions of disease-bearing germs.

With the advent of the self-propelled vehicle, the horse was on its way out, but which technology to choose, and why not reliable steam or electric power? As early as 1839, Robert Morris and Salom Anderson of Scotland had built a workable electric carriage. And in the blizzard of 1897–1898, a fleet of Electrobat Morris & Salom taxis were the only vehicles able to operate on the streets. But change had to be somewhat gradual for public acceptance to be incorporated in the evolution of progress. As another example, steam fire engine pumpers, which had been horse-drawn, were first replaced by two-wheel motorized tractors built by such companies as A&B, Christie and Ahrens-Fox before being entirely replaced by self-contained motorized fire engines.

The steam engine's flexibility in fuel sources was an advantage up to a certain point. Early vehicles used coal or coke to heat up the boiler, later ones kerosene and gasoline. Designers and entrepreneurs clung to the notion that steam engines, with their very high torque characteristics, could eliminate expensive transmissions, clutches and differentials while maintaining speed and pulling power. The idea of a puff of clean water vapor exhaust had its obvious allure even though it was overlooked that some kind of fuel still had to be burned to heat the water for steam to be produced, and this created remarkable quantities of gaseous by-products during the combustion process.

Steam vehicle builders such as Stanley and White were concerned that unsavory fumes would pollute the mostly urban surroundings where their vehicles would be used. James Halsey, a designer and inventor, claimed his steam wagon would be "free from odors, have no ashes ... no dangerous gasoline lamp, require no stoking." In early periodicals White advertised that its radiator's purpose was "to avoid the appearance of steam in crowded traffic."

Another problem with steam-powered vehicles was the complexity of their actual operation. Flash boilers made it possible to obtain steam power rather quickly—in some vehicles within a minute or two, but during World War I it became clearly apparent that moving out, even with such a short delay, might mean life or death. Operating steam vehicles required a number of time-consuming steps. The fuel had to be pumped up to a certain pressure (30 psi, for example) or whatever was specified for the particular vehicle. The boiler had to be filled. After steam was up, the engine had to be carefully bled of condensed water to avoid water-hammer damage. In most steam-powered vehicles of the World War I era these procedures would take 20 minutes or more. Steam vehicles required faithful proponents when even harnessing and hitching a team of horses required about the same time before being able to roll forward.

Abner Doble of the San Francisco Bay area has been cited as one of the few, perhaps only, builder of more easily usable modern steam vehicles. But the few dozen vehicles his company built, mostly luxurious cars, were hand-fabricated at a very high cost and were quite complicated. Nevertheless, old notions die hard, and steam power enthusiasts have continued to extol the elegance of steam engine motive power in a romanticized form of thoughtful wishing. Unless the problems of combustion by-product emissions, heat transfer, weight reduction and metal corrosion can be solved, the steam engine will remain essentially a technology of the past, though many fine restored steam-powered vehicles are still extant.

In the development of chemistry before World War I, it was understood that the oxidation (rusting) of steel not only turns it brown but also brittle and porous. To prevent this, brass, nickel, chrome, cadmium, zinc and copper plating were effectively used over the years, until the cost of such processes increased dramatically. At the same time, aesthetics of visible components have shifted reflecting increasing availability of paint, glass and plastics, the latter of which was just beginning to be developed in World War I.

No doubt the fascination with such naturally found material as transparent quartz, the new manmade materials were dubbed "Icinglass" and "Bakelite." Bakelite was the first successful synthetic resin, developed in 1909 by Belgian-American chemist Dr. Leo Hendrik Baekeland, who developed the polymer of phenol and formaldehyde with fiber fillers and pigments. Because it was almost noncombustible, except at very high temperature, it gradually replaced celluloid, sometimes commercially called "Icinglass" (sometimes spelled "isinglass"), as it was considered nearly transparent, at least translucent enough to permit adequate visibility.

Celluloid was the first plastic, synthesized in 1869 by John Wesley Hyatt from cellulose nitrate and camphor, nearly as combustible as its related substance, the explosive nitrocellulose. Some of the first photographic transparency material for still and moving film used celluloid, and its sudden and sometimes unpredictable combustibility resulted in the interruption of moving picture programs with an admixture of considerable panic. Of considerably better structural integrity, glass was used as a substitute for daguerreotypes, albeit not for moving film.

Glass made from melted silicon had been in existence for centuries, developed by 1500 B.C. in what is now called the Middle East. However, what is known today as safety glass, a fused laminate of two layers of glass and a central layer of plastic that shatters into large granules instead of sharp sheathes, daggers and ragged plates, was developed after World War I. That meant being thrown through a real glass window back in the First World War, whether due to explosive concussion or accident, could mean lacerations of life-and-death proportions.

Other significant advances during the Industrial Revolution were in the area of explosives. Like nitrocellulose, other explosive materials had been gradually developed since the first fireworks were created in the 10th century in China. "Black powder," eventually called gunpowder, although in different granulations and formulations, was described by Roger Bacon in the 13th century. Also sometimes called brown powder, it was a mixture of charcoal, potassium nitrate and sulfur. Guncotton was introduced in 1845 but proved to be too powerful for use in firearms. In the 1880s, smokeless powders were developed for firearms, which entirely superseded black powder, except for hobbies and special demonstration purposes.

Detonating explosives have been subdivided into basically two types: initiating explosives and high explosives. Initiating explosives, such as fulminate of mercury, are highly sensitive. The high explosive nitroglycerin was invented in 1846 by Italian Ascanio Soberro. This material was later combined with siliceous earth; then in 1867, Alfred Novel combined nitroglycerin with wood pulp to create dynamite. Nobel also invented another type of smokeless powder called Cordite.

By the turn of the century, trinitrotoluene was developed, known simply as TNT. Its explosive force is the standard by which all explosives are measured. The original grenade, a 16th century invention of unknown specific origin, consisted of a hollow iron ball filled with gunpowder and a lit fuse—now the classic stereotype of the round, black bomb. In addition to the gamut of artillery shells (mentioned further on), which all used explosive material, by the time of the "Great War" various grenades were also invented and developed, such as the British "Grenade No. 1," which was a cast-iron explosive on an 18-inch stick. It was known for its bouncing back tendencies.

The German stick grenade was more complex and had a string detonator. The Mills bomb had a spring-loaded firing pin, and due to accidental detonations was modified with a spring-loaded lever locked by a pin that actuated a four-second delay fuse. The surrounding metal was intentionally designed to fragment. Thirty-three million Mills bombs were manufactured, including the Martin Hale type, which could be fired from a rifle, sending it 600 feet and detonating with the use of an impact fuse. Compared to any previous wars, explosives packaged in all forms were a very significant "main feature" of World War I.

In addition to the rapid development of metallurgy before World War I, one of the most significant elements of industrial and technical progress was in electricity. Electricity was known to ancient humans in the form of lightning, which rightfully inspired much fear and was the source of considerable mythology due to the many mysteries of its essential physics not understood without scientific tools or knowledge.

Even small bits of amber when rubbed by fur produced static electrical current that attracted tiny particles, known in Greece as early as 600 B.C. *Elektron* was the Greek word for amber. It took nearly two thousand years before William Gilbert proved many other substances also had the same electrical properties.

The experiments of Benjamin Franklin have now become famous bits of historical trivia. He is said to have obtained sparks from a key tied to the string of a kite flying during a storm. Like Benjamin Franklin, William Watson of England theorized in 1847 the existence of a type of electrical static "fluid" that could be found in many substances. But practical application of static electricity proved elusive except for starting a fire.

Static electricity became the source of much amusement in the 1700s to the extent that small static-electricity mechanisms using turning wheels produced visible miniature sparks and glows used for visual awe and entertainment. The Smithsonian Institution even has a replicated 19th-century house parlor in which a man would touch a static electricity generator while transferring the palpable current through a kiss upon the lips of the humored visitor.

The essential challenge was how to store electricity in some form without continuously rubbing substances to form static. The Leyden jar was a primitive method of storing static electricity. This problem of storing electrical current was finally solved from a scientific perspective by Italian physicist Alessandro Giuseppe Antonio Anasastsio Volta, who was the inventor of the first electric battery in 1800. He called it a voltaic pile, which was made of alternating metals submerged in a mild acid. The unit of the electrical potential "volt" was therefore named in his honor.

Still, the challenge of harnessing electrical energy would not be of real practical value until Danish physicist Hans Christian Oersted in 1819 demonstrated that electricity and magnetism were directly related, and two years later in 1821 the English scientist Michael Faraday demonstrated the magnetic power of a free-hanging wire dipped into a pool of mercury. When an electric current was applied to the wire, it would turn, showing that there was a rotating magnetic field around the wire, essentially demonstrating the possibility of building an electric motor.

The first practical DC electric motor capable of work in practical applications was built by American Thomas Davenport, a Vermont blacksmith without education, though he had knowledge of the work by Joseph Henry and Michael Faraday. Davenport patented his electric motor in 1837. Numerous electrical motor and dynamo inventions cascaded from the minds of British, American and European inventors in the 1830s and 1840s, undoubtedly requiring an entire set of books on the subject itself.

By 1860 Gaston Faure invented the secondary cell, which would be the first rechargeable battery; this was unlike Volta's earlier battery, which needed to have the active elements replaced. With Faure's rechargeable battery, portable, renewable electric power was now available for a variety of mechanisms. Until then the problem had been the availability of electric current, which had no built distribution networks until the great inventions of Thomas Edison, among others.

Then in 1873, Zeobe Gramme combined a dynamo he had invented with a second similar unit driving it as a motor, and this became the first successful electric motor used in industry. Experiments by A.L. Ryker and William Morrison in the United States and by many in Europe led to the creation of the electric vehicle. Morrison's electric surrey, built in 1891 and showed by Harold Sturges and John A. Qualey, was used to carry visitors at the Chicago Columbia Exposition in Chicago in 1893. Without metal rails to carry electrical current, but based on lead-acid batteries, it made quite an impression on thousands of visitors. For a brief period, J.B. MacDonald made copies of the vehicle using a Siemens armature at the American Battery Company.

Numerous others followed in the production of electric motors, for various purposes such as tram and vehicle propulsion, including Thomas Edison, Siemens in Germany, United States Electrical Manufacturing Co., and Carl and Paul Bodine, whose first practical electric motors were used by dentists by 1907. The electric motor became a source of motive power for countless vehicles and mechanisms around the world, especially with the use of suspended wire electrification, which provided a continuous supply of current, in cities and later in rural areas, in addition to the development of reliable and rechargeable batteries. In addition to steam and internal combustion power, along with progress in chemistry, electrical power was undeniably one of the greatest contributions of the Industrial Revolution.

As important as electric motors, generators, solenoids and related mechanisms eventually became, the first truly practical application of electrical current was in the development of the telegraph, which used a primitive electric printer and a signaling code devised by Samuel F.B. Morse in 1837; in that year, Morse installed England's first railway telegraph system, which improved continuously for decades. In 1843 he received $30,000 from the United States Congress to create an experimental telegraph line between Washington, D.C., and Baltimore, Maryland. The first message was transmitted in 1844 and consisted of the sentence, "What hath God wrought?"

Morse's system of dots and dashes representing letters and numbers allowed for instant long-distance communication. The Morse Code was used in various forms through wires, and by using lights between ships and on land.

The next type of electric motor came into existence when Nikola Tesla patented the

William Morrison built this jitney in 1891 and made quite an impression when it was used to carry visitors at the Columbia Exposition of 1893 in Chicago.

alternating (AC) current type in 1888. Due to the simplicity of building batteries using lead and acid, lights, instruments, and devices such as horns, DC electrical systems were in use by World War I. The AC system's main advantage was in distance of transmission, and today's power lines, which can span hundreds of miles, all use AC electric power. Nikola Tesla spent many years developing the AC motor at the Westinghouse company, among many other inventions, some of which he did not have time to finish according to some historians.

Having beaten Edison for the huge contract, Tesla went on to light the 1893 Columbian Exhibition, his most famous accomplishment. Along with the AC motor, the basic ignition system, essentially used to this day, was perhaps Tesla's most useful invention.

One of the factors in the development of electrical innovations that made a gradual but very significant impact in World War I communications was the invention of the "wireless." Guglielmo Marconi, born in Italy, studied earlier experiments, such as that of

Once the telegraph and telephone were invented, Guglielmo Marconi developed the short-wave radio system along with other scientists of the era. "Wireless" communication technology was already in use by World War I, as seen here being set up with a White truck in 1916.

British scientist James Clark Maxwell in the 1860s, and those of Heinrich Hertz twenty years later. Maxwell predicted the possibility of generating electromagnetic waves for a type of "radiation," hence "radio" broadcasting. Both men were fascinated by the idea of eliminating wire in the use of the telegraph. Improving greatly on Hertz's experiments, Marconi offered his wireless communication system to the Italian government after William Pierce presented his version in 1892. By 1894 a British scientist, Oliver Lodge, sent Morse-code signals over half a mile, and in 1895 Russian physicist Alexander Stepanovich Popov also built a receiver that could detect electromagnetic waves in the atmosphere. He predicted that these waves could be generated and the signals picked up effectively over great distances.

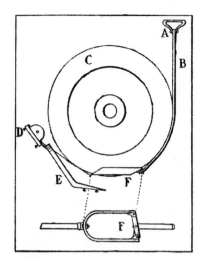

Marconi obtained a patent in England in 1896, and once securing his device as his own invention, he obtained financial backing and founded Marconi's Wireless Telegraph Company. In 1898 he transmitted a message across the English Channel. By 1900 when Marconi's four-circuit tuning system was proved to be entirely functional, it quickly became widespread in use, whether ship-to-shore or between antennae on the ground. It was especially proven by the 1901 experiment in which he received a radio-wave message at St. John's in Newfoundland from Cornwall, England. Marconi shared the Nobel prize in physics in 1909. By World War I the "wireless" was commonly used by the military for short-distance

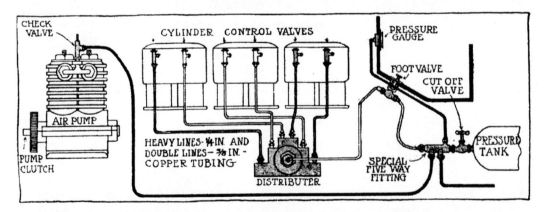

Top: What continued to plague the popularization of the internal combustion engine was how to get it started. The Kimball Pull starter was the simplest of all starters if not the most effective, especially with large motors. *Middle:* As World War I began, different starter mechanisms were still being offered, such as this attachment of the Ever-Ready Mechanical Spring Starter from 1914. *Bottom:* A schematic-type technical drawing of the Jenn-Steinmetz compressed-air starter.

J. L. LAKE & G. W. BEYERLE.
ENGINE STARTER.
APPLICATION FILED MAY 1, 1914

1,125,130.   Patented Jan. 19, 1915.

A complex kick-starter patent of 1914 with over-riding clutch was useful for small motors such as on motorcycles, but not for large engines.

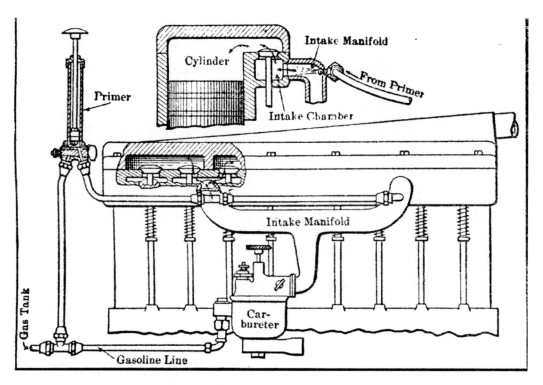

The K.E.W. Motor Primer, which injected an explosive mixture into the intake chamber, was yet another method of starting the internal combustion engine when engineers assumed it was near impossible to use an electric motor.

communication. Marconi himself represented Italy at the Paris Peace Conference in 1919 when the war ended.

During World War I, communication became the new imperative in terms of wide-scale operations as never before in the theater of combat, and it involved new technology that had never been used before this global conflict. Wireless communication was the latest and most versatile method of relaying vital information, yet German wartime message transfer was effectively blocked by intentional interference from the Eiffel Tower, which has been called the earliest form of radio jamming used in combat. On the western front, telephone cables were buried eight feet deep so that bombardment would not break the actual cable lines. At the end of the war it was calculated that the U.S. Signal Corps had strung approximately 100,000 miles of wire throughout France alone. According to historian William Dooly, Jr., at the peak the Signal Corps was "operating 282 telephone exchanges and 133 telegraph stations with nearly 15,000 telephone lines and 9,000 stations; and 47,555 telegrams a day averaging 60 words each were sent."

Another challenge in the field of electrical engineering just before World War I, largely overlooked but quite essential, was how to start up the internal combustion engine and continue its operation as long as fuel was supplied to the engine. The magneto had been developed in the 1890s and required no storage battery as it generated and distributed current to fire the spark plugs. The intensity of the voltage increased as the engine speed increased. But the problem of starting the engine, basic as it may seem, was one that had not been solved even in the first decade of the 20th century. Because of the complexity of approaches by numerous persons involving several patents, it may be worthwhile to look at this technical problem in some detail.

Most motors in those days had to be hand-cranked. But first the ignition had to be retarded or the motor would very likely backfire, often times spraining or breaking the person's wrist or thumb. There was a special "over-the-top" way to hold the crank to help prevent this hazard, but many thousands of people had serious injuries from starting an engine back then. There were even some deaths associated with this "kick-back" phenomenon that manufacturers were in a quandary as to how to resolve.

Hand-cranking also limited the size of the motor. With a large motor it was almost impossible to overcome the compression in the cylinders by arm strength alone. Hence the hand-crank was nicknamed the "armstrong" starter. Early on, there were several different inventions that attempted to resolve the problem of "firing up" the internal combustion engine.

Electric vehicles had the distinct advantage of needing only the flip of a switch and the push of a lever to get moving. For pickup and delivery work it was especially convenient to shut off the electric motor at each stop rather than having to crank-start the motor each time, or be forced to leave it running. *Motor Age* stated in the October 12, 1911, issue, "The self-starter is one thing that is badly needed. Once it arrives it will place the gasoline car on an equality with the electric car."

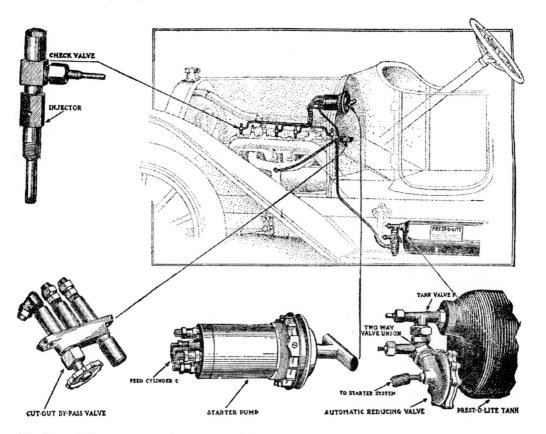

The Prest-O-Starter measured an amount of Prest-O-Lite gas into each cylinder in order to begin combustion and turn over the motor.

Curiously, the actual development of electric starter motors (or self-starters as they were called) began earlier without much notice or special inspirational impetus toward manufacturing or mass production. According to the Society of Automotive Historians, an automobile called the Armstrong, built in 1896 in Bridgeport, Connecticut, had an electric starter motor built into the clutch. Over the years this car was erroneously called an electric car, which it was not. The vehicle has remained extant in England.

Another early patent was issued to Clyde Coleman in 1903 (No. 745,157, Means for Operating Motor Vehicles) and later to the same man in 1907 (Patent No. 842,627, Starting Means for Internal Combustion Engines). Both patents were assigned to companies for which Clyde Coleman worked, and that is perhaps why his name was not readily recognized until he began working alongside Charles Kettering at General Motors.

Steam-powered vehicles took time to get warmed up, but no hand-cranking per se was necessary, except for pumping up the fuel system to a determined pressure. However, the energy density of gasoline, as well as its availability and storage convenience, made gasoline the most effective fuel for vehicles as well as aircraft, which were usually started by throwing over the propeller, another dangerous proposition. But once the Model T arrived in 1908 and the oil industry gained momentum, the internal combustion engine was here to stay.

Some of the first self-starters used compressed air to turn over the engine. Two methods were used. One used a separate compressor; the other used exhaust gasses. As early as 1904, William Forest Meserve built a passenger car with a four-cylinder two-cycle engine that had a compressed-air starter. In 1905, the successful Alexander Winton offered

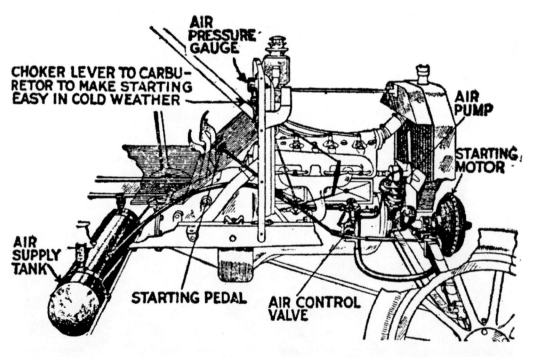

As difficult as the compressed-air starter was to manufacture in the early days, it was ahead of its time and has been used in recent times now that compressors and air tanks can be manufactured with reliability.

a Model C car with a 2-cylinder engine that had an exhaust gas starter device that could also be used to fill the pneumatic tires. The Triumph Motor Car Company of Chicago offered a compressed-air starter on their Model A in 1907.

According to the *Horseless Age,* the first Chevrolets had compressed-air starters. John Walter Christie was another early inventor who designed and used a compressed-air starting system. Christie formed the Front Drive Motor Company, which built the Christie Tractor. At least 600 were used by several fire departments as successor to the horse when fire apparatus were too expensive to replace with new trucks.

Other designs were more unusual but used quite commonly before the arrival of the electric starter motor. The most widely used at one time was the explosive gas method. The *Automobile* of January 4, 1912, stated, "The type which appears to have the most extensive adoption is the first-named, the acetylene gas starter." Presto-O-Lite used this method, which involved a hand pump that introduced acetylene gas into the cylinder before a spark exploded it, moving the pistons down and starting the motor.

An earlier method called the Ignition Starter required the driver to shut off the motor with the throttle open, leaving raw gas in the cylinders. If the pistons were in the right position, the ignition spark would cause the gas/air mixture to explode, which would start the motor. A priming pump was devised later, the so-called Priming Starter. The Christensen Gasoline and Air Starter went one step further with the use of a compressed-air tank and separate carburetor/distributor unit along with valves and gauges. The simplest starter was the Kimball Pull Starter, which used a handle and strap.

In the early days, the electric motor had not been successfully applied as a starter for the internal combustion engine only because of scientific and engineering naysaying. Everyone who had even contemplated the idea of using an electric motor to start a gasoline engine could prove on paper that it was impossible. According to all the expert calculations, it

Once the electric self-starter was invented before World War I, the military could use large Caterpillar tractors, such as this 5-ton artillery tow vehicle.

This 1918 Maxwell 25 was built in cooperation with Chalmers Motors of Detroit. The leased Maxwell factories would also build the American Buda-powered M1917 tank towards the end of the war.

would take an electric motor nearly the same size as the engine itself to be effective, and this was obviously highly impractical.

History has a way of taking strange turns. It was 1908 and Byron J. Carter, known for the Cartercar and inventor of friction drive, who was vice-president of the Motorcar Company of Detroit at the time, was on his way to Belle Isle on the Detroit River. On the bridge ahead of him a woman had stalled her car and was blocking his way. Carter got out to crank-start her engine but was unaware that the ignition advance had not been retarded. As was the case so often, the engine backfired and the motor crank hit Carter in the face, shattering his jaw. Contrary to much rumor and misinformation, Carter died on April 6, 1908, from pneumonia and other complications of his painful injury. Although some historians are not convinced of this tragic scenario, the *Cycle and Automobile Trade Journal* of May 1908, *Motor Field Magazine* of May 1908 and the *Horseless Age* of April 15, 1908, each carried an obituary, among other publications citing this episode.

Carter's death apparently had an effect on Henry Leland. He entrusted the challenge of resolving this technical problem to Charles Kettering, one of his engineers.

Kettering was already an accomplished designer who had just solved the problem of using an electric motor to operate cash registers. It was a similar case in which engineers could use calculations to prove it was impossible to resolve the problem unless the electric motor was the same size as the cash register. Kettering had also developed a successful battery ignition system for Cadillac. He correctly deduced that the electric motor, just as in the cash register design, did not have to operate continuously but only for a short moment. A small motor could be overloaded briefly as long as it cooled down between uses. He first installed an electric starter on Christmas Eve of 1910 and drove the Cadillac to Detroit to show Leland. Leland kept the car for further testing and Kettering installed an electric motor in another Cadillac in Dayton. After further testing, all 1912 model year Cadillacs had electric starters.

Cadillac received the Dewar Award in 1913 for the greatest contribution in automobile progress for the year. Other manufacturers quickly followed suit, with Ford and some truck builders holding out the longest before incorporating a battery and starter motor system of their own. Patent infringement lawsuits were abundant and other companies claimed to have the first electric self-starter. But the invention would change many people's attitudes regarding ease of operation, expanding the market much further.

However, many, if not most, of the vehicles used in World War I had to be hand-cranked to start, even with motors of over 400 cubic-inch displacement such as the Liberty B truck four-cylinder. With a primitive ignition system, uncertain carburetor, and damp magneto on a cold day, it would have posed a challenge to even the strongest man in the battalion.

Following along with the hypothesis that the Industrial Revolution was the precursor to World War I, the subject of medicine and medical practice must be addressed, at least very superficially in the context of the discussion of modern invention and scientific progress in general. Following the Age of Enlightenment of the 1700s, during which secular views on human reason and scientific discovery were emphasized, philosophers alongside inventors and industrialists as well as those in the field of medicine began focusing on the improvement of human life through empirical study and science, rather than basing their well-being on religion, metaphysics or superstition.

The discovery that the human body responded and functioned by stimulation of electrical current was a milestone that paralleled the interest in dissection of bodies. However, this also resulted in some remarkable practices such as body snatching, both dead and alive, during the 1800s as regulations were placed restricting schools of medicine to a small number of cadavers that could be autopsied for the education of its students. In the United States and Britain, for example, only four bodies per school were allowed, leading to night-time grave robbing and even murder. A pinnacle of science fiction, the apotheosis of Dr. Frankenstein, caught the imagination of the public in a novel written by Mary Shelley (wife of Percy Bysshe Shelley) in 1816 after decades of fascination with the idea of "resurrectionism."

For the purpose of this discussion, the subject of military medicine and nursing is most specifically pertinent. For example, of the 6,000,000 soldiers that died in the Napoleonic Wars it is impossible to determine how many died from wounds and what number died from other causes such as disease. Death as a result of wretched hospital conditions was common in ensuing conflicts, particularly during the Crimean War of 1854.

In general, the medical advances necessary to care for those most severely affected by war lagged behind other technological and scientific progress. An exceptional example in the realm of compassionate medical practice was the tireless work of Florence Nightingale, who devoted her life to nursing and helped change the backward attitudes toward the care of the sick and wounded. A school for nurses at St. Thomas's Hospital in London was opened on June 15, 1860, in her name. But progress along these lines was quite

Of the numerous health issues in addition to wounds and injuries was infestation by vermin. This truck was one of many that carried de-lousing equipment to rid soldiers of so-called "cooties." Antisepsis had been developed by Louis Pasteur and Joseph Lister.

slow overall. For example, in the American Civil War, the mortality rate from disease was double that from battle wounds.

In 1862, Swiss philanthropist Henri Durant published a book on the tremendous suffering of soldiers he witnessed in the Battle of Solferino. The popular reaction to his writing resulted in the International Conference of Red Cross Societies of 1863. Each nation's participants set up associations for the purpose to aid the wounded, and at the beginning fourteen nations signed an agreement to the Geneva Convention, allowing all those who were sick or wounded and army and medical staff to be treated as neutrals in the battlefield.

What was available in the way of inoculation and anesthesia became imperatives in the saving of lives that would otherwise perish as an outcome of battle (and later natural disasters, as the Red Cross was organized more broadly). The quick evacuation of the wounded by motor vehicle became essential in saving lives. However, medical practice was still rather primitive. It would take another decade after World War I that the first real antibiotic in the form of penicillin to be discovered by Scottish biologist Alexander Fleming. His work would not be put into truly practical use until a group of biologists, including H.W. Florey, would first purify penicillin in 1941, establishing its effectiveness in treating infectious diseases without serious side effects. The most common disfigurements and maladies of World War I veterans were infections, amputations, blindness, untreatable venereal disease, as well as what was then labeled "shell shock," which in actuality was a euphemism for profound mental and psychological trauma.

Bacteriophage was discovered during World War I but not put into use until the 1930s, and then only in isolated parts of the world. Perhaps the most significant advance

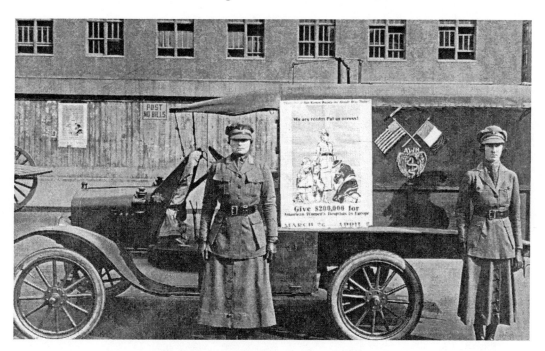

Following in the footsteps of Florence Nightingale, nurses were the main caregivers of the sick and wounded. Here, using a 1918 Ford ambulance, two women representing America Women's Hospitals raised $200,000 through the Medical College of Pennsylvania.

prior to World War I in the field of medicine was the discovery of the X-ray by Wilhelm Roentgen, who received the Nobel Prize in 1901.

Medicine was also advanced indirectly (at first) by the discovery of vulcanization of rubber. Of all the advances, vulcanization could be considered the most widely influential fluke, in that its discovery could be called accidental as well as tragic for the inventor himself. Some of the first useful applications of rubber were also in the field of medicine in the form of tubing, bottle stoppers, gloves, rollers, et cetera.

Until the discovery of vulcanized rubber, wheels were made of wood or metal (stone was used much earlier), and the word *tire* referred to the "attire"—an outer leather or metal hoop—worn by the wheel. Rail wheels used pressed-on metal hoops. For road uses, leather softened the contact as it rolled. After vulcanization was discovered, rubber-covered wheels allowed vehicles to roll faster, quieter and longer with better traction.

Documented usage of rubber goes back to the Orient in the middle of the second millennium. For centuries rubber was known in Europe as a gummy and gooey substance derived from the sap of rubber trees and rubber plants, such as the *Havea brasiliensis* and *Ficus elastica*. In the 1700s and 1800s Brazil was the main producer before production shifted over to Asia and Africa.

Rubber treated with nitric acid was used to make coated shoes as early as 1836. This was the year that Edwin M. Chaffee of Roxberry, Massachusetts, developed a calendaring machine, which applied rubber directly to fabric in a uniform coating without the need for solvents.

Charles Goodyear discovered vulcanization by accident in 1839. Goodyear was a persevering inventor who believed that rubber could be cured or tanned much like leather.

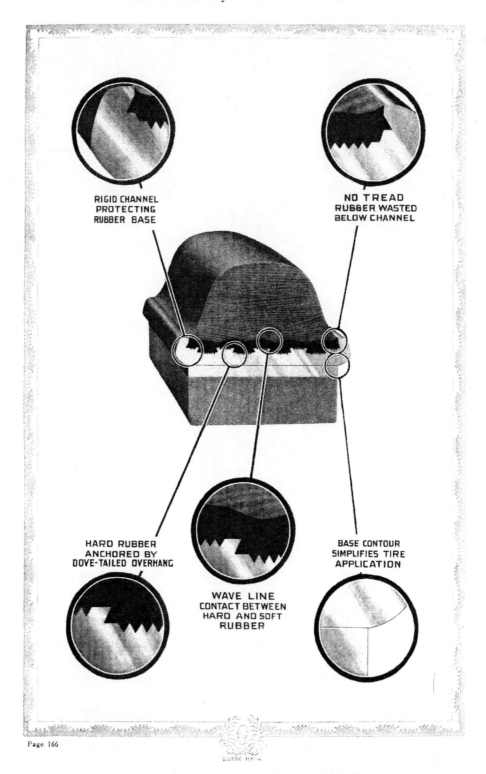

Once rubber vulcanization was discovered, hard rubber tires for heavier vehicles were molded onto wood or metal wheel rims. This technology's design complexities are shown here in magnification.

While adding different substances to a batch of rubber, a mixture of sulfur and rubber sap fell onto his hot kitchen stove. Goodyear left the spilled rubber to melt and congeal and the stove to cool before cleaning it up. When he did scrape up the rubber spill, he noticed that it was smooth, dry and flexible. He nailed the piece of rubber to the door outside in the cold winter air overnight. The next morning he was ecstatic to find it was not brittle at all, but fully pliable and flexible, yet structurally congealed and intact.

The accidental combination of sulfur and heat had "cured" the rubber, and the term *vulcanized* was derived from the name of the blacksmithing Roman god Vulcan. Charles Goodyear patented the vulcanizing process in 1844, but financial success eluded him completely. His experiments had cost him his entire savings, and perfecting the vulcanization process had sunk him deeper into debt. At one point, according to his book *Gum-Elastic and Its Varieties*, Goodyear was even forced to pawn his children's school books, justifying his actions by stating that "the certainty of success warranted extreme measures of sacrifice." Instead, he was sent to debtor's prison. When Charles Goodyear died in 1860, his family was left with $200,000 in bills and unpaid loans.

The patent on vulcanized rubber sat forgotten for ten years after Goodyear's death. In 1870 Benjamin Franklin Goodrich, who had been a Civil War surgeon, turned his attention to vulcanized rubber for use in medical applications and in industry. Goodrich had no problems persuading investors to help build his company, the B.F. Goodrich Company of Akron, Ohio, the predecessor of the Goodyear Company founded later in honor of Charles Goodyear.

Cotton-covered rubber hose became the first best-selling product, especially for fire fighting. By 1871 there were also rubber gaskets, jar rings, bottle stoppers, clothes wringer rollers, shoes and tires, among other items.

Invention of the inflatable rubber vehicle tire was a separate development, most of which took place in England. The pneumatic tire was first patented in 1845 by Robert W. Thomson. He called his tire "elastic bearings for carriages," which consisted of several layers of rubber-saturated canvas with air pockets, rarely used on carriages.

His first tires were made from leather with an internal coating of rubber to create an air-tight chamber. In 1846 Thomson was granted a patent in France, and in 1847 he received a U.S. patent. But his efforts stalled and the pneumatic tire sat forgotten for decades, just as the patent for vulcanization had also been neglected.

In 1888 John Boyd Dunlop tested vehicles with both solid rubber and inflated tires. He received a patent later that year, and investors poured money into his venture. In 1890 the Thomson patent was uncovered, and the discovery of "prior art" resulted in Dunlop's patent becoming instantly unenforceable.

Within a few years, hundreds of companies in Europe and America sprang up to manufacture inflatable rubber tires. These were at first intended for the lightest applications, which at the time was specifically for the newly invented modern-type bicycle. "Servicing the ruptured tire" was something inventors such as Dunlop had overlooked in terms of practicality. Dunlop's tire, for example, was attached to the wheel with 70 bolts.

The first wire-bead tire was invented by Charles Kingston Welsh in 1890. Later that year the design was refined by William Bartlett, who was first to obtain a patent on a detachable pneumatic tire called a "clincher" because wires in the molded rubber would fit into flanges of a wheel. His design was similar to Thomas Jeffery's "clincher" tire.

At that time the Michelin Brothers, Andre and Edouard, were already in the rubber

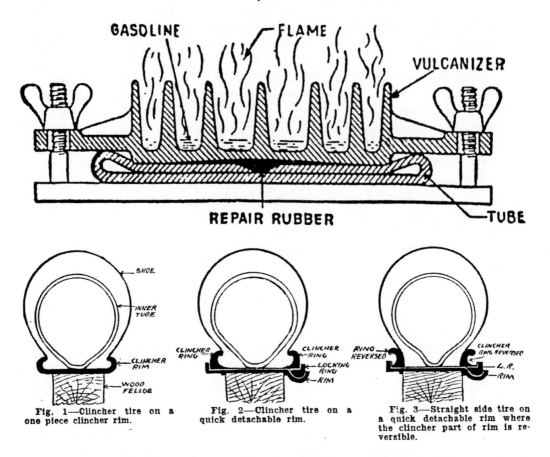

Top: For pneumatic tires, inner tubes were patched using a disc of rubber and a "vulcanizer plate," which had a small reservoir of gasoline or other flammable liquid. *Bottom:* This illustration shows a cross-section of three types of pneumatic tire rims from 1918.

and leather business. They patented a pneumatic tire in 1891 in Europe. Their demountable tire was intended especially for bicycle wheels at a time when bicycles became extremely popular across the world. That same year, another important advance in pneumatic tire design became available: the two-way tire valve, which was invented by Charles H. Woods. The first Michelin automobile tire was introduced in 1895.

Meanwhile, in the United States the first inflatable tire was built by the B.F. Goodrich Company for Alexander Winton of Cleveland, Ohio, builder of the Winton automobile. This was on a special-order basis. It was in 1891 that a company by the name of New York Belting and Packing began manufacturing pneumatic tires for bicycles. Charles R. Flint bought this company while building up the Rubber Trust. After the enactment of various anti-trust laws at the turn of the century, the Rubber Trust turned into the United States Rubber Company, which would later absorb the Morgan and Wright Company of Detroit, Michigan, in 1914. Up to that time Morgan and Wright held about 70 percent of the bicycle tire market in America.

The rubber curing press, which allowed molding of tread patterns and lettering directly into the tire during vulcanization, was invented by H.J. Doughty in 1896. A dozen years later, Firestone offered a tread pattern that literally spelled out "NON SKID." Addition-

Thomas B. Jeffery built Rambler bicycles and was also the inventor of a clincher tire before building his first automobile in 1897, shown here.

ally, in 1908 George H. Schrader invented the screw-in tire valve, which, essentially in its basic form, has been used to the present time.

A couple of years into the 20th century, Harley-Davidson, Indian and other companies began manufacturing motorcycles, so a new market quickly sprang up, and at the same time over 200 bicycle companies expanded into some type of automobile development. One of the best known was the Gormully and Jeffery Company, which eventually became American Motors Corporation. The first Rambler was actually a bicycle.

Tires were originally reinforced with linen, then later with cotton fiber. For more than a decade, tires were the color of natural rubber, which was milky white. By 1904 it was discovered that adding carbon black to the rubber helped its structural integrity. This innovation was first accomplished by Sidney C. Mote in Silvertown, England. Another significant improvement took place in 1906 when George Oenslager of the Diamond Rubber Company discovered chemical accelerators for the curing time of rubber.

Tires for heavy-duty applications, including most trucks and commercial vehicles, remained composed of solid rubber without any tread pattern. Many battery-powered electric vehicles benefited from the lower rolling resistance of very narrow hard rubber tires, and at that time heavy steam-powered trucks competed with internal combustion–powered vehicles as well as electric battery-powered vehicles. Ten-ton capacity trucks were available by the end of the century's first decade, but none could use pneumatic tires.

Another in a series of milestones in development was the invention of the Banbury Mixer in 1916. The Banbury Mixer, which speeded up the manufacturing process dramat-

ically, has been used to the present day much as the calendaring machine. Hard rubber tires were most commonly held by embedded wire and later molded into a dove-tail groove of the wheel. By 1917 the Goodrich hard rubber tire had been greatly refined, with side-removable molds for simple treads, but all solid rubber tires were known for their lack of cushioning. Because vehicles had very stiff suspensions, some soldiers during World War I wore kidney belts to withstand the jarring and hammering of a truck on rough roads.

In pneumatic tire development up to World War I, a significant patent by Christian Hamilton Gray and Thomas Sloper in 1913 remained forgotten for decades. Their design used radial-ply construction, which literally radiated from the inner diameter, as opposed to the simple bias-ply that held on for many years, until Michelin introduced their own radial ply called Michelin X, but decades later.

After World War I, tire technology continuously improved, and the Goodyear Tire and Rubber Company of Akron, Ohio, embarked on an effort to engineer a pneumatic tire for heavy-duty applications. The company had pioneered in the development of pneumatic tires for five-ton capacity at the end of World War I in 1918. Goodyear built several of its own six-wheel three-axle trucks to prove a point. By April of 1917 Goodyear organized a fleet of Mack, Packard and White trucks and embarked on a 740-mile journey to test the new tires from Akron, Ohio, to Boston, Massachu-

Molding a tread pattern was important for better traction, such as this Firestone "Non-Skid" tire developed prior to World War I.

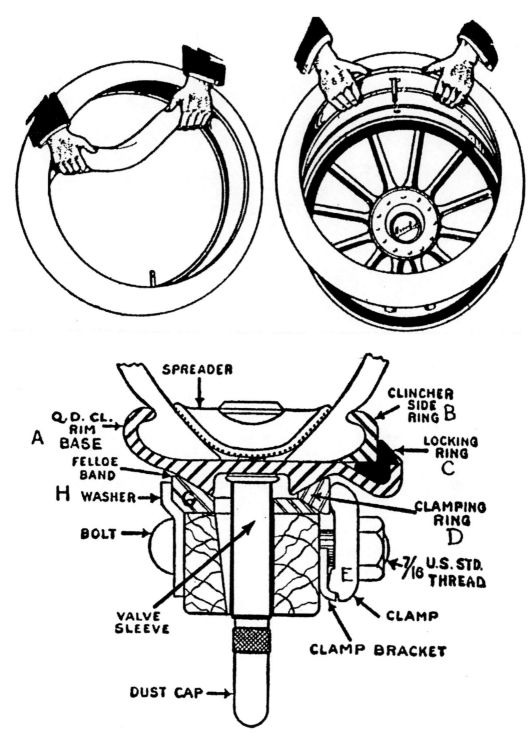

Top: "Tire ruptures" were an everyday occurrence and involved replacing the inner tube by hand, which required technique, hand strength and dexterity. *Bottom:* The tire valve of 1918 was patented, and it greatly simplified the inflation of motor vehicle inner tubes before "tubeless" tires were invented.

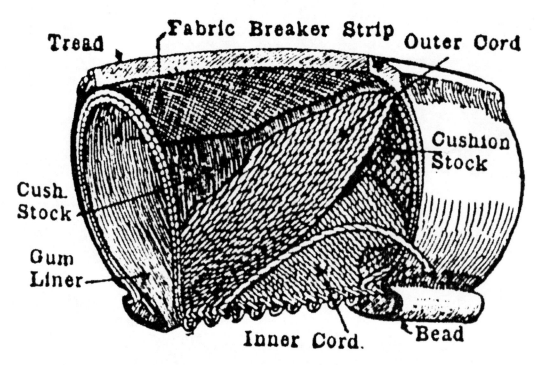

Tread   Fabric Breaker Strip   Outer Cord

Cushion Stock

Cush. Stock

Gum Liner

Inner Cord.   Bead

The first radial tire was invented in 1913 by Christian Hamilton Gray and Thomas Sloper, but it remained forgotten for decades until Michelin made it famous.

setts, over the Allegheny Mountains. These heights could not be crossed in bad weather without pneumatic tread-pattern tires, which were also capable of withstanding 35 mph on a flat solid road. Specifically, these tires were called "balloon tires" and were 38 × 7 in front and 44 × 10 in the rear.

One of the first problems was the mismatch of the truck's cargo surface area and that of the loading dock. Goodyear used the tandem bogie, which was a non-driven third axle, to solve this problem. Automotive engineer Ellis W. Templin helped in the design of the Goodyear trucks. At this time Harold Gray at B.F. Goodrich and Sidney M. Cadwell at United States Rubber Company were both credited with the discovery of antioxidants for rubber, which further advanced their strength and durability at a time when punctures, ruptures and blowouts were a regular occurrence.

Kicking tires became a well-known sight among truck drivers. With multiple tires at the rear of the truck, either with duals or multiple axles, the driver could tell which tire was deflated by its soft "thunk" sound, as opposed to the more solid "thud" sound of an inflated tire. Since the punctured tire was still lifted off the ground by its adjoining good tire, a visual inspection was not enough. With only four tires on a vehicle it was easy to see which tire was literally flat. Passenger car drivers rarely understood this significance, and "tire kicking" became a sort of contemporary urban mythology as well as an idiom meaning "casual testing."

In military service, tires were only second to problematic components such as U-joints, which were the weakest link in the drive-shaft mechanism. Lubrication of bearing surfaces and the sealing from abrasive sand and dirt, at first performed by leather, were gradually developed from the experience of extreme conditions.

A fairly thorough analysis of tire problems was published by *Automotive Industries* as well as by *Commercial Car Journal*, among other periodicals, in July of 1917. Problems with the adopted American-designed type SAE rims became apparent quite rapidly, even though the locking rings, bolts and nuts were thoroughly galvanized and fitted with wooden center struts to prevent distortion of the outer rims. The muddy conditions in Europe quickly proved that this design type resulted in so much rust that the tires could not be removed even in a tire press.

It was also strongly advised to limit the number of sizes for truck tires. Universal diameter and five-inch width were the recommended size, although when used as duals in the rear they developed problems with uneven wear due to concentrated weight distribution on the outer wheel, whereas on heavily cambered roads the weight would be concentrated on the inner wheels. The engineer and author of this analysis, Owen Thomas, advocated the use of single, wider rear tires, and pointed out that American tire manufacturers were over-curing the rubber, making them more liable to crumble. He also recommended abandoning wooden wheels in favor of cast or pressed steel, standardizing hubs to fit all makes of ball and roller bearings, and avoiding the use of a separate flanged hub in favor of a smooth disk due to the wet and muddy conditions.

But the development of the motorcar in America and its role in World War I would have had an entirely different complexion had it not been for George B. Selden's monopolization of *all* automobiles through an inauspicious patent. Having obtained the all-inclusive patent on November 5, 1895, Selden was in the position to control all motor vehicle companies that used an internal combustion engine and was doing business in the United States. They were forced to apply for a license to manufacture or distribute gasoline-powered cars and trucks and pay a licensing fee through the Association of Licensed Automobile Manufacturers (ALAM).

It should be noted that ALAM was instrumental in adopting universal specifications, such as for a motor's horsepower (referred in these pages simply as "hp," and also cubic-inch displacement, abbreviated "cid"). ALAM differentiated a motor's bare power (brake horsepower) from final output horsepower, which was measured along with all other components and friction-producing, power-robbing mechanisms of the vehicle. This type of power measurement differentiation was adopted by SAE and in Europe as the DIN specification. For example, an engine producing 100 brake horsepower may in reality be worth only 50 hp when all its additional components and accessories are taken into account. A decimal point usually indicated detailed SAE specs.

George Baldwin Selden was a Rochester patent attorney whose interests included mechanical inventions. At an exposition during 1876 in Philadelphia, Selden took notice of a two-cycle Brayton engine, and drew up a vehicle with this type of motor in mind the following year. The idea was in fact quite progressive. Selden kept a close eye on the technology as it evolved and kept the patent from being issued by filing amendments until 1893.

Patent No. 549,160 was issued two years later, just 23 days before the famous Times-Herald Race of 1895. What made the contest well known was the entry of the Duryea Brothers' Motor Wagon, which was considered one of the first, if not the very first, of America's internal combustion–powered vehicles. Despite the rapid proliferation of motor vehicles in the late 1890s, no companies were interested in buying the rights to the U.S. Selden patent.

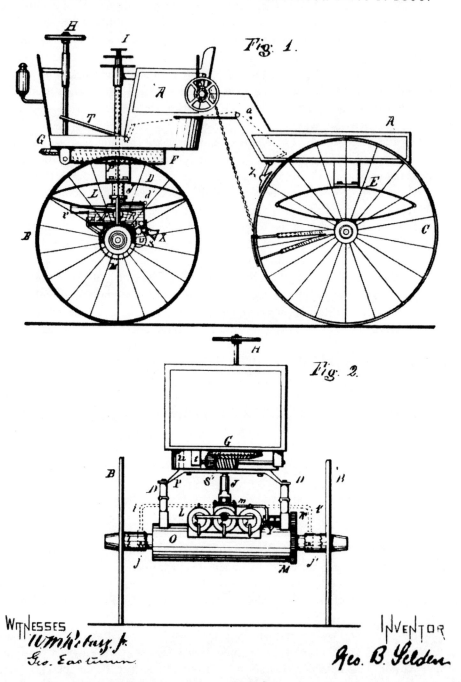

One of the most remarkable patents of all time was granted in 1895 to George Selden for his "Road Engine," which allowed him to monopolize the automotive industry until Henry Ford challenged him.

Henry Ford in his later years showing his first car, the Quadricycle of 1896. Ford would not go along with the Selden Patent when he was refused a licensing agreement to build automobiles.

Meanwhile, Colonel Albert Pope was building Columbia bicycles in the early 1890s. Intrigued by the development of motorized transportation, Pope decided to enter the field, and his company began building Columbia electric vehicles in 1897, and an assortment of gasoline-powered vehicles as well.

Colonel Albert A. Pope was a very successful businessman for a number of years before his small industrial empire fell apart. The complexity of his investments and involvements illustrates the inception of motorized transport in America when the "horseless carriage" was considered merely a novelty and a fad.

After the Civil War, Colonel Pope started his Pope Manufacturing Company in Boston during 1876. The company was established to manufacture small patented articles, which included sewing machines. Colonel Pope designed a bicycle in 1877, which was consigned to the Weed Sewing Machine Company in Hartford, Connecticut, for manufacturing. Pope took over the company in 1880.

By 1899 Pope had bought out or merged with 45 bicycle manufacturers to create a

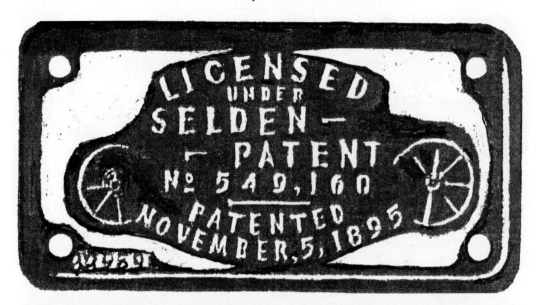

Top: An enlargement of the brass plate issued by the Association of Licensed Automobile Manufacturers (ALAM) to all those who manufactured or imported a motorcar in America. This was proof that a company had permission to build gasoline-powered cars, but ALAM had connections to electric vehicle and battery companies who had other interests in mind. *Bottom:* As early as 1907, Anheuser-Busch bought thirteen Pope-Waverly electric trucks at a time when it was uncertain whether steam-, gasoline- or battery-powered vehicles would dominate the transportation industry.

THE POPE-HARTFORD THREE-TON TRUCK

Chassis Only		Complete Truck
$3,350	For 14-foot Platform and Stake Body, The Standard Size.	$3,550
$3,350	For 12-foot Platform and Stake Body, Optional Size.	$3,550
$3,475	For 16-foot Platform and Stake Body, Special 160" Wheel Base	$3,675

For specifications, see page 3.

This factory illustration of a Pope-Hartford 3-ton truck shows one of the vehicles produced by a company that was part of Albert Pope's short-lived manufacturing empire at a time when electric and gasoline vehicles in particular competed for the rapidly emerging market.

"Bicycle Trust." Trusts were a free enterprise business phenomenon that were eventually dismantled by the federal government (i.e., President Theodore Roosevelt) to undo monopolies of certain industries; the Oil Trust was the most famous of them all, but there were many others (Lead Trust, Sugar Trust, Beef Trust, et cetera).

Bicycle components, especially wheels, bearings, chains, axles, frames and tires, became important in the development of motor vehicles. The Pope empire was as complicated and financially precarious as it was lucrative and widespread for a brief period just before World War I.

Pope had used the name *Columbia* for one of his best-selling bicycles, taking advantage of the widespread popularity of the 1893 Columbian Exhibition in Chicago. In 1896 the company developed an electric vehicle by that name, and Colonel Pope hired Hiram Percy Maxim to head the motorized carriage part of the business. His claim to fame was having invented one of the first mufflers for motor vehicles as well as silencers for guns. His uncle, Sir Hiram Stevens Maxim (of U.S. birth but British Knighthood), invented the machine gun in 1884, which the British adopted in 1897. In 1898 the company built 500 Columbia electric vehicles, along with forty gasoline carriages designed by H. P. Maxim.

The Pope enterprise history got more complex when financier William Collins Whitney bought the Electric Vehicle Company owned by Isaac Rice, brief operator of taxis in

List of Early Electric Vehicle Manufacturers

American Electric (1896–1902)
Argo (1912–1916)
Babcock (1906–1912)
Bachelle (1900–1903)
Bailey (1907–1916)
Baker (1899–1916)
Borland (1910–1916)
Broc (1909–1916)
Buffalo (1901–1906) (1912–1915)
Buffalo Rochester (1899–1900)
Chicago (1913–1916)
Cleveland (1909–1910)
Columbia (1897–1913)
Commercial Truck / C.T. (1908–1928)
Detroit Electric (1907–1938)
Eastman (1898–1900)
Edison (1913)
Electra (1913)
Electric Carriage (1896–1897)
Electric Vehicle / E.V. (1897–1899)
   (1904–1906)
Electrical (1906)
Electricquette (1914–1915)
Electrocar (1922)

Electroc-Coach (1913–1914)
Electromobile (1906–1907)
Flanders (1912–1914)
Fritchle (1905–1919)
General Electric (1898–1899)
GMC (1911–1915)
Grinnell (1912–1915
Hupp-Yeats (1911–1919)
Kimball (1910–1912)
Milburn (1914–1916)
Morris and Salom (1895–1897)
National (1900–1908)
Ohio (1910–1918)
Pope-Hartford (1906–1914)
Pope-Waverly (1904–1908)
Rauch and Lang (1905–1928)
Riker (1897–1902)
Studebaker (1902–1912)
Tiffany (1913–1914)
Ward (1905–1934)
Walker (1906–1942)
Waverly (1898–1903) (1909–1916)
Woods (1898–1918)

New York. Whitney got financial backing from Pope, and the Columbia Automobile Company was formed to build Columbia electric vehicles, while the Electric Vehicle Company continued in business to build taxis and electric vehicle (EV) trucks and buses. In 1900 the entire enterprise under Pope's control became known as the Columbia and Electric Vehicle Company of Hartford.

At the turn of the century the Electric Vehicle Company acquired the Selden patent for all gasoline vehicles. As an attorney, Selden was clever enough to have kept his patent alive, asserting that he had built an actual Selden vehicle. It resembled a wagon/light truck, having a small bed in the back and a carriage seat for two up front. His 1877 prototype was later proven to have been built years later.

At the turn of the previous century, the Lead Trust had acquired many electric vehicle manufacturers, electric streetcar franchises, battery manufacturers and electric taxi service companies. Among the firms that had been acquired was the Columbia and Electric Vehicle Company, which owned the Selden Patent. Now the patent on all "hydro-carbon" powered vehicles was in the hands of the so-called competition.

Because electric vehicle sales were not expanding, the Electric Vehicle company began a program of collecting on the Selden patent under the auspices of the Lead Trust and ALAM. Every gasoline vehicle manufacturer had to get a license and pay a royalty to build gasoline cars, trucks and buses to whomever owned the Selden patent, of which George Selden got a percentage.

One of several who refused to pay was Henry Ford. The Selden Patent covered two-cycle engines, while Ford's vehicles were powered by four-cycle engines, the attorneys argued. Meanwhile, Ford portrayed himself as David battling Goliath, which didn't hurt the sales and marketing of his cars.

There were six specific claims in the Selden Patent. Each paragraph noted the use of a "liquid hydro-carbon gas engine." If for no other reason, Selden and his partners were delineating the nomenclature of the patent as a warning.

In the *Cycle and Automobile Trade Journal* of December 1900, it was announced that a lawsuit was brought against the Winton Motor Carriage Company for infringement of the Selden Patent. Judge Coxe of the U.S. Circuit of Appeals overruled a demurrer filed by the defendants stating, "The Bill, in the usual form, is based upon letters patent No. 549,160 granted November 5, 1895 to George B. Selden for a road vehicle, the motor being a liquid hydrocarbon gas engine."

Given the fact that gasoline-powered cars were gaining a sure foothold in the marketplace among electric- and steam-powered vehicles, ALAM was enforcing the collection of licensing fees. Most car and truck manufacturers went along with the licensing arrangement and paid their dues rather than get into expensive court battles. Every vehi-

Opposite, top: As shown by this list, numerous companies believed the future was based on battery technology, not on gasoline. Many of these vehicles still traversed the roads in America by World War I, and due to their mechanical simplicity and high quality, they often outlasted their petroleum-based competitors even if the vehicle manufacturers themselves were defunct by the end of the war, or soon thereafter. The ability to "refuel" in minutes, as opposed to hours, gave petroleum-powered vehicles a distinct advantage once the infrastructure of filling stations and repair shops was established. *Bottom:* The Woods Motor Vehicle Company of Chicago began manufacturing early on in 1898 and stayed with electric vehicles until the end of World War I, although the military did not use such trucks and autos in the field due to lack of electricity for recharging and the time it took to accomplish it.

Food companies such as Heinz far outlived the electric vehicle companies that distributed their products, such as this 1918 General Vehicle (GV) electric truck built in New York City.

cle was issued a brass plate with a serial number that had to be affixed as proof of complying with the patent license process. It was not only expensive, but the licensing applied to both imported and domestic companies, which could be denied a license if ALAM so decreed (Ford being one of them).

At the age of forty and on his third such business venture, Henry Ford had established Ford Motor Company in 1903. ALAM hesitated to grant Ford a Selden Patent license on the grounds that Ford's company was merely an "assembler" of automobiles and not a true manufacturer. Ford had begun experimenting in earnest with motor vehicles a decade earlier, and he decided to challenge the Selden patent. In the meantime, Winton had given in, but a few "independent" companies were willing to join with Ford.

Ford placed a full-page ad in the October 24, 1903, issue of the *Automobile Magazine* stating, "Notice to dealers, importers, agents and users of our gasoline automobiles—We will protect you against any prosecution for alleged infringements of patents.... The Selden patent is not a broad one, and if it was it is anticipated. It does not cover a practicable machine, no practicable machine can be made from it and never was so far as we can ascertain."

Ford and his attorneys pointed out that George Selden had never actually built a working prototype of his "Road Engine." Ford's ad was a mocking response to a notice in the *Motor World* which had been placed by ALAM on July 23, 1903. It listed 26 manufacturers that had not obtained the patent license and were continuing to do business. The ad read, "No other manufacturers or importers are authorized to make or sell gasolene [*sic*] automobiles, and any person making, selling or using such machines made or sold by any unlicensed manufacturers or importers will be liable to prosecution for infringement."

American officers used Cadillac open touring cars extensively in combat, as this photo shows at Vimy Ridge.

And so the court battle began. Ford's main advantage was his image that as underdog trying to protect innocent citizens against lawsuits brought on by a huge, greedy conglomerate that was trying to monopolize the industry. The legal fight hit the press internationally, since the lawsuit was extended to importers of foreign-made cars, which were numerous. At the time there was no clear evidence that gasoline-powered vehicles were superior or that they would dominate over those that were electric- and steam-powered.

Almost immediately in the litigation the question was raised of who was the originator of the first gasoline-powered road vehicle. In the January 28, 1904, issue of *Motor Age*, the French Lenoir patent was cited from March 22, 1860. It was compared to that of Selden's. The article quoted George Prade in *l'Auto* as stating, "The value of the Selden Patent is ... based upon very little, if upon anything at all. Furthermore, it has no influence upon automobile construction, because it was in Cannstadt, Germany that Daimler took up the question without even knowing of the existence of the Selden patent."

Prade went on to point out that Lenoir had actually built a vehicle in 1862 with an internal combustion engine; his highly detailed patent included a description of a clutch (*l'embrayage*), ignition system and carburetor. The differential had also been invented in France, as mentioned.

But rather than lose money and time, companies such as Panhard and Mercedes also gave in by 1905 and obtained licenses. At that time thirty-one U.S. manufacturers had complied. But Ford resisted with the help of a few supporters, and the drama unfolded in

Top: A photograph taken in 1906 of the patented vehicle that George Selden claimed he had built in 1877. It turned out that when asked to show an actual working example of his patent, Selden cobbled together this vehicle much later. *Bottom:* After years of after-market conversion, Ford began building its own factory-produced trucks such as these in 1917.

Rauch & Lang began building electric cars in 1905. This Model BX-7 was offered in 1918 and like a few other electric cars, could be steered from the back seat. The company built taxis and lasted until the stock market crash of 1929.

the court as well as in the press. A letter from the Ford Company published in *Motor Age* during the initial stages of the legal battle stated, "In taking this stand we can not conscientiously feel that Mr. Selden ever added anything to the art in which we are engaged. We believe that the art would have been just as far advanced today if Mr. Selden had never been born, that he made no discovery and gave none to the world ... and that he and his assignees cannot monopolize the entire trade."

The battle was not only a personal and professional one, but it involved considerable sums of money. The *Horseless Age* of July 4, 1906, stated that members of ALAM had thus far paid over $800,000 in licensing fees, and that three-fifths of this money went to the Columbia and Electric Vehicle Company, owners of the Selden Patent. That year, Selden had been induced by attorneys to prove out his patent by showing the actual vehicle he had drawn and described. On May 19, 1906, he had invited the press, lawyers and experts representing both sides to a demonstration of his Road Engine.

George Selden's son, Henry R. Selden, had assembled the described vehicle using a two-cycle three-cylinder engine that was alleged to have been built by the patentee in 1877. There was considerable suspension of disbelief over this matter. The vehicle itself, photographed for the May 24, 1906, issue of *Motor Age*, had the date 1877 painted on its side. The demonstration was successful as the witnesses "were given a ride in the car for 100 yards or more."

In response R.A. Parker, attorney for Ford, wrote in a letter that was printed in the press as follows:

This 1918 CT electric was one of a fleet of 22 such trucks that served Curtis Publishing in Philadelphia until 1962, silently delivering magazines in the early morning hours with nary a puff of smoke.

> Few people realize how much is at stake in the Selden litigation. One hundred million dollars is a conservative estimate.... Of the independent makers there are now considerably over 100 concerns producing automobiles; and the independents now make over 60 percent of all the automobiles in America and Europe. Should the ridiculous claims of Selden to a basic patent which would apply to every automobile today—thirty years after the patent was originally applied for—be sustained by the higher court, all these concerns would be bankrupt.

Raising the stakes, lawsuits against fifteen more independent manufacturers were instituted in 1907. On September 15, 1909, Judge Hough of the U.S. Circuit Court of the Southern District of New York rendered a decision in favor of the plaintiffs, sustaining the validity of the Selden Patent. Ford immediately appealed and placed ads in periodicals stating, "There are many reasons why anyone should NOT buy a car licensed under the Selden Patent, because by doing so Trust methods are encouraged, the evolution of the industry curtailed, and the maintenance of high-priced and poor quality cars assisted, because it is obvious that a protected monopoly does not try to please the public."

On appeal, Ford and his attorneys finally won on January 9, 1911, when Judge Noyes of the U.S. Circuit Court of Appeals handed down the decision that the Selden Patent applied only to vehicles using two-cycle (2-stroke) "constant pressure" engines. Although the patent was valid, it was announced that Ford and others had not infringed upon it. At that point some $3,000,000 would have been due to Columbia and the Electric Vehicle Company.

The final decision broke the back of the latter company, and Charles Kettering's invention of the electric "self-starter" that year (adopted for 1912 Cadillac and others thereafter) amounted to a nail in the coffin for most electric car manufacturers, whose one major boast in terms of convenience was that their vehicles did not need to be crank-started—a

Top: The Ford Model T was a simple machine, and as men went off to war women had to learn how to repair and maintain such motor vehicles on their own. *Bottom:* The Ford Model T was popular for being affordable and easy to drive, and some models such as this open touring model were exported to England with right-hand steering, as used by these two officers shown with their dog.

real chore, and often enough, a dangerous one. But several companies continued to build specialized electric cars and trucks, as well as burden carriers, tow vehicles, forklifts, golf carts and other mostly short-range conveyances. Until the storage capacity of the electric battery was to increase tenfold, the energy density of liquid petroleum-based fuel would continue to have the advantage, until the advent of fuel cells.

The Selden Patent would have expired in 1912. During the Great War more electric vehicle and steam vehicle manufacturers went out of business. With the lessons of World War I, it became apparent that power, range and instantaneous ability to operate, along with rapid refueling capability, were not only advantages but essentials in vehicle operation and survival, especially in the most severe conditions.

George Selden died in 1923, but his own Selden Truck Corporation (which had assembled the Liberty truck during World War I), along with the licensing fees he had collected (which he did not have to reimburse on so many makes of motor vehicles), had made him and his family quite wealthy and famous, even though he was overshadowed by Henry Ford.

It was Henry Ford's challenge to the Selden Patent that made history, and by winning in court on appeal, the monopoly over the motorcar industry was broken. By the time Ford won the Selden Patent lawsuit, the electric car companies who had acquired the patent in an underhanded fashion lost millions of dollars as a result of the court battle, contributing to their demise in the following years. The challenge to the Selden Patent had undoubtedly been one of the most important litigations in the history of patent law and the automotive industry.

By the time the electric starter motor was invented, and it was proven that cheap gasoline could be carried by tanker quickly and efficiently into the field almost anywhere, the motor vehicle of World War I proved that the truck and automobile powered by refined petroleum was here to stay.

Chapter VI

NEW ALLIED VEHICLES DOMINATE

War has always tended to accelerate technological development, but World War I dragged on before the U.S. military decided to adopt standardization and interchangeability of parts. Undoubtedly, the major development was the design and quick manufacturing capability in the United States, especially of the "caterpillar" type tractor turned into a "tank."

Turning the so-called tank into reality for the first time may have been a milestone, but the concept was rather ancient. Leonardo da Vinci wrote in 1482 at the age of 30: "I am building secure and covered chariots and when they advance with their guns into the midst of the foe even the largest of enemy masses must retreat and behind them the infantry

In a photograph from a personal album, Private Erdman poses in front of a Liberty Model B truck in 1918. The emblem U.S.A. was used on the standardized 4 × 2 truck powered by a 424 cubic-inch-displacement (cid) four-cylinder engine.

can follow in safety and without opposition." This among numerous of da Vinci's ideas did not come to fruition, although a drawing does exist.

The invention of a continuous track to propel a vehicle, later called the Caterpillar Track, has been attributed to Richard Edgeworth in 1770. He was born in Bath, England, in 1744 and lived in Edgeworthtown, Ireland. Among the earliest steam engines ever built for military use, a few were successfully employed to power tractors during the Crimean War of 1853–1856. In 1855 James Cowan built a Steam Powered Land Ram in England, essentially a steam tractor with a cannon and rotating scythes on the sides, which was called "barbaric" by Henry John Temple, 3rd Viscount Palmerston. However, another implication was that this vehicle was too impractical and unreliable.

An inventor named David Roberts who had studied early Holt tractors, as head of Sons of Grantham, built tractors with patented "chain-tracks" at the turn of the century. His first patents in England were granted in 1904. Lack of funding prevented Roberts from continuing to experiment with tractors having armor. A working example of the Roberts Military Tractor was completed and shown in July of 1905 to the British War Office, without any orders being placed. Further interest came about from a demonstration in 1906, after which Roberts applied for more patents, particularly on the chain, which was the essence of most tank functionality in addition to armor and weaponry. In obvious terms, if the chain or "track" had no grip or broke, the tank, or crawler tractor, was stranded.

The Hornsby-Akroyd Company with which Roberts was affiliated continued to build oil engines. The Roberts machine was especially unusual in that it was the first tractor to use the differential method to steer the vehicle, in which brakes were applied to either side of the differential, causing one side to roll faster and therefore turn the tractor.

Experiments in other countries such as that of Gunther Burstyn of Austria in 1911 were ignored. Lancelot De Mole of Australia showed proposals beginning in 1912, and even demonstrated a working model in 1917, but the British War Office cast this aside, even though the Commission on Awards of Inventors in 1919 recognized De Mole with a payment of 987 pounds to cover part of his expenses. His friends had urged him to approach the German government before the war began, but he refused, referring to his patriotism. Not all inventors, engineers and scientists held such strong ethical beliefs, even in times of war.

The especially momentous if not imperative development of tracked "crawler" vehicles as tow vehicles, weapons and transporters, to be discussed further, was preceded by the realization of the necessity of standardization in Great Britain's military circles as well as in the American military and such engineering circles as the newly formed SAE in the U.S. At this point it may be best to delineate the tremendous impact and significance of the "engineering philosophy" of standardization before continuing with the history of the development of tanks.

There were finally several standardized truck type designs, including a Class A and LA trucks (the latter being the Light Aviation), but these particular models were not built in any significant numbers. The LA truck was built by GMC, Denby, Paige and Republic under license and war-time contracts. It was a shared design and the truck was powered by a C2 Continental 35 hp engine with a four-speed transmission. It had a 149-inch wheelbase and used a Hotchkiss drive. According to the *Automobile and Automotive Industries* of July 12, 1917, a meeting at Columbus, Ohio, on July 9 resulted in an agreement pertaining to nearly all the Class A truck design features and specifications.

That issue of the highly influential magazine went on to editorialize,

All Washington is talking about this work. Even the aircraft progress, wonderful as it is, also, has paled a little in comparison with the accomplishments of the truck industry. The spirit of the thing cannot be realized except by participation. That more of the right men were not at Washington, June 27, is regrettable; that more were not at Columbus July 9, is shameful. Granted the notice given was short, granted that work has not been helped up to enable polite letters to written to all, this is no time for the ordinary usages of society or business. Today every minute of delay on work of national importance is paid for by lives. For every hour of delay men will die sudden and horrible deaths.

In other words, there was a type of mass epiphany in recognizing the importance of the standardized motor truck as an essential part of the war effort.

The Liberty Class B and Militor were also standardized trucks. Once the military created specifications, a rapid course of development was set in motion. Up until then, inventory records required a twelve-story building in Paris with hundreds of clerks managing the part numbers of 2,000,000 types of components for all the motor vehicles in use.

In August of 1917 the relatively new SAE met, and eight teams went to work designing standardized trucks, among them the 3- to 5-ton Liberty Truck. It took 69 days for a team of fifty men in eight groups from SAE to complete the design of the Model A and Model B Liberty trucks. A 424 cid, four-cylinder engine would power the 160-inch wheelbase Model B truck, which soon went into production.

Continental manufactured the block, while the cylinder head was from Waukesha and the pistons from Hercules. The transmission was a four-speed. The dry-disk clutch was amidships. Rear axle used a worm drive. Two separate ignition systems, one magneto and one battery type, improved reliability at a time when electrical systems were primitive. All in all, 150 companies built the multitude of components for the Liberty B trucks, which had "U.S.A." emblems on their radiators. The entire Liberty truck was made up of 7,500 parts.

The lighter 1½-ton was called the Standard A. The Standard A was built by Autocar, Denby and White only in prototype form, and it is documented that only one each were produced by these three companies. It was powered by a smaller 27.23 hp, 312 cid motor built by Buda and had a three-speed transmission. Its wheelbase was shorter than the Model B's at 144 inches.

The 1½-ton Mode CC4 Dart trucks, which served in the Punitive Expedition, were also referred to as "Class A Type" and were powered by the Buda engine with a Muncie three-speed transmission, but these had a 150-inch wheelbase. Many of the Dart trucks ended up at Ft. Snelling in Minnesota as the war ended.

The very first Liberty B trucks were presented to Secretary of War Baker on October 19, 1917, after a 450-mile trip from Rochester to Washington, D.C. A.W. Copeland was the chairman of the production schedule committee for what was called the "experimental" trucks as late as the end of 1917. Full production was not expected to begin until January of 1918, which it did under engineer Christian Girl, in charge of truck production; W.T. Norton, chief engineer at Selden; and SAE engineers Coker F. Clarkson, H.L. Horning and A.W. Copeland. As the two examples of the "First Heavy Duty War Truck, Standard Military Class B" truck traveled along with banners proclaiming this feat, they made their way down to Washington, and huge crowds gathered along the way to see and honor them with signs and applause.

The Society of Automotive Engineers designed the standardized Model B Liberty truck, and it was first manufactured in 1917 using 150 different companies in the U.S. after such companies had built their own non-interchangeable vehicles for a number of years.

Much of the route that was selected included dirt roads (part of the highway system across Pennsylvania and Maryland) and included bridges to see how the trucks would perform on them or if they could pass under them. Minimum bridge capacities and underpass dimensions were yet to be established nationwide in the U.S., so it was not possible to carry all loads across the country. One journalist observed the Liberty B truck "[t]aking a railroad crossing at 15 mph without a jar." Even on a smooth, hard surface road with well-graded tracks, that was considered remarkable at the time.

Fifteen different companies were final assemblers of the 3-ton Model B body/chassis/engine/transmission/axles assemblies: Bethlehem, Brockway, Diamond T, Garford, Gramm-Bernstein, Indiana, Kelly, Packard, Pierce-Arrow, Republic, Selden, Service, Sterling, U.S. Motor Truck and Velie. But after only 9,364 Liberty trucks were produced, the remaining order for 43,000 was canceled after the Armistice.

Standardized trucks were built separately for the Signal Corps. The press explained in November of 1917 that there were "two types of standardized motor vehicles which the Signal Corps is now testing in and around Washington ... due to the different work which the Signal Corps trucks will be called upon to do, they vary in quite a few details from the Quartermaster Corps Class A and Class B vehicles. The Signal Corps trucks are standardized, however, and were worked out under the direction of Captain Arthur J. Slade."

The Signal Corps Class A was rated at 1½-ton and the Class B at 3-ton. The lighter

The Signal Corps' 1½-ton standard truck could easily be distinguished from the heavier Signal Corps truck by its single rear wheels. Both had a heavy radiator guard.

trucks were ordered from General Motors while the heavier types were placed with Federal Motor Truck of Detroit, Kelly Springfield Motor Truck of Springfield, Ohio, and Velie Motors Company of Moline, Illinois. The Signal Corps trucks distinguished themselves from others in tire equipment, which consisted of

> Goodyear straight-sided, cord-construction casing with all-weather treads on both front and rear wheels. The front are 35 × 5 and the rears 38 × 7 pneumatics. In brief, the light truck has a unit power plant with a four-speed gearset and a final worm-drive employing radius rods to take the driving propulsion. The standard parts included in the truck make-up are a special Continental truck engine lubricated on the combination forced-fed and constant-level splash system, Marvel carburetor, an Eisemann high-tension magneto, a tubular radiator with water circulated by means of centrifugal pump, a Monarch suction governor, a multiple-disk clutch, a Brown-Lipe four-speed gearset, a solid propeller shaft in two parts, with three universals and supported in the center on a self-aligning ball bearing, and a Timken-David Brown worm-driven axle.

The 3-ton trucks were "similarly made from standardized parts" but of heavier construction, including dual rear wheels. Both trucks had heavy angle-iron radiator guards and featured a single searchlight at the open-cab dashboard.

Some companies did very well as a result of war production. Mack became internationally known for its sturdy "bulldog" trucks, which were even used to transport Renault and Whippet tanks directly on their chassis in an enclosed steel bed. The "bulldog" name was given to the trucks by British engineers, who arrived in New York in 1917 on a pur-

Top: Giant components for electric elevators could be carried in 1908 by trucks such as this Mack five-ton model. *Bottom:* In addition to motor vehicles, the cavalry got involved in nearly all aspects of the war, even in such operations as washing this Cadillac staff car in a French river.

chasing mission. They immediately ordered 150 of the Model AC Mack, stating, "In appearance these Macks, with their pugnacious front and resolute lines, suggest the tenacious quality of the British Bulldog." The name stayed, although the canine logo wasn't registered until 1921 and the hood ornament got installed a full decade later.

When Mack merged with Saurer and Hewitt, the founder of the latter company, Edward R. Hewitt, joined the ranks of the Mack team and became an important designer of Mack trucks, albeit briefly. He was responsible for the design of the AB Mack prior to his departure in 1914. The AB was introduced before World War I, but most of the Mack trucks that were shipped to Europe were the AC Model, with the swept-back "sculpted"

Top: This four-ton Mack Type Two of 1910 was built with a "Special Designed Bottler's Body" with three doors on each side for delivery of Seitz Mineral Water. *Bottom:* This 26-passenger sightseeing car was photographed at the Golden Gate Park in San Francisco in 1910. Mack trucks and buses were gaining popularity and trust across the entire nation.

Opposite, top: This four-ton Mack Type Two of 1909 was sold to Puerto Rico where it transported pineapple, coffee and grapefruit from the interior of the island nation to San Juan over grades up to 22 percent. *Bottom:* Along with the other factory illustrations, this one shows all lighting and controls of the four-ton Mack Type Two with a "Special Beef Body" built before World War I began.

Top: The three-ton Mack Type One of 1910 with special double body was built for Dupont to carry explosives before Mack started building the AB year-around body for the same purpose. *Bottom:* The 1½-ton Mack AB worm-drive chassis was used to build the year-round cab from 1916 to 1918, in this case to carry explosives for Dupont in a more efficient manner.

Top: Traffic jam during the Meuse-Argonne Battle shows truck, horse-drawn transport and soldiers on foot. Almost at the very center of the photograph is a nearly lost detail—the unmistakable emblem and hood of a Mack AC returning from the front. *Bottom:* This photograph from 1918 (noted on the back as "CB—1st Detachment") shows soldier mechanics learning their skills with a variety of trucks and touring staff cars at a time when those who knew how to repair and maintain motor vehicles were a new, highly desired workforce.

Top: This early Mack AC from 1917 was built as an Army transport truck and featured louvers instead of screens on its hood, which were less expensive and cheaper to make in the long run. The truck was built for demonstration purposes to obtain additional contracts. *Bottom:* Once America entered the war, Mack built thousands of trucks in Allentown, Pennsylvania, as this photograph clearly shows, with many rows of the Mack AC model ready to be shipped from the factory in 1918.

Top: The Mack AC 7½-ton truck could carry a Renault FT-17 tank or an American-made M1917, which was nearly identical. *Bottom:* Mack developed this experimental small crawler, calling it the AB tractor, at the end of the war.

Top: Holt Manufacturing of Stockton, California, and later Peoria, Illinois, built tractors named Caterpillar and at the beginning of World War I experimented with tank design. *Bottom:* Another view of the Caterpillar tank from Holt dubbed the G-9, which did not go into production.

hood similar to Renault and IHC, among others. The Mack AC was introduced in March of 1916. Mack was building its own engines, transmissions and axles by that time.

In November of 1917 the U.S. military ordered 900 of the heaviest Macks, which were rated at 5½-ton (AB) and 7½-ton (AC) respectively. The AB used a spiral bevel differential, whereas the AC continued with dual chain drive, largely due to metallurgical inadequacies of the era that limited the size of spiral-bevel drive at the differential. A 7½-ton rated Mack could carry a tank weighing twice that much as a benefit of engineered limit allowances, but it could do so only for a limited time and at very slow speed.

The Mack engine, cast in cylinder pairs, was first rated at 30 hp and transmissions were three-speed selective sliding-gear type. Although much heavier, these Macks were similar in appearance to other trucks, which had radiators efficiently located behind the engine, such as the ¾-ton IHC Model H and 1-ton Model F, of which over four hundred served the military during the war. Just as with many American military vehicles of World War I, only a portion were actually shipped overseas. Many remained on American soil in use at the hundreds of military installations across the country.

The final testing of American World War I trucks was conducted by the U.S. Ordnance Department beginning late in 1917. The U.S. Army had specified a standardized truck to replace the 4 × 4s such as FWD, Winther, Duplex, Walter and Nash Quad. Two companies received a contract to build this heavy duty 4 × 4—the Militor Corporation of Jersey City and the Sinclair Corporation of New York City. The Militor also had its radiator behind the engine, used a 36 hp Wisconsin four-cylinder power plant and a four-speed transmission with internal gear drive.

This 1915 Militaire four-cylinder motorcycle with floor shifter and drop-down rear auxiliary wheels was developed by the Sinclair Corporation of Jersey City and tested by the U.S. military, but purchases in quantity did not follow.

The Ordnance Department tested the standardized Militor truck in Nyack, New York, by towing a Nash Quad and Renault truck uphill at Hook Mountain.

The Militor corporation was also placed in charge of building a powerful, standardized military motorcycle. As the war came to an end, the Militor, renamed Militaire (back again from an earlier 1915 Militaire effort by N.R. Sinclair), was then intended for commercial use. These motorcycles were produced in small numbers as prototypes and not in the least were unusual in design. They were powered by an in-line four-cylinder motor and had a floor shifter for the three-speed gear box, electric starter and foot-operated brakes. They had retractable stabilizer wheels at the back so that the driver need not worry about propping up the very long, cumbersome, heavy machine. Later models used side-cars instead of the side wheels. The U.S. Army bought very few Militor motorcycles, which were shipped to France in 1918. By all accounts they were nearly impossible to ride in the muddy lanes where they were intended for courier work. Eventually, they were powered by a 1435 cc overhead-valve in-line four-cylinder engine and were available only with a sidecar. Troubles with reliability put an end to the Sinclair company within a couple of years. Harley-Davidson became the primary motorcycle for courier work.

Meanwhile, grueling tests at Hook Mountain in Nyack, New York, were set up during which the Militor truck prototypes had to tow a Nash Quad and a Renault uphill, dig themselves out of wheel-high mud and climb stairlike boulders. The trucks performed very well but after 150 were built, orders were canceled as the war ended. Militor merged with Knox in order to survive and moved to their facilities in Springfield, Massachusetts.

Returning to the subject of tanks, by far the most remarkable advances in vehicle development as a result of World War I was in their design. At the time, tracked vehicles of

Top: The 1918 Militor was the culmination of efforts by the Society of Automotive Engineers and the Ordnance Department after the U.S. military had used several different makes of 4×4 trucks. *Bottom:* The Militor 4×4 was thoroughly tested by the Ordnance Department at Hook Mountain in August of 1918 but never went into mass production before the war ended.

the "caterpillar" type were also referred to as "creepers" and even "centipedes." The Allies, especially among the British military, were highly motivated to create a machine to overcome the continuous impasse of trench warfare, which may have been won by one side or the other eventually, through years of attrition. However, even with the use of heavy artillery, mortars, grenades, poison gas and aircraft, once the large fortresses had been

Top: In 1918 the Militor was to be the finalized standard Army 4 × 4, which appeared similar to the Mack AC with radiator behind the engine. This version with smooth hard rubber tires and tire chains was to be used for towing artillery. *Bottom:* In August of 1918, the Ordnance Department wrote a complete evaluation of the Militor using detailed photos such as this one of the rugged internal gear drive, which performed very well.

destroyed along the borders, the front lines fluctuated and seesawed back and forth without any substantial conclusion in sight while tens and even hundreds of thousands of casualties piled up on both sides. Such enormous loss of life in a single war was unprecedented in the history of what is often referred to as human civilization.

Prior to World War I, tanks simply did not exist as vehicles ready for battle. Engi-

Benjamin Holt and Daniel Best both had designs for a crawler tractor such as this Caterpillar 18 of 1915. Note position of driver's seat.

neers calculated that using a 13-inch-wide "endless sectional track" on a vehicle weighing several tons resulted in ground pressure that was a mere 6.25 pounds per square inch. With a 30-inch-wide track, that ground pressure fell to about three pounds per square inch, which was still less than the foot pressure of a man or a horse. This was exactly the type of machine that could "crawl" or "creep" across the swampy miles of open land where buildings and trees had been already decimated and the muddy killing fields were criss-crossed with trenches, rivers and bomb craters that no horse, car or truck could overcome.

Although tracked vehicles had been developed as functional vehicles in the U.S. as early as 1904 by Benjamin Holt in Stockton, California, little credit has been given to Frederick Simms, who built a similar type of vehicle in 1899, which he called a "motor-war-wagon." It had a bullet-proof shell surrounding it and two machine guns on revolving turrets, and was powered by a Daimler engine. The British War Office rebuffed the obscure Simms vehicle.

By 1914 the Killen-Strait armored tractor with three tracks was shown to David Lloyd George and Winston Churchill, and most likely had a convincing effect on the British leaders, although the vehicle itself did not progress past the prototype stage. Two American Bullock tractors coupled together also failed as a prototype.

When Benjamin Holt bought into Best Manufacturing in nearby San Leandro, California, in 1908, which had built steam traction engines, out of these early machines evolved the first tracked "crawlers" nicknamed "caterpillar" before the title stuck as a company name. However, the *Engineer,* publishing a series of articles between August 10 and September 14, 1906, claimed that the "caterpillar" designation was already applied by British soldiers when they observed the Roberts tractor that year. These types of details may never be sorted out, and perhaps do not really pertain to the overall picture that is being drawn here for the purpose of general historical significance.

Clarence Leo Best, son of farm equipment builder Daniel Best, designed and built some of the first successful "caterpillar" tractors, which very much resembled the modern two-tread tractors that did not rely on an enormous front wheel to steer the vehicle, and which usually left the ground in any climbing maneuver whatsoever. They instead relied on varying the drive to the two tracks separately. Benjamin Holt continued to use this design after Clarence Leo Best started C.I. Best Gas Traction Company (later C.I. Best Tractor Company) after the designer resigned from Holt in 1910.

Tracked vehicles were partially derived from Hornsby-Ackroyd tractor patents in England (by Ruston Hornsby), so there was significant interaction between inventors and manufacturers in both countries. The invention was moving ahead so quickly at this time that the sequence of events is not as pertinent as their actual impact.

Focusing once again on the contribution of American ingenuity and manufacturing in this discussion, it should be noted that another invention patented along the lines of tracked vehicles was undertaken by the Phoenix Manufacturing Company of Eau Claire, Wisconsin, during 1906. The company began building "locomotive sleds" primarily for log hauling. Instead of link-coupled drive wheels as on a standard rail locomotive, which it otherwise resembled, this vehicle had chain track drive on either side. Two long ski-

This Caterpillar 5-ton crawler tractor of World War I was both armored and finally camouflaged for the first time, but the driver sat on top completely unprotected.

Like other Caterpillar tractors, the armored 10-ton Model 55 did not have protection for the driver that even light tanks provided.

type skids in front were used for steering, intended for the snowy and icy conditions found in Wisconsin's forested terrain. The one ingenious element of the Phoenix was that its weight-bearing chain (track) was separate from its driving chain.

P.J. Diplock was another early inventor who took out a patent in 1910 for a "chain track machine." He incorporated a "pedrail" system with triple roller chain, and his later tractors used four tracks, resembling trucks with crawler chains at each corner.

A similar machine was patented during 1907 by Alvon L. Lombard, who also separated the driving chain from the weight-bearing tread chain. Aside from the unusual and perhaps obscure advances by companies that did not intend to build war machinery, it was Holt Manufacturing that commenced series production of chain track tractors as early as 1908. Some of the crawler tractors had been exported to the U.K. as early as 1912, perhaps ironically in that Holt had bought patents from Hornsby in November of the same year. Although the company carried the Holt name, the vehicles were soon called Caterpillar, and eventually the entire company became Caterpillar, moving to Peoria, Illinois, in addition to the Stockton, California, factory, the latter being eventually phased out entirely. The first actual Holt military sales were to the French government in 1914.

Originally, the vehicles were designed for road building and agricultural work, but a few military leaders realized these heavy-duty, go-anywhere vehicles could be suited for warfare. The early Holt crawlers were used to tow heavy guns by the British Royal Artillery from the outset of the war.

The application was derived from recommendations by Lieutenant-Colonel Ernest Dunlop Swinton. Before traveling to the U.S., Swinton was a frontline correspondent at the start of the war, often also referred to as a propaganda officer, having obtained an inspiring letter in July of 1914 from a South African engineering colleague named Hugh Merriot who drew attention to the idea of using armored tractors in warfare. Swinton wrote in November of 1914 that what was needed was a "power-driven, bullet-proof, armed engine capable of destroying machine guns, of crossing country and trenches, of breaking through entanglements and of climbing earthworks."

At first Swinton's proposal was sent to the British Royal Engineers, and Colonel Maurice Hankey proposed it to Lord Kirchener. He, General Sir John French and his scientific advisers rejected the idea. With the help of Colonel Hankey and a memorandum to the Committee of Imperial Defense and First Lord of the Admiralty, Winston Churchill, the project got started.

The first idea of using a giant metal roller pushed by tracked vehicles to protect advancing infantry was not considered feasible, but Winston Churchill wrote to Prime Minister Herbert Asquith that the enemy could soon produce a similar device. The Inventions Committee was organized by January of 1915 and headed by General Scott-Moncrieff, but the idea floundered for weeks before Winston Churchill took it upon himself to form the Landship Committee in February of 1915.

Specifications were drawn up that included a top speed of 4 mph on flat ground (approximate walking speed of a soldier); capability of a sharp turn at full speed; ability

A Signal Corps photograph of a Holt 75 towing caissons in France, which was the best use for the Caterpillars, in addition to towing supply trailers.

This Illinois National Guard Holt 75 was photographed towing a tracked Holt 20-ton wagon from Eckwood Park to Glen Oak Park circa 1918.

to travel in reverse, to climb a five-foot bank (parapet), and to cross an eight-foot ditch or gap with a crew of ten men; and to carry two machine guns and one two-pounder cannon.

Despite much opposition, Lieutenant Walter Gordon Wilson and William Tritton of Foster and Co. Ltd., who were manufacturers at Lincoln, England, were handed the task to built a small "landship." Holt indicated his company was not prepared to mass produce the type of tractor required by the Landship Committee but provided some samples.

The Royal Artillery had ordered two crawler tractors in 1914 after having seen some 75 hp Holts (Holt 75) in agricultural work. Both the Holt 75 and Holt 120, in addition to smaller units, would be used in France to tow artillery as well as various wagons and trailers. The Foster Company used a lengthened Bullock tractor chassis from the U.S. for its proof-of-concept unit. However, Holt Caterpillars, as well as wheeled American tractors from several different manufacturers, were used to tow several types of artillery.

Because the mass development and manufacturing of artillery essentially preceded the steam or gasoline machines that would eventually tow them in and out of battle, it may be appropriate to mention what type of heavy guns would require such vehicles once the horse was relegated to other burdens.

Although a few thousand American-built tractors of different types towed artillery pieces of various sizes, including heavy machine guns, howitzers, anti-aircraft guns, mortars and other guns, the United States was caught amazingly unprepared, and in 1917 when they entered the war they could count up only 900 pieces of artillery in total, most of them 3-inch guns. In contrast, in August of 1914, the Germans had 5,000 77 mm guns,

1,260 105 mm howitzers, 1,360 150 mm heavy artillery and eventually nine "Big Bertha" 420 mm howitzers.

The French had the best field gun in the form of the "magnifique" 75 mm rapid-fire cannon capable of fifteen to twenty rounds a minute or even more. But they had only 250 heavy guns, mostly 155 mm and very few howitzers. They ramped up production in order to supply their own artillery as well as that of the AEF, which used mostly French artillery pieces during 1917 and 1918. By the end of the war the French were manufacturing over 51,000 shells of various types per day.

By mid–1914, the British were also notably in short supply of artillery pieces, and by summer of 1915 could count only 1,400 guns in France, of them only 71 larger than 5-inch. There was also a national scandal, as countless artillery shells turned out to be "duds" due to slipshod manufacturing. Some blamed sabotage.

In the spring of 1915, the Ministry of Munitions was formed in England, headed by Lloyd George and ultimately by Winston Churchill. Production increased from 400 tons of ammunition per week to 4,000 tons per week, and artillery went into production at a remarkable pace.

American AEF caissons often consisted of the French "75," developed in 1897 by Captains Sainte-Claire Deville and Emile Rimailho. At the beginning of the war, the "75" was considered superior in its class of weapons. The gun's shell attained a muzzle velocity of 1,805 foot-seconds, and its projectile hit a target as far away as 10,000 feet at nearly 1,000 feet per second.

In the Battle of Grand Couronne on September 5, 1914, the Kaiser himself waited with his white-horse *cuirassiers* at the outskirts of the town of Nancy preparing for a triumphant entrance. The following day, correspondent Gerald F. Campbell, writing for the *London Times* summed up the battle:

> From the woods a mile away, headed by their fifes and drums, wave upon wave of Germans advanced as steadily and pompously as if they were on parade, to the attack of the French infantry positions on the side of the hill.... The Germans advanced six times towards the deadly hill, and were driven back to the sheltering woods. At some places at its base the bodies were piled up five or six feet high, and when the survivors took cover behind the heaps of dead and living in a mire of flesh and blood, the "75s," firing over the heads of the front ranks, finished off the work further back.... Thousands of German dead were left lying on the plain, and in the evening they asked and were granted a few hours' to bury them.

One of the more noteworthy features of the French "75" was its hydro-pneumatic recoil system and recuperator. These were combined in one cylinder instead of the usual two. It could also fire a shrapnel shell, a fragmentation type of projectile invented in 1784 by Lieutenant Henry Shrapnel of the British Army. The 16-pound shrapnel shell held 300 lead balls weighing 12 grams each that were hardened with antimony and mixed with compressed black powder so that, aimed at the opposing infantry, the resulting damage may well be beyond one's imagination.

The other artillery piece that was most effective and manned by American soldiers was the "155," which was the answer to the German 150 mm. The French 105 mm Schneider gun had a similar range of 10 miles but its projectile was too light. The solution was soon provided by the Saint-Chamond 155 *Grande portee filoux*, or "Great Range Filoux." The abbreviation GPF was commonly used, which also meant "Great Power Filoux." The cannon's length was 232 inches and it weighed 20,100 pounds on a wheeled mount, undoubtedly needing a tractor for hauling unless it was mounted on a flatbed rail car. It

spat 95-pound projectiles as far as 21,000 yards, over 3,000 yards farther than the Schneider gun mentioned above. The French "155" went on to be used in World War II as the U.S. M12 Gun Motor Carriage, mounted on a Sherman tank chassis. It was that powerful and durable.

Many disastrous battles convinced the Allies of the need to bring in howitzers, which could hurl an explosive shell at a high angle over a hill, forest or set of buildings; a low-angle "straight-shot" artillery piece could not accomplish this feat. For example, at the Battle of Artois-Loos beginning on September 15 of 1915, the French officers were convinced that a three-day shelling with their "75s" would allow a straight-forward bayonet-fixed charge over the slope. However, the German position on the reverse slope was entirely intact, safe from anything but the plunging shells of the nonexistent howitzers. The ensuing attack was met with a very well prepared and entirely whole German second line. The resulting charge was not an initial success as might be presumed. French 155 mm howitzers were finally built at the end of the war by Saint-Chamond, and even heavier ones by Schneider, but too late, as they were needed earlier on in various battles in the hills of France.

When the war began, the British were not far better prepared than the U.S. in terms of artillery forces. The British divisional artillery was composed of three brigades of three batteries each of 18-pounders, with a total of 54, plus eighteen 4.5-inch howitzers in one brigade of three batteries as well as four 60-pounders and a siege train of six 8-inch howitzers. The 13-pounder, also used in the navy, was eventually replaced by the 18-pounder as an anti-aircraft weapon. The 60-pounder, which had a 5-inch bore and a range of 15,000 yards, was a rare item. As the war progressed, six-inch cannon were developed as well as 6-inch howitzers along with a heavy 9.2-inch howitzer. Shrapnel shells were gradually replaced by explosive shells, especially after the Battle of Loos.

The advocates of preparedness in the United States saw only the need to equip a 500,000-man army, but the sudden expansion to a number ten times higher than that, as direct involvement in World War I was no longer avoidable, created a dramatic deficiency in artillery. Of the 900 working pieces there were 544 three-inch guns of 1902 vintage, 64 M1906 4.7-inch guns, only a few of which were shipped overseas, and some newer 4.7-inch and 6-inch howitzers, most of which were used for training purposes.

The urgency of the situation prompted the re-boring of the 3-inch guns to use the French 75 mm shells, and the U.S. versions were known as the M1916 75 mm. The British 18-pounder was also produced in the U.S. with a similar design improvement by adding a block-type breech mechanism and a hydro-spring recuperation system. This was designated as the M1917 75 mm, not to be confused with the M1917 tank. Once American factories got into full production mode, thousands of artillery pieces were ready to be shipped to France, but the war was over.

Smokeless powder was one materiel that could be quickly manufactured in America, and by November 11 of 1918, in just 18 months, the U.S. had produced 632 million pounds of this explosive substance needed for ammunition and projectiles. The U.S. also got involved in producing poison gas shells, which were assembled at the military Edgewood

Top: A Holt 75 captured by the German Army gathers a curious crowd of onlookers. *Bottom:* In some instances Holt 120 tractors were the only vehicles capable of towing large artillery across dirt paths in France.

Gas masks from United States, Britain, France and Germany, from left to right, each had their disadvantages in that they were not foolproof against poison gas and greatly restricted the vision of
the soldier, many of whom survived but were blinded by the new weapon first devised by the German army in an attempt to break the trench warfare stalemate.

Arsenal complex of factories at Aberdeen Proving Ground in Maryland, which manufactured 10,000 tons in 1918. The entire toxic gas and gas shell filling operation was performed under the U.S. federal government's auspices, as no private interest found it
palatable enough from an ethical perspective to become engaged in mass production of
this type. There was no doubt that, despite the carnage caused by bullets and explosives
of all types and sizes, poison gas was considered the pernicious invention of German science and the newest evil that had emanated from a war of previously unimagined proportions and dire consequences.

More to the subject of motor vehicles, despite heavy artillery, reconnaissance aircraft,
spies, the mining of waterways, published propaganda and other execrable methods of beating the opponent, what was typical of the entire war was that the western front shifted
back and forth only a few excruciating miles, eventually at the cost of literally millions of
casualties. New weapons were being developed to terrorize civilian populations, including the use of zeppelins and winged aircraft capable of dropping bombs. Poison gas was
invented on the German side, but it would be highly improbable that it could become the
break-through weapon, no matter its horrific disabling effects. Moreover, the prevailing
westerly winds would carry the poison gas back to the German side, which occurred on
more than one occasion.

Aircraft of that day could not effectively attack miles of trenches. Purpose-built
bombers were only beginning to metamorphose from the drawings and materials in
machine shops into actual flying aircraft. Occasional strafing from biplanes was more of a
way to intimidate and interrupt the doughboys, or enemy, and then only temporarily, as
the aircraft's ammunition quickly ran out for the wrong purpose, taking on machine gun
and anti-aircraft fire from the ground. Meanwhile, thousands of bogged-down soldiers
continued to decay in muddy ravines, dead or alive, strewn throughout the rotting landscape.

"Little Willie" was one of the first "tank" prototypes begun in 1915 based on tractors such as the Holt Caterpillar. The name *tank* originated from Winston Churchill and General Swinton to ensure security of the project. The rear wheels seen in this photograph were eventually superseded by braced tail bars for trench crossing and tracks were as tall as the entire tank for better center of gravity.

On the Allied side, the tracked armored vehicle became a source of hope as the one new weapon that could overcome this tragic impasse. Under top secrecy, the new motorized weapon was dubbed a "tank," the name attributed both to Swinton and Winston Churchill, describing a "water container for use in Mesopotamia." This was to ensure security of the project, which was not finally adopted until December of 1915, and even by then the secret had not leaked out.

The unit nicknamed "Little Willie" was first tested on September 10–11, 1915, in front of the entire Landship Committee. It was powered by a four-cylinder 105 hp British Daimler motor (in 1896 Gotlieb Daimler sold rights to build motors under that name in England). The tracked vehicle weighed 14 tons, had track frames twelve feet in length and a ten-foot-tall armored box. It could reach three mph and held a crew of three.

The British Pedrail Transport Company also provided prototypes of very small crawler tractors even earlier in 1915, but these were not successful. The "Little Willie" design did not meet specifications and was not accepted at first, but it quickly evolved into a tank prototype known as "Big Willie," also known as "Mother," which became the Mark I tank. The original sketch of the Mark I has been attributed to British Lieutenant W.G. Wilson. He redesigned the Bullock track system to be much more robust, so that a gun and rotating turret's weight could be added.

Wilson's drawings also involved a rhomboid shape with tracks surrounding the entire machine whose size precluded a rotating turret per original concept. Instead, naval six-pounder cannon were mounted in sponsons on each side: armored bubblelike rectangular protrusions described as "blistering out" on the hulls. This greatly helped with the center of gravity, which a top-mounted turret would diminish. The first Mark I tanks were capable of only two mph in the field (four mph on road surface), which made them vulnerable to artillery, as well as lacking in any real element of surprise.

The first fifty Mark I tanks were shipped in disguised crates to France on August 30, If they used the 57 mm guns they were called "male" and if fitted with Hotchkiss or Vickers machine guns they were dubbed "female." Both Sir William Tritton and Major Walter Gordon Wilson, as well as the managing directors, would eventually receive commendations from the Royal Commission on Awards to Inventors for the development of the tank.

The first ones were prone to mechanical breakdown and had a very short range. Out of a crew of eight it took four men to control the 30-ton machines: the driver up front, a man for changing gears and one for "braking" each track, plus gunners. One correspondent described the "men in their unlit steel boxes, filled with fumes and exposed working parts, jerked to-and-fro as unsprung suspension heaved them across country, deaf from the din of engines and armament and practically unable to communicate among themselves or with the infantry outside." Finding and training capable crew members turned out to be a bigger challenge than designing and building the vehicles.

Nevertheless, in January of 1916 successful trials took place at Hatfield Park in England, with a nine-foot ditch crossing and a climbing of a six-and-a-half-foot bank. Bolstered by the new vehicle's convincing performance, the engineers invited British military and political top brass—Lord Kitchener, Secretary of War David Lloyd George and Reginald McKenna—to a demonstration under the utmost secrecy (which was still not leaked by the press). Lord Kitchener stated that "the war would never be won by such ... mechanical toys." But George and McKenna were duly impressed and initiated an order for 100 tanks, according to official records.

A number of tanks were built by August of 1916 in England and finally put into action for the first time. Forty-nine Mark I tanks, of which seventeen broke down, startled and terrified the enemy in the attack at Flers-Courcelette and consequently in the Battle of the Somme on September 15, 1916

However, General Sir Henry Rawlinson, with 12 divisions and 49 tanks, had too small a number of the armored vehicles and therefore they were basically not effective in the battle, confirming the doubts that British General Douglas Haig, a cavalryman, had regarding motor vehicles and machine guns as well. Indeed, many of the tanks broke down or were bogged down in the deepest trenches. Reports of the tanks' reliability varied as to exact numbers and statistics, depending on severity of mechanical trouble and timing of the situation taken into account.

The French military were quite critical that the British had prematurely unveiled their secret weapon, held very closely at the time, and that there were not enough tanks to have a decisive victory based on the invention itself. On the plus side, the British engineers quickly learned the weaknesses of the new machines and the overall soundness of the concept. The positive outcomes were that the tanks could indeed cross nine-foot ditches and bomb craters, were bullet- and shrapnel-proof, could crush barbed-wire entanglements with ease and had a terrifying effect on the enemy soldiers.

General Haig had strongly believed in the cavalry. Despite serious doubts, Colonel John Fuller, chief of staff of the Tank Corps, was quite sure of the tanks' eventual effectiveness and persuaded General Haig and the British government to plan on supplying 1,000 tanks.

Designed by Pliny E. Holt, this Caterpillar gun mount called Mark I carried an 8-inch howitzer and was built in 1918.

As a frontline correspondent earlier, Colonel Maurice Swankey wrote on the Somme Battle later in 1919:

> Although the day was not unexpected, it proved to be a dreadful surprise to the Germans. They had taught the Allies so many fearsome tricks of modern warfare that they regarded almost as an impertinence the mechanical monsters which now came lolloping from the British front; land Dreadnaughts which took shell-holes and trenches in their stride as though in the manner born, spreading death from armour-plated sides, and crushing everything which barred their passage like veritable juggernauts.

Whatever effect the formidable tanks had at the time, the fighting at Somme would nevertheless result in more than 600,000 casualties.

One of the most significant developments of the Great War in terms of large hardware was the Caterpillar Self-Propelled Gun Mount, developed by Holt, and in particular Pliny E. Holt who was the primary designer. The Self-Propelled Gun Mount solved several problems. One was the difficulty of towing a large gun through terrain where the caterpillar tractor was at ease but the gun itself was reluctant to go due to surface conditions. It also solved the problem of moving the entire artillery piece back and forth as the conditions of the battle changed. In essence, having a large cannon mounted on crawler treads was the optimum solution and one of very potent versatility.

Holt built the Mark I, II, III and IV versions while the war still continued, but by the Armistice put an end to production, although not development. Additional, larger versions were built through 1921. One revolutionary idea was to have the motor and electrical system so well waterproofed that the entire vehicle could submerge itself up to the gun mount, thereby hiding, shielding and taking advantage of the recoil-absorption characteristics of the water at the same time.

Caterpillar continued to build tracked gun mounts such as this Mark III of 1918, which carried a 240 mm howitzer. The whole tractor weighed 53 tons.

Under Pliny E. Holt, the U.S. Ordnance Department built the Mark I using an eight-inch British howitzer, which itself weighed 7,728 pounds. The whole vehicle weighed 58,000 pounds. The gun itself fired 200-pound projectiles at a range of 12,000 yards. Only two such vehicles were built. The Mark II carried a 155 mm gun built in 1918. This howitzer fired a 95-pound projectile 17,000 yards. The Mark I and Mark II were capable of 4 and 5 mph, respectively. The Mark III was even heavier and was designed to carry the 240 mm howitzer, which weighed 10,000 pounds by itself. It fired a 356-pound projectile a distance of 1,700 yards. Now the weight of the whole vehicle was up to 106,000 pounds.

Interest in building tanks continued in the U.S. It also formed through an improbable cooperation among the U.S. Army Corps of Engineers, under General John A. Johnson, Boston bankers Phelan and Ratchesky and the Endicott and Johnson Shoe Company. The Stanley Motor Carriage Company of Watertown, Massachusetts, famous for their Stanley Steamers, was employed as a consultant. Two Unit Railway Car kerosene-burning steam engines with a combined power of 500 hp were built into the experimental vehicle, intended for use as a flame thrower against pillboxes and fortified bunkers. As a steam vehicle it was unusual in that it had a two-speed transmission, both forward and reverse, when steam vehicles most often did not need any transmission or differential. The tank was based on a British Mark IV, although it had mud-clearing spikes mistaken for battering rams on the unsprung suspension, which altered its appearance superficially. The prototype named America cost $60,000 to fabricate. The crew was to have been eight men: commander, driver, four machine gunners, mechanic and flamethrower operator. After being completed in April of 1918 it was shown in parades, minus flame thrower demon-

In an unlikely collaboration, Boston bankers Phelan and Ratchesky, the Endicott and Johnson Shoe Company and General John A. Johnson teamed up to build this American-made steam-powered tank, which was designed to carry a flame thrower.

strations, then shipped to France for testing. However, the total weight of 50 tons and length of nearly 35 feet limited this tank to 4 mph, and no further manufacturing in the series took place.

This tracked vehicle had $^1/_2$-inch plate for armor and also carried four machine guns. The flamethrower used a 35 hp gasoline engine to compress its weapon's fuel mixture to 1,600 psi, which could then be projected up to 90 feet, producing an approximately twenty-foot diameter ball of flame. Although flamethrowers were used at the end of World War I in combat, this tank remained only a prototype.

One other steam armored experimental vehicle was produced by Holt, starting in late 1916 and completed in February of 1918. This vehicle was called the Steam Wheel Tank, 3-Wheeled Steam Tank or Holt 150-Ton Field Monitor, the last name referring to some imaginary number since the whole contraption weighed 17 tons. There was also the possibility that this was the next number to be used after the Holt Model 120, or a number to confuse enemy spies, according to a few writers, or simply a typographical error. Confusion in nomenclature aside, the tank actually came into existence as a prototype.

Using the original "Big Wheel" Landship concept from England, Holt (Caterpillar Inc.) built it with two eight-foot-diameter agricultural Holt factory tractor wheels, which were three feet wide and were located at the front of the chassis outside the armor on each side. At the rear was a large roller wheel for steering; this included a skid plate for crossing trenches, a common feature at a time when follower-wheels were too complex and costly to produce. This Holt tank was armed with a 75 mm howitzer mounted low in front. Each armored side also carried a ball-mounted Browning machine gun. Armor was between $^1/_4$-inch to $^3/_4$-inch, depending on the area of the vehicle.

The Holt Three-Wheel Steam tank was another American prototype using tractor components without tracks. The wide roller was at the rear and was used for steering with a braced fin to aid in trench crossing.

Each front wheel was driven by a two-cylinder 75 hp Doble steam engine using a Doble kerosene-fired boiler. Since Holt and Caterpillar had used gasoline engines almost from the outset, Doble of San Francisco luxury motorcar fame was hired for this project. But Doble had also built railroad steam machinery and trucks and buses as well, and his steam-powered vehicles with their flash boilers, ready within a few minutes, were of a very high standard, so steam engine application itself was not necessarily the problem with the prototype. The horsepower-to-weight ratio was 9.8 to 1, which seemed adequate, but traction and steering probably were the culprits. So was the weak cooling system. In May of 1918 the vehicle was tested at Aberdeen Proving Ground where it became stuck after fifty feet of movement, which ended the project. Apparently, substituting large wheels for caterpillar tracks was not the answer for such a heavy vehicle. However, as with most prototypes, without plenty of additional vision and funding, the brand-new machine would soon end up in a scrap yard.

The Rock Island Arsenal designed the smaller crawlers, and Cadillac powertrains, including the V-8 engine, were used for these tractors. The largest production number was for the 10-ton Model 55, of which 2,103 were delivered out of an original order for 11,150. Combined, Holt also delivered 1,810 Model 75 and 676 Model 120 to the U.S. British,

French and Russian armies. It should be noted that during the war, Reo, Federal, Interstate and Chandler Motor Companies each manufactured Holt tractors under license. In total, 4,689 tractors were built under license by other companies under the supervision of the Holt company. Holt also built the Model 18, Model 45 and Model 60. Many of the different size tractors, including the 5-ton, were also built in long-track version and in other variations. Although many had their motors and running gear protected by armor, the drivers sat in the open breeze, and this was the primary difference between the armored tractor and the armored tank at the time.

The British belief in the heavy tank was due to the impasse posed by endless trenches and barbed wire. In the battle of Ypres in April of 1917, the British tunneled deep under the dug-in German positions at Messines Ridge, trying a different tactic to overcome the stalemate. They simultaneously set off nineteen mines and blew up the entire set of German trenches, instantly causing 20,000 enemy casualties. Using General Haig's doubtful planning, under General Sir Hubert Plumer the British advanced slowly and encountered six lines of entrenchments with numerous machine gun lunettes in reinforced pillboxes surrounded by water on three sides.

The Germans also had a new weapon: shells filled with mustard gas. After heavy artillery bombardment disgorged 1.5 million shells, continuous rain began falling on July 30, adding to the quagmire comprising stagnant ponds filled with the excrement of soldiers and animals in addition to the decomposing corpses of man and beast alike. Only forty-eight tanks were organized for a further attack, of which nineteen actually were able to move under their own power. Seventeen were quickly destroyed with artillery.

After an advance of two or three miles across a front of some fifteen miles, a German counterattack caused a retreat and everyone basically returned to their original positions. British casualties amounted to 32,000 in this battle alone. Here the destruction of so many lives, along with the complete devastation of the Flemish village of Passchendaele, would stand as an exercise in mass futility.

Lloyd George, who was to become prime minister and was an adversary of General Haig, wrote, "Ypres with the Somme and Verdun, will rank as the most grim, futile and bloody fight ever waged in the history of war ... a result of stubborn and narrow egotism, unsurpassed among the records of disaster."

At the Battle of Cambrai on November 20, 1917, under General Julian Byng and General Elles as commanders, 422 tanks went into action. The plan was kept as secret as possible and no tanks were allowed within a mile of the staging point. The British used low-flying aircraft and machine-gun fire to mask the rumble of the tanks' approach to create more of a surprise attack. A new approach was also adopted in the use of camouflage painted by artists to help conceal the "landships." In anticipation of anti-tank trenches that were twelve feet in width, the tanks carried long fascines of brushwood encircled with chain that were dropped into the newly made ravines to act as bridges. The attack was quite successful in taking the Germans by surprise and in breaking through the German lines. In the attack, 65 tanks were destroyed and 114 broke down or were stuck in the terrain.

After much celebration of the victory by the Allies, the forward progress of the battle was good only for less than a fortnight, as the Germans counterattacked under General Erich Ludendorff. The Germans regained the front line, still called the Hindenburg Line, and the positions ended up nearly the same as they had been earlier at the cost of

British officers inspect a German anti-tank rifle, which could pierce thinner armor, especially around the engine, but was largely ineffective and unwieldy.

45,000 British casualties. However, the initial success was largely due to the strategic and well-planned deployment of the new war machine: the armored tank. Hindenburg himself would write, "The English attack at Cambrai for the first time revealed the possibilities of a great surprise attack with tanks ... that they could cross our undamaged trenches and obstacles and did not fail to have a marked effect on our troops." (Paul von Beneckendorff Hindenburg was German Field Marshal and Chief of Staff, later President of Germany who appointed Hitler as Chancellor in 1932. Hindenburg died in 1934. The Hindenburg Zeppelin, which exploded in New Jersey in 1937, was also named after him.)

By January of 1918, the Germans had also invented an anti-tank rifle, which fired a five-inch-long (125 mm) and approximately $1/2$-inch-bore (13 mm) projectile that could pierce certain sections of many tanks, especially around the engine, which had thinner gauge plate, as opposed to the sides, which had up to $3/4$-inch plate. The rare rifle's 35-pound weight and heavy recoil made it unwieldy. Most light tanks of the day were vulnerable to artillery fire (for example the wheeled German 77 mm gun), large ditches and mechanical breakdown. Comparatively speaking, the standard-issue rifles for American infantry were the Springfield and Lee-Enfield, both bolt action with magazines carrying five rounds, the latter actually an English rifle chambered to take the U.S. .30-caliber ammunition. There was also the Short Enfield, which could use a 10-cartridge magazine but was less accurate. The anti-tank land mine had yet to be put into action.

A hanging-chain-visor tank helmet was invented to help protect crew members, but it was quite unwieldy, uncomfortable and made vision extremely difficult. Other body armor invented at the time for soldiers was too bulky due to a lack of availability of any light dense material at the time.

The U.S. Tank Corps had its inception when then–Captain George Patton transferred, applying to General Pershing on November 10, 1917, in order to start a tank school for the U.S. 1st Army. In February of 1918 the Light Tank School was established at Bourg near Langres in France. There was only one problem: The school had no tanks. Patton directed that plywood mock-ups be built, and these were constructed, complete with a turret containing a Hotchkiss 8 mm machine gun. A rocking device to simulate terrain was also added. Training began.

On March 10, 1918, the school obtained ten 7.4-ton Renault tanks. On April 28 the First Light Tank Battalion was established under Colonel Samuel D. Rockenbach, who had been appointed on December 22, 1917, and whose right-hand man was Captain George Patton. In June the designations 326th and 327th were established under Captains Joseph W. Viner and Serreno E. Brett, respectively. However, before the St. Mihiel offensive, Captain Ranulf Compton took over the 327th.

To protect a tank crew man's head and eyes, a hanging-chain-visor helmet was invented, but it was uncomfortable and interfered with vision.

Stateside, Captain Dwight Eisenhower was involved with the 65th Engineer Regiment at Camp Mead, Maryland, under Lt. Colonel Ira C. Welburn (appointed by Secretary of War Newton D. Baker) in order to organize the First Battalion, Heavy Tank Service, as it was called. Again, having only one Renault tank sent from France for training purposes, Eisenhower employed a flatbed truck with a three-inch naval gun that was driven over moguls for the soldiers to practice their aim in rough terrain. In mid–March this battalion was ordered overseas, and although Eisenhower was preparing to ship out, he stayed behind to further organize logistics training at Camp Colt in Gettysburg, Pennsylvania. Eventually, there were two American Tank Corps: one under the AEF and one known as Tank Corps, United States. They were first involved with the Meuse-Argonne and St. Mihiel offensives along with the U.S. First Infantry.

The operation was spearheaded by Corps I, IV and V of the U.S. First Army, with Patton part of Corps I. They were accompanied by two battalions of the 304th Tank Brigade composed of 144 Renault tanks and supported by two groups of Schneider and St. Chamond heavy tanks (14.9 and 25.3 tons, respectively), the latter manned by French crews. A total of 419 tanks were used. Ten percent of these broke down or bogged down. Only three were hit by enemy fire.

Seeing action in France, this tank belonged to the James L. Noble Post No. 3 of Altoona, Pennsylvania. It was captured by the Germans and then recaptured by the AEF. Weighing seven tons, it was transported on the back of a 1917 Federal truck.

On September 26 the Meuse-Argonne offensive began. From previous experience it became apparent that one of the biggest logistics problems with tanks was keeping them fueled up, because once out front in the field there was little anyone could do to bring additional gasoline to them. Captain George Patton ordered his crews to strap two fifty-five-gallon barrels to the back of each tank. The potential for disaster was obvious in case the extra barrels were hit, but the probability of tanks running out of gas was even more of a possible nightmare. The barrels were tied on with ropes so that any fire would allow them to break loose and fall away.

Keeping the tanks in good repair and running condition out in the battlefield was another enormous challenge. At the suggestion of one of his men, Patton turned a tank in each company into a mobile repair shop complete with such things as drive belts, parts, hardware and towing capability as well as one good mechanic in the crew.

In the Meuse-Argonne offensive, only 27 tanks were lost to enemy action, but breakdowns left only a total of 50 still operational on November 11, 1918, which heralded the end of the battle and essentially the war. However, that was enough to arm the AEF on a practical basis to continue the entire operation with the help of the British 301st Heavy Tank Battalion under Commander Ralph Sasse using the British Mark V tanks.

Another logistical challenge was contact between tanks before the advent of effective radio communication. Battle plans were drawn up ahead of time but would remain highly inflexible unless unit commanders and messengers were forced to run between and among the tanks to deliver tactical maneuver changes, if there were any. At first, carrier pigeons

Yet another tank prototype was the "skeleton tank" of 1918 built in the United States. It was mostly composed of iron pipe with an armored box for the crew, the advantage being there was a lot less to hit, and weight and cost were greatly reduced.

in bamboo cages were employed, but this was highly impractical with predictable results. Finally, junior officers were delegated to scramble alongside the tanks, which was quite easy to accomplish in terms of speed since top clip for any World War I tank was no more that 5 mph in open terrain. Safety was another matter altogether.

Two Medals of Honor were awarded in the American Tank Corps, both in Patton's brigade. Corporal Donald M. Call was the driver of one Renault tank when it was hit by a 77 mm shell on the first day of the Meuse-Argonne offensive. The vehicle began burning and he hopped out onto the road. However, the tank's commander, 2nd Lieutenant John Castles, got stuck trying to climb out of the turret. Corporal Call jumped back into the flames, was hit by machine-gun fire and severely wounded. However, he dragged his commander to the side of the road before the gasoline tank exploded. He then carried Lieutenant Castles to safety a mile away. Both men survived.

The second Medal of Honor went to Corporal Harold W. Roberts, who was the driver of a tank on October 6, 1918. Trying to get away from enemy fire, he accidentally drove his tank into a deep, water-filled ditch. The tank began to sink rapidly. "Only one of us will get out," were his last words. He told his commander to leave and pushed him out of the hatch as he himself drowned. He was awarded the medal posthumously.

Toward the end, one unusual bit of strategy the Germans employed at this time was to build plywood mock-ups of Allied tanks. They would place them on their own side of the front line in order to fool Allied aviators into thinking this was the farthest point of the advance. Pilots would fly off looking for the enemy somewhere else. In the final tally, 20,000 men served in the combined United States Tank Corps and AEF Tank Corps.

In the Battle of Amiens, 400 of the faster and more durable Mark V tanks were used to break through the German lines successfully. Many tank designs were developed from this pioneering effort.

Among the most unusual designs was the Skeleton Tank, which was developed by the Pioneer Tractor Company of Winona, Minnesota, in 1918. Much of the tank's structure was of regular iron plumbing pipe joined by standard plumbing connections. It had a relatively small cubelike body made of $1/2$-inch armor and carried a .30-caliber machine gun between the two 25-foot-long tracks powered by two 50 hp Beaver four-cylinder engines allowing for a top speed of 5 mph. The Skeleton Tank was specifically designed for crossing trenches and was considerably less heavy, weighing 9 tons (one-third that of the Mark IV and Mark V), and a harder target to hit. Although a prototype was built, which is still extant, it never went into production.

The Allied or Liberty tank, as it was known, had been derived in design from earlier tanks, especially the Mark V. Also called the Mark VIII tank, and sometimes referred to as the International tank, because of the cooperation of the Anglo-American Tank Committee, a design was completed late in 1917. It was first built in the U.S. as a prototype, and the large manufacturing capabilities in America were earmarked for mass production.

The program was chaired jointly by Lieutenant Albert Stern from the U.K. and Major J.A. Drain of the United States, a representative of General Pershing, and also with industrial expert, H.W. Alden. The plan was to build 1,500 Mark VIII tanks, 300 per month in order to mechanize five heavy American battalions (in addition to 20 light battalions). A factory was built 200 miles south of Paris at Neuvy-Pailloux, but it was not completed until the Armistice. Sir Albert Stern's book titled *Tanks 1914–1918, The Logbook of a Pioneer*, published in 1919, is the definitive document on the history of this very complex engineering development.

Under Major J. A. Drain of the United States and Lieutenant Albert Stern of Great Britain, the Mark VIII Liberty tank was developed as a prototype in America during 1918.

This Renault FT-17 was photographed on American soil, as suggested by the signs in the background. It was used for training as well as for the purpose of being copied as the American version called the M1917.

In his memoir Sir Albert Stern extols the cooperation of the American military only after June of 1917, even though much design work had been shared two years earlier, including the creation of Little Willie and the wholehearted involvement of Holt Caterpillar, later personally acknowledged by General Ernest Swinton. Apparently Stern had some trouble getting everyone on the same page and was only able to get the American Colonel Lassiter to visit the experimental ground where the British tanks were being developed. Colonel Lassiter was the sole representative of the United States in London at the time.

Without much interest from the U.S. Army, Stern invited the Navy, including Admiral Sims and Admiral Mayo as well as Ambassador Page along with forty naval officers. Ambassador Page stated that "he would cable President Wilson that he considered it a crime to attack machine guns with human flesh when you could get armoured machines." General Pershing quickly expressed his support of the tank project. A joint venture was proposed that include 1,500 tanks in cooperation with the U.S. These included the Mark IV and Liberty Type. Winston Churchill approved the venture after some delays in communication. A new department called Mechanical Warfare (Overseas and Allies) was created.

Because the U.S. Tank Corps Depot in France was already largely manned by Chinese laborers in 1917, it was planned that the tank factory would also use Chinese workers. Aside from the factory, the French ended up having little to do with the Anglo-American Tank Program due to lack of men and resources.

In a separate effort, the French government did eventually loan a couple of Renault FT-17 tanks for training purposes, resulting in American tank crews handling French tanks in battle. And finally, FT-17 tanks were loaned to be reverse-engineered under license in the United States, where manufacturing capacity far exceeded that what was possible in war-ravaged France.

All these efforts were regrettably far too late on the calendar, whether or not due to America's reluctance to officially join in the war with its allies until mid–1917, individual egotistic men in politics and the military and engineering fields trying to elbow each other out of the way, or to entire military branches wasting time competing with one another for glory and recognition, primarily, and for a true and final victory, secondarily. This last point would not only be controversial but specious.

As an example, on Christmas Eve of 1914, French and English soldiers in many trenches climbed out to meet German soldiers on no-man's land, in order to smoke, drink, eat and play cards together. By midnight both sides retreated to their literally old entrenched positions and began shooting at each other again, once the Christian holiday was over. Such an account may seem superfluous on the surface, but on either side of reasoning, the delays and reluctance to do battle, the bureaucratic delays in decision-making and manufacturing new and effective weapons by the Allies only resulted in countless more casualties on the ground.

Meanwhile, the enemy was not wasting time in developing new weapons such as submarines with torpedoes, high explosives, poison gas, enormous artillery, zeppelins for bombing civilians, highly effective aircraft, the practice of torturing and executing prisoners of war including medical staff, or planting expert spies, such as the famous Dutch dancer Mata Hari, who was executed by the French in October of 1917 after years of passing vital strategic information. It was gleaned from naïve or treacherous Allied officers who were willing to trade dire military secrets for a few moments of sexual bliss and a bit of false companionship in a tryst of utmost treachery, on one side or the other, or both.

And among the American Tank Corps and U.S. Army officers, the *French-English Military Technical Dictionary* by Colonel Cornelis De Witt Willcox, published by the Washington Government Printing Office in July of 1917, was not an unusual handout at a frontline desk, albeit the English-French version did not appear as a companion translation from English to French.

Yet it was with American cooperation, determination, productivity and boots on the ground that the French, English and Allies smothered the unrepentant aggressors who were transfixed in a regimented, meaningless evil bent on domination. This would not be the first or the last of its type across civilized Europe.

It was not until the end of 1917 that a Council of National Defense was coordinated, calling for a weekly conference of the "war-making activities" according to Washington reporters. The collaboration brought together Secretary of Treasury William G. McAdoo, Edwin N. Hurley of the Shipping Board, Food Administrator Herbert C. Hoover (who would become U.S. president in 1929), Fuel Administrator Dr. Harry Garfield, Chairman Daniel Willard of the War Industries Board, Director Walter S. Gifford, Secretary of War Newton D. Baker, Secretary of the Navy Josephus Daniels, Secretary of the Interior Franklin K. Lane, Secretary of Agriculture David F. Houston, Secretary of Commerce William C. Redfield and Secretary of Labor William B. Wilson.

Regarding the first Council of National Defense a month before the end of the year,

Factory workers using a large cart to move a Liberty V-12 engine ready for installation. Several automotive companies built the Liberty engine under license.

Automotive Industries stated: "This means that we will now have a war council, so to speak, and that the country's resources will be used in an intelligent manner and that there no longer will be any such lack of coordination as will bring about the haphazard orders that were originally issued and which were contradictory between departments."

Meanwhile, the United States and England were continuing the latest cooperative venture in the design and manufacturing of a larger, more powerful tank. The Liberty Mark VIII design differed from the earlier British designs in several significant details. First, the motor and crew compartments were separated by a bulkhead to reduce danger and noise to the crew, although one engineer-mechanic sat inside the engine compartment and communicated with the driver and commander in front via an "inter-phone." Also, a ventilation system raised the internal air pressure slightly higher in the crew section to prevent fumes and exhaust from entering easily as in the earlier British tanks, which even in moments of peaceful maneuvering made hell for the crew members, occasionally rendering them semi-comatose from carbon monoxide and other exhaust gases.

The armor was increased to 16 mm thickness on the sides and front, with 12 mm on the rear and 6 mm on top and bottom. Total track width was widened now to 26 inches. The tank still carried two six-pounder cannon on each side in addition to seven machine guns, each with its own gunner; hence there were 12 crew members in total.

The Mark VIII was to be powered by a 300 hp V-12 Ricardo motor or a 338 hp aircraft V-12 Liberty engine using a two-speed planetary (epicyclic) transmission (similar but much heavier than those in Fords of that time) with gear reduction and final chain

Top: The Liberty Mark VIII tank was so much bigger than the FT-17 and M1917 that the smaller tank could climb on top of the back of this prototype. *Bottom:* The Liberty or International tank, as the Mark VIII was called, was going to be built at 300 per month in a new factory 200 miles south of Paris. This cross-section of the prototype shows the V-12 Liberty engine that could power the giant 34-foot-long tank that had a crew of twelve. It did not go into series production.

drive. Previous tanks had used sliding-gear transmissions. The first hull was fabricated in England yet shipped all the way back to the United States to be fitted with a Liberty V-12.

The new tank was 34 feet 2 inches long, 10 feet 3 inches tall and 11 feet 8 inches wide. It could cross a trench of 14 feet and weighed 37 tons dry. It was capable of crossing a 15-foot gap. The prototype was completed in the U.S. and also tested with a Rolls-Royce engine. All the rest of the mechanical components were assembled by Locomobile in Bridgeport, Connecticut, where the first unit rolled out on September 29, 1918.

The North British Locomotive Company in Glasgow, Scotland, built seven more of these tanks using paired 6-cylinder Ricardo engines in V-12 configuration producing a total of 300 hp. With a 338 hp 12-cylinder Liberty engine, which had twin cams and overhead valves, the power-to-weight ratio was slightly better at 8.66 lbs/ton.

Once World War I ended, the French immediately canceled orders except for three units to be used for experimental purposes, so that the consortium collapsed virtually overnight. Out of seven built in Scotland, one Mark VIII tank survived overseas at the Royal Army Corps Tank Museum in London. The United States built the rest of the order, changing some details, and the tanks were used for training. One hundred sets of parts had been finished in the United States by the end of the war, and these were used to build the Mark VIII tanks, which served the Army into the very early 1930s before the M.2 tank was to arrive. (The Mark IX tank was built by the British—also known as the "Pig" and the "Duck.")

The French FT-17 and FT-18 had the highest production numbers at a total output of 3,700 by war's end, and continued to be built and assembled in other countries, used even into the beginning of World War II. It is believed that 4,500 were eventually built in all. It was the brainchild of Frenchman Rudolphe Enst-Metzmaier and was shepherded through the Renault factory by General Jean Baptiste Eugene Estienne.

It has been said that Americans did not build any tanks during World War I. Aside from all the design and prototyping involvement, the M1917 was built in the United States in considerable numbers. It was almost entirely based on the FT-17 (and very similar FT-18) Renault two-man light tank.

The FT-17 was nicknamed the "mosquito tank" primarily because of its small size compared to other tanks, and perhaps because of its small engine unmuffled exhaust. It had just one gunner and one driver. The July 1918 counterattack at Soissons involved the largest number of FT-17 tanks, 480, making it the largest tank battle of World War I.

The FT-18 differed in that it had a round, cast turret, instead of a riveted, octagonal one, but it would also be armed with a machine gun, such as the 7.62 mm Hotchkiss (transformed into the .30 caliber also) or a 37 mm gun.

Both the FT-17 and FT-18 were powered by a 35 hp four-cylinder L-head Renault engine. Armor consisted of 6 mm to 22 mm in thickness depending on the area. Top speed on level ground was 8 kph (no more than 5 mph in reality) with a 30-mile range. Real speed on soft ground was more like 3 mph, and at the time all the tanks' slow speeds were acceptable because of equally slow marching or walking speed and technical limits. The early FT-17 had front-sprocket idler wheels made of steel-rimmed wood, which were not very durable, and the whole tank was driven at the rear by a 15-tooth sprocket on each side.

The M1917 was produced in mid–1918 by Maxwell Motor Company, C.L. Best Company and Van Dorn Iron Works. C.L. Best, already working in conjunction with Holt Caterpillar, produced the track system, while the armor plating was fabricated at Van Dorn Iron Works, and the vehicles were assembled at Maxwell at its huge new plant in Detroit, Michigan. Maxwell-Briscoe was considered one of the top three in manufacturing capacity size at this time.

Jonathan Dixon Maxwell had experience with working for Oldsmobile, having started as a machinist and helped build Elwood Haynes' first car in 1893 (extant, now in the Smithsonian). The Briscoe Brothers Metalworks had their own large company. After fire destroyed the Tarrytown, New York, factory in 1907, Maxwell constructed what was considered at the time the largest automobile factory in the world, which was located in New Castle, Indiana. But by the time Maxwell was working with the U.S. military, the company's assets had been acquired by Walter Flanders, and it was at that time that the company once again moved—to New York City. There was also a plant in Dayton, Ohio.

General Swinton visited Benjamin Holt in Stockton, California, to salute him for his contribution to the war effort and to inspect the Holt one-man tank prototype. Because the war ended, the tank was never manufactured.

However, the Maxwell Motor Corporation, financed by Walter Flanders, had also leased factories from the Chalmers Motor Company in Detroit to augment their Highland Park plant to fulfill their World War I government contracts.

The M1917 had all-steel wheels, and the one exterior recognizable feature was an additional vision slot on each side for the driver. In all, 952 were placed on order, but because production did not begin until October of 1918, none ever saw action in World War I in Europe. They differed slightly in dimensions, having been translated into inches, and were 16.5 feet in length. They were powered by a modified 42 hp Buda HU four-cylinder motor, which made it just a smidgen faster. Width was 5 feet 7 inches, height 7 feet 6 inches.

It was claimed that the M1917 could climb a 70 percent grade, but there were not many opportunities to prove this out over any significant stretch of actual terrain. The

Opposite, top: From the Jacques Littlefield tank collection, this is one of the very few remaining American-built M1917 tanks, which could be immediately distinguished from the Renault FT-17 by its extra visor slits for the driver. It was powered by a Buda engine, with all fabrication dimensions in inches and other minor changes. *Bottom:* Another view of the Jacques Littlefield Collection M1917 shows the removable tail; it was otherwise identical to the FT-17.

One unusual American prototype of the tank was the gas-electric hybrid built by Holt. It had a crew of six and used a Holt four-cylinder motor to turn a generator in order to power two electric track motors. This design was later used for giant mining trucks and highway construction vehicles.

driver's area, sides and turret were armored with .60-inch-thick (approx. 15 mm) hardened steel and the motor with .25-inch-thick (approx. 6 mm) steel. An unarmed signal M1917 for radio communications was also built, and the M1917, which had a lengthened rear hull to accommodate larger motors, became the M1917A1, which often used a lighter Franklin six-cylinder air-cooled motor when assembled in the U.S. and elsewhere. These latter versions also had an electric starter motor replacing the hand crank. Total weight of the M1917 was 7.3 tons (6,580 kilograms). The M1917 was also armed with a 37 mm M1916 cannon or a M1919 7.62 mm caliber (.30) machine gun. All the versions of this tank ended up in many different countries all the way up into World War II.

Most tanks used in World War I were of European manufacture, but the Caterpillar and Bullock tractors had much influence on some designs. In France there were differences and conflicts in the approach to tank design. As an example, the French Schneider Company bought two 45 hp Baby Holts (Holt 75) in April of 1915 and used these as a basis for their versions, which had one 75 mm gun and two Hotchkiss machine guns. The whole tank weighed 13.5 tons. It was first tested at the Aberdeen Proving Ground in Maryland.

General Ernest Swinton traveled to Stockton in 1918 to meet with Benjamin Holt to express his gratitude for the company's contribution to the war effort. Holt had also built a gun-mount Caterpillar tractor capable of carrying a 75 mm gun at the then unheard-of speed of 28 mph. Advances in metallurgy made this a possibility so that transmission components would not disintegrate from heat and friction, but it would be a number of years before this would be proven in the field. A one-man tank prototype was also developed by Holt/Caterpillar in Stockton, but it never went into production. Existing photos show General Swinton thanking and shaking hands with Benjamin Holt surrounded by Stockton factory workers in front of a wooden mock-up of the tiny one-man tank.

Another single prototype was built by Holt in conjunction with General Electric Company (GEC). It was completed in January of 1918. It used lengthened and upgraded iterations of the Holt tractor with pivoting track frames on vertical coil springs and ten road wheels on each side. The Holt Gas-Electric used a 90 hp Holt four-cylinder motor to drive a GEC generator that powered two electric motors, one for each track. By varying the current in addition to the brakes on each shaft, the tank could be steered more easily. This vehicle had a 75 mm gun in the nose and a .30-caliber Browning machine gun on each sponson. The engine and transmission at the rear nearly blocked the only door in and out of the tank with a crew of six: commander, driver, gunner, loader and two machine gunners. Only a prototype was built, but with its weight of 25 tons it had considerable shortcomings in climbing and speed, which was about 6 mph at best. Armor was between $^1/_4$-inch and $^3/_4$-inch thick depending on section area.

This design was later used by a few companies, such as Caterpillar, to build huge road-building trucks and graders, even up to this day. There was also a 20-ton tractor mounted with a truck body, and this crawler was used to build yet another prototype also called the "American Tank."

Holt also provided "self-propelled Caterpillar mounts" for carrying 8-inch Schneider long-range guns (known as Mark I) or heavy 240 mm Schneider howitzer (known as Mark III). Both of these were built in prototype form only, as the U.S. Army switched to lighter, faster and more mobile vehicles.

Toward the end of World War I, Caterpillar began to experiment with different tractors, including this one fitted with a truck body for carrying ammunition and heavy equipment.

HARLEY-DAVIDSON
MILITARY MOTORCYCLE

The first Yank and Harley to enter Germany 11/12/18

As the war ended, a photograph was taken of this motorcycle and rider who were called the "First Yank and Harley-Davidson to enter Germany 11/12/18."

Once the German army was stopped on the eastern front by March of 1918, the Germans returned to the west and overran the British 5th Army again at the Somme. Pushing to the Marne, newly arrived American soldiers stopped the German troops at Chateau-Thierry. Here, in one of the most dramatic examples of motorized firepower, 354 tanks of various types rolled over barbed wire, machine guns, trenches and obstacles, breaking the German line and the troops' morale and resulting in a requisition for the Armistice on October 4. With the fighting finally ended, the Armistice was signed on November 11. The Treaty of Versailles was not actually signed until June 28, 1919.

Despite the many technical advances in the development of tanks, trucks, cars and motorcycles during World War I (in addition to aircraft, submarines, et cetera), the majority of photos from the actual battlegrounds show men traveling on horseback and attacking on foot at close quarters in vast numbers in the midst of barrages of machine gun and artillery fire along with poison-gas attacks up until the war finally came to a close.

One of the last innovators of tank technology during World War I was John Walter Christie. He had founded the Front Drive Motor Company in 1912, having pioneered front-drive since 1904 through several different iterations of his engineering firms under different names. He concentrated on racing at first, and entered the 1907 French Grand Prix with a car that had two 19.88-liter V-4 engines, one fore and one aft.

Gaining notoriety but lacking success in racing, Christie turned to utilitarian front-drive machines, and he designed two-wheel tractors that could substitute for horses on steam pumper fire engines, which were quite common at the time. These tractors were very successful and Christie sold some 600 before building a prime mover to haul artillery in 1916. This latter vehicle, which featured a transversely mounted 60 hp engine, did not go into series production, but Christie's creativity continued, and by war's end he also designed and built a tank, calling it the M1919. Its main innovation consisted of center bogies so that the tank could be driven on wheels, achieving slightly higher road speed and prolonging the life span of the tank treads. The tank track bands themselves could be removed and replaced in 15 minutes at a time when losing or breaking a track on a tank or crawler tractor would disable it and usually required major repairs. The Christie tank prototype had $\frac{1}{4}$-inch armor and weighed 13.5 tons with a 360-degree turret, which could be mounted with a .30-caliber machine gun or 57 mm OQF gun. It had a crew of three, top speed was 7 mph, and it had a 35-mile range on flat ground. But as the Treaty of Versailles was signed, this machine became one more of Christie's experimental vehicles, only preceding continuous efforts in various innovations such as half-tracks and further tank development in World War II, before his death at age 80 in 1944.

It is noteworthy to tally the final number of killed in that war to end all wars: Russia (including Poland, Slovakia and Czech under Russian rule), 1,700,000; France, 1,375,000; Great Britain, 908,400; Italy, 650,000; U.S., 126,000 (including 112,432 military plus civilians); Germany, 1,773,000; Austria-Hungary, 1,200,000; Turkey, 325,000; Bulgaria, 87,500; plus another 400,000 divided up among Japan, Rumania, Serbia, Belgium, Greece, Portugal and Montenegro.

World War I compelled American vehicle manufacturers to accelerate their rate of production and advanced U.S. wheeled and tracked motor vehicle technology, in addition to many other innovations often cited as the "silver lining" of competition in war. Although World War I resulted in tremendous human losses and destruction, it was the impetus for rapid and substantial progress in the design and manufacture of motor vehicles (as well as advances in medical treatment).

American truck companies had built 227,000 trucks in 1918 alone, a ten-fold increase in just six years. The entire automotive industry made major advances in design and engineering, and motor transport changed forever during World War I. Military leaders would never again look at motor vehicles with such skepticism as during the post–Victorian (and Edwardian) era. The tens of thousands of surplus vehicles left over after the global upheaval also had a tremendous influence on leaving the horse behind as the primary mode of transportation on the ground.

By November 15, 1918, telegrams from the AEF were sent out to all companies that had provided vehicles to cease war production and convert back to civilian manufacturing. As could be expected, canceled contracts throughout the country caused disruption in the operations of hundreds of industrial plants.

Ford replied that it had 25,000 cars on hand for military delivery. Some of the smaller companies had their contracts continued, but the upheaval in the American motor vehicle industry resulted in the demise of numerous manufacturers, while others banded together. Wartime material shortages had also proven lethal to some smaller companies. Expectations were that the war would continue into 1919. Of the 40,000 passenger cars that were ordered from Cadillac, Dodge, Ford and White, at least half had been delivered by November of 1918 (with numbers rounded off because of lack of accurate documentation).

These particular companies had kept producing their standard line of vehicles with only minor modifications for military use, such as extra running board gas tank, olive drab paint, search lights, heavier wheels, gun mounts, et cetera. Converting back to civilian production was fairly straightforward for these four large companies, and all four thrived after World War I, having made a marginal but solid profit throughout their wartime output.

The motor vehicle industry in Europe had been so transformed for the war effort that there was a large-scale shortage of cars and trucks for civilian use, so those American vehicles that were not crated and ready to be shipped back remained as surplus vehicles, especially throughout France and Belgium, but also throughout the Continent and Great Britain. Those that were still crated and were shipped back, as well as the thousands of vehicles that had not yet been shipped overseas were declared surplus by Act of Congress and distributed among such government agencies as the Post Office Department, Department of the Interior and the Department of Agriculture, in addition to various local governments.

Surplus nonstandard vehicles and those in disrepair were auctioned off to the highest bidder by the end of 1920. The recession of 1920 was partially related to the rather sudden return to peacetime industrial production as well as a plethora of surplus machinery, equipment and vehicles for the war effort.

As opposed to a dramatic slump in the economy of such nations as Germany and Austria after World War I, America's economy rebounded during the Roaring Twenties.

The first Cadillac in Germany was also the first Allied car across the Rhine River, seen here at Alt Breisac on the German side. It was known as the Cadillac M. Broad Arrow, and was under the command of Lieutenant Colonel George H. Johnson, who was present on November 18, 1918, seven days after the signing of the Armistice.

In what became the Soviet Union, a new political philosophy, in large part following ideas promulgated by Karl Marx, created an artificial social and political system that could not go the distance by design. However, it has been argued that Marx's social and political ideas were influenced by what he had seen with his own eyes as the obvious side effects of the Industrial Revolution: numbing urbanization, disease, pollution, child labor and a multitude of dehumanizing "work-till-you-drop" policies in various industries. Out of the bitter punishment that the losers of World War I received, a new, more potent militarization and industrialization emerged during the next two decades, resulting in another soon-to-be global upheaval of cataclysmic proportions in the form of World War II.

In a sense, the twenty years between 1919 and 1939 were only an intermission after which the same nations, with few exceptions such as Japan, took up the same sides in order to destroy each other in a more lethal and large-scale manner, involving exponentially more civilians and even more efficient industrial participation.

CHRONOLOGY OF THE WAR, 1914–1919

1914

06/28   Archduke Ferdinand of Austria-Hungary and his wife are assassinated in Sarajevo by Gavrilo Princip, a member of the ultra-nationalist group named the Black Hand.

07/05   Kaiser Wilhelm of Germany promises to aid Austria-Hungary in case Russia and France interfere with a possible Serbian war.

07/23   Austria-Hungarian government insists that the Black Hand ultra-nationalist group in Serbia be arrested and blames the Serbian government in complicity with the assassination. The ultimatum is set.

07/24   The day after the above accusation the Serbian government appeals to czarist Russia for protection.

07/25   The Serbian government pleads innocent regarding the assassination and refuses to extradite members of the Black Hand who are in custody. The reply is rejected.

07/27   Germany rejects Britain's offer at mediation.

07/28   Austria-Hungary declares war on Serbia.

07/29   Russia mobilizes its army. Austrians shell Belgrade.

08/01   Germany declares war on Russia.

08/02   Germany invades Luxembourg.

08/03   Germany declares war on France.

08/04   German troops invade Belgium after General Moltke orders the Schlieffen Plan to be put in motion, which includes invading France and approaching Paris from the north. Great Britain declares war on Germany and passes the Defense Realm Act, giving government control over railroads and supplies. France recruits 3.5 million men, leaving women and children to work in agriculture and other professions. Greece declines offer of alliance with Germany and remains neutral.

08/06   Mobilization of 750,000 men begins in Great Britain and recruitment posters go up throughout the country. Austria-Hungary declares war on Russia while Serbia declares war on Germany.

08/07   One hundred thousand soldiers are called up by Lord Kitchener in Great Britain. Portugal announces collaboration with Allies but does not declare war on Germany. British troops land in France while French troops invade Alsace-Lorraine.

08/10   Austrian army invades territory of Poland from Galicia.

08/12   Germany employs Big Bertha artillery against the Liège Forts, decimating the fortifications and Russian troops including Slavic nationalities under the Czar. The same day Austro-Hungarian troops invade Serbia. Great Britain declares war on Austria-Hungary.

08/13   France declares war on Austria-Hungary.

08/14   Lorraine is occupied by French troops. A series of encounters called the Battles of Frontiers develops along the western front and continues until August 25th.

08/16   Germany takes over Liège. Serbians rout Austrians at Battle of Jadar.

08/17   Russian troops invade East Prussia in first clash with German army.

08/18   Russians invade Galicia.

BUICK SEARCHLIGHT CAR

Buick

Send for Catalogue to
General Motors (Europe) Limited
136 Long Acre, London, W.C.
Phone: Gerrard 9626 (3 Lines). Telegrams: "buickgen, London."

Buick built Searchlight Cars, as this ad for General Motors (Europe) announced from London.

(1914)

08/19   With the full support of Congress, President Woodrow Wilson declares the U.S. to be neutral in the war in Europe.

08/20   German forces enter Brussels.

08/22   British Expeditionary Forces (BEF) arriving in France engage German forces of 160,000 with their own 70,000 men in the Battle of Mons.

08/23   Japan declares war on Germany. Battle of Mons in France commences.

08/24   Plan XVII is abandoned by the French Army.

Top: Before refrigeration compressors and cooling systems were developed, sealed box vans with plenty of blocks of ice were used to transport food in trucks such as these built by White. *Bottom:* The Mark VIII tank was built in prototype form in the United States, with several more built in Scotland, such as this example shown with factory engineers in 1918.

Factory literature from Cadillac used this Hoffman painting to illustrate the cooperation of officers in a limousine and a lone courier on a motorcycle.

(1914)

08/26   Beginning of the Battle of Tannenberg in which Russian forces in East Prussia are defeated as a result of personal enmity between Russian Generals Rennenkampf and Samsonov, uncoded radio messages and discovery by Germans of a dead Russian officer with entire military plans in his pocket. Battle of La Cateau.

08/28   Battle of Heligoland takes place as well as Battle of Lemberg, forcing Austro-Hungarians to retreat to Carpathian Mountains.

Uncle  Sam Uses 5000 Harley-Davidsons

Harley-Davidson and Indian prided themselves for producing thousands of motorcycles for the war.

(1914)

09/02   Conference of War Propaganda Bureau Writers.
09/03   French government leaves Paris for Bordeaux. Russians capture Lemberg.
09/06   Beginning of the first Battle of Marne when French commander-in-chief held the line on the river and attacked, forcing the German army to withdraw.
09/08   Second invasion of Serbia by Austrian army fails.
09/09   The Crisis of the Marne, in which the British Expeditionary Forces (BEF) use Paris taxis to bring up 6,000 reservists to the frontline, breaking the German attack.
09/10   First Battle of the Masurian Lakes.
09/11   Battle of Rava Russkaya in Galicia. Russians send Austrians back to the Carpathians.
09/13   German troops are attacked by the French Army at River Aisne, beginning the "race to the sea."
09/22   U-boats sink British warships for the first time.
09/25   Battle of Albert begins.
10/01   Battle of Arras begins.
10/05   The first German aircraft is shot down by an Allied plane.
10/06   Germans drive Russians back in Poland and Galicia.
10/09   Germany invades Antwerp.
10/11   First Battle of Ypres.
10/12   Germans advance on Warsaw.
10/15   The Battle of Ypres begins. After four weeks the Allies continue to hold ground around the Belgian town, effectively defeating the Schlieffen Plan.
10/16   Troops from Canada arrive in Britain.
10/21   German troops withdraw from Warsaw area.
10/31   Turkey joins Germany and Austria-Hungary, declaring war on the Allies.

As the Army expanded its Motor Transport Corps, new careers were created for those inclined.

(1914)

11/01   Russia declares war against Turkey. British are defeated at sea by German ships near Coronel, Chile.

11/02   German army repelled from Poland. Russians invade East Prussia. British begin mining North Sea.

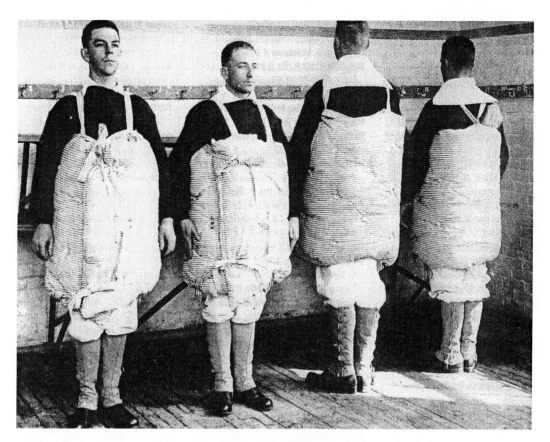

Top: No matter which military branch a soldier belonged to, by 1916 body armor was something to be considered for every one of them; yet as shown here, it was unwieldy, made running difficult, did not cover the upper torso and virtually nobody wore it. *Bottom:* Several branches of the military began buying large numbers of motorcycles such as this 1916 Indian, which was swift and advanced in design.

Harley-Davidson sidecars were mounted with machine guns in 1916, shown here on training manuevers.

(1914)

11/05   After a short delay, Great Britain and France declare war on Turkey.
11/07   Having sided with the Allies, Japan seizes German Western Samoa, Caroline, Marshall, Mariana Islands and finally port of Tsingtao by this date.
11/11   Third invasion of Serbia by Austrian troops fails.
11/21   English and Indian troops invade Mesopotamia. British troops occupy Basra in then–Mesopotamia with a plan to attack Baghdad. On the same date the first night-time bombing is performed by a Farman MF-11.
12/02   Austrian troops enter Belgrade after its evacuation.
12/03   New Serbian attack forces Austrians back across the border.
12/08   Battle of Falkland Islands begins with Vice-Admiral von Spee's squadron being sunk.
12/18   Egypt becomes a British protectorate.
12/25   A truce is announced by both sides and soldiers emerge from their trenches and celebrate Christmas for one day before the war restarts.

1915

01/12   Przemysl surrenders to Russian Army on the eastern front where Central Powers using Austro-Hungarian forces concentrate.
01/14   South African forces occupy Swakopmund.
01/24   The Battle of Dogger Bank.
01/31   First use of poison gas by Germans at Winter Battle of Masurian Lakes.
02/18   Germany declares waters around Great Britain to be war zones.
02/19   British Navy raids Dardanelles and opens fire on Turks. Rear Admiral Robeck sails for Alexandria after three British battleships are sunk and three damaged. British Army takes over without plan.
02/28   German army retreats from Upper Poland.
03/01   Allies blockade Germany.

Opposite: A 1918 poster announcing "An Opportunity for Mechanics" showed both infantry and a truck to promote the First Replacement Regiment of Engineers.

The **U.S. ENGINEERS**
NEED YOU

**AN OPPORTUNITY FOR MECHANICS
and MEN WITH TECHNICAL TRAINING**
Be a **FIGHTING ENGINEER** by joining
The **FIRST REPLACEMENT
REGIMENT** *of* **ENGINEERS**
Address: **Headquarters Room 107, Washington Barracks, D.C.**

Inadequate transportation was one reason these captured German soldiers had to march for many kilometers in France amid a mix of horse-drawn wagons and truck traffic.

(1915)

03/03   Dardanelles landing repelled.
03/10   British Expeditionary Forces attack at Neuve Chapelle begin.
03/14   Battle of Saint Eloi.
03/18   Dardanelles are attacked by Allied naval forces after Turkish forces closed the area. Four British and French warships are sunk.
03/28   Przemysl in southern Poland falls to the Russians.
04/12   Turkish attempt to take over Basra fails.
04/22   German troops resort to the first use of gas in France, attacking Ypres for the second time, but despite initial panic, the Allies recover.
04/25   Allied forces land at Gallipoli.
04/26   Secret Treaty of London is signed by Great Britain, France and Russia promising territory as payment to Italy to join the Allies.
05/04   Austro-German offensive begins against Russian front at Gorlice and Tarnow.
05/07   The German submarine U20 torpedoes the passenger ship Lusitania on the Atlantic Ocean, galvanizing public opinion against the Central Powers in Europe.
05/09   The Artois offensive begins with British attack in the Battle of Aubers, but an acute shortage of artillery shells and bad planning cause many casualties with few gains. Outrage over shortages is seen in British press.

White trucks were used extensively in Europe, such as this one shown in 1918 being given the "thumbs up" by a solider as the truck passes over a dirt road.

(1915)

05/16	Main assault on Vimy Ridge begins by the Allies in the second Battle of Artois. Lack of Allied reinforcements and German counterattacks allow the Germans to regain lost ground in more than six weeks. Also, the Battle of Festubert begins with German line pushed back less than one mile lasting until May 27.
05/23	Italy declares war against Austria-Hungary.
05/25	Germany abandons the Ypres attack. Also, Asquith forms a coalition government.
05/29	French Army reaches Vimy Ridge in third Battle of Artois. To the north French begin second Battle of Champagne.
05/31	Germany bombs London using a Zeppelin.
06/01	German offensive into Galicia, the Gorlice-Tarnow Offensive, becomes a major victory for the Central Powers and forces Russian Army to withdraw.
06/02	German troops enter Przemsyl in southern Poland.
06/03	British take over Amara on the Tigris River.
06/09	British General Swinton agrees on first specifications of tanks to be built, including top speed of 4 mph, the ability to climb 5-foot parapet, cross 8-foot gap, work in a 20-mile range radius and contain a crew of ten men.
06/22	Germans retake Lemberg.
06/23	The first Isonzo Offensive commences in Italy to be followed by ten more battles in this area.
08/05	Warsaw falls to German Army with Russian retreat.
08/06	The Suvla Bay Offensive begins at Gallipoli.
08/21	Italy declares war against Turkey.
09/05	Grand Duke Nikolai is removed from the position of Commander-in-Chief and Czar Nicholas takes command of Russian army.
09/11	British military leaders are shown the first motorized tank prototype.

Top: Being photographed in and around automobiles was prestigious, as with these members of the Red Cross Motor Corps in April of 1917. *Bottom:* The American Ship Building Company used trucks such as this 1917 White in its shipyards. Note long bulb horn and acetylene lamps.

(1915)

09/25   British and French forces begin offensive at Artois-Loos.

09/26   Czar Ferdinand of Bulgaria finally commits alliance to the Central Powers after playing to both sides.

09/28   British capture Kut-el-Amara on the Tigris River in Mesopotamia.

10/05   Allied troops arrive at Salonika.

Top: The Harley-Davidson with sidecar like this 1917 example became commonly used for dispatch and courier work and for transporting officers. *Bottom:* American vehicles were occasionally used by the enemy, and like Riker in the U.S., the Austrian Army mounted railroad flanges on this 1917 Locomobile touring car.

White trucks are being used here to transport soldiers from an American troop carrier, which was painted ship camouflage to confuse German submarines.

(1915)

10/07	Austro-German forces invade Serbia.
10/12	British nurse Edith Cavell is executed, causing extreme public reaction.
10/14	Bulgaria declares war against Serbia, which is defeated.
10/15	Great Britain, France and Serbia declare war against Bulgaria.
10/19	Sir Douglas Haig becomes the new British Expeditionary Force commander. Italy and Russia declare war against Bulgaria.
11/06	Second Battle of Champagne ends.
11/22	Battle of Ctesiphon where Anglo-Indian troops are forced to withdraw to Kut-al-Imara.
12/07	Kut-al-Imara surrounded by Turkish troops as British relief fails.
12/10	Britain's Field Marshal John French is replaced by General Douglas Haig after a series of failures due to poor strategy, inability to exploit advantage, materiel shortages, lack of reserves and large casualty figures.
12/19	Anzac and Suvla Bay are evacuated.
12/31	Under Britain's War Minister Horatio Herbert Kitchener, 2.6 million men have been recruited since war began.

1916

01/15	After Turkish reinforcements arrive under Mustafa Kemal around Gallipoli and the Dardanelles, with no breakthrough in sight, the Allies withdraw in defeat.
02/02	The draft (conscription) begins in Great Britain.
02/21	The German Verdun Offensive begins under Falkenhayn with huge artillery barrage.

After being unloaded from trains, tanks had their protruding sponsons assembled at a "Tanka-drome," here at Rollencourt in June of 1917. Although this photograph shows British tanks, it makes clear how the military avoided depot container explosions and made gasoline portable by using 5-gallon canisters.

(1916)

02/26	Fort Douaumont near Verdun is captured by Germans with enormous numbers of casualties on both sides.
03/09	Germany declares war on Portugal.
03/16	The French cross-channel ferry *Sussex* is sunk with loss of civilian life, further enflaming opinion in neutral countries against the Central Powers.
03/18	After a request from French military leadership, the Russian Army attacks Germans at Lake Naroch to alleviate pressure at Verdun, but Russian losses are very serious without any real strategic gains.
04/29	After the British and Indian troops occupy Kut-el-Amara in late September of 1915, the British suffer a major defeat two months later and surrender after starvation, illness and devastating deprivation.
05/05	British begin construction of rail and water lines on the Sinai coast.
05/31	The Battle of Jutland begins.
06/04	The Russian Brusilov Offensive begins and south of Pripet Marshes.
06/05	Lord Kitchener is killed at sea. Sherif Hussein of Mecca organizes revolt against Turkey.
07/01	Beginning of British and French Somme Offensive under General Haig with the intent to capture German trench system. Counting both sides, 60,000 casualties within 48 hours.
07/25	Capture of Pozieres by Australian troops as part of Somme Offensive is considered actual but limited success. Remaining Serbian forces arrive in Salonika.
08/09	The Italian Army begins the Gorizia Offensive.
08/27	Romania declares war against Austria-Hungary. Germany declares war against Romania. Italy declares war against Germany.
08/29	Hindenburg becomes German Chief of Staff.
08/30	Bulgaria declares war against Romania.
09/01	Troops under Field Marshal August von Mackenensen invade Romania.
09/15	Tanks are used for the first time at Flers-Courcelette with only limited effect, with element of surprise, but slow speed and lack of firepower accuracy.

Top: Stateside, local governments had well over 100 makes of trucks to choose from for such work as police patrol, as with this 1918 Republic paddy wagon in San Francisco. *Bottom:* The Virginia Shipbuilding Corporation used trucks like this 1918 White in their huge operations on the East Coast, keeping up with demand for more supply ships as they were sunk by German submarines.

(1916)

09/20   Russian advance is halted by Austro-German forces.
10/24   Douaumont Fort at Verdun is recaptured by the French Army.
11/05   Fort Vaux recaptured by French.
11/18   The Somme Offensive ends with 550,000 French casualties and 435,000 German casualties. Falkenhayn is replaced by Generals Hindenburg and Ludendorff.

Top: The Jeffery Quad became the Nash Quad when Charles Nash bought the company in 1916. The Nash Quad joined the Four-Wheel-Drive (FWD) and Walter trucks as some of the most important 4 × 4 Allied vehicles of World War I. *Bottom:* This photograph of General Pershing sitting in the back of a 1918 White staff car in a parade exemplified the heroic image he had acquired as World War I ended.

(1916)

11/29	Jellicoe is replaced by Beatty as Commander-in-Chief.
12/06	Lloyd George becomes British Prime Minister.
12/12	General Nivelle becomes French western front Commander-in-Chief, replacing Joffre.
12/19	British intelligence intercepts Zimmermann telegram attempting to draw Mexico and Japan against the U.S. Also, Battle of Verdun ends.
12/21	British capture El Arish in the Middle East.

1917

01/30	Rail and water lines completed by British to Rafah.
01/31	Germans officially announce unrestricted submarine attacks beginning the following day.
02/04	German U-boat resumption of unrestricted sinking of ships results in U.S. breaking diplomatic relations with Germany.
02/24	British forces retake Kut-el-Amara.
03/11	British and Indian forces win the Battle of Kut and Baghdad falls to the Allies.
03/12	Russian Revolution begins and the Czar abdicates.
03/26	First Battle of Gaza begins.
04/02	President Woodrow Wilson petitions the Senate to declare war.
04/06	United States declares war on German government.
04/09	Allied Arras Offensive begins. Vimy Ridge captured.
04/12	Vimy Ridge recaptured by Canadian Army as part of Arras battle.
04/16	Second Battle of Aisne begins, also known as the Nivelle Offensive in the Champagne region, and first time French used tanks in battle.
04/17	French tanks are used in battle for the first time. Second Battle of Gaza begins.
04/20	Strong German resistance at Aisne causes 118,000 French casualties.
04/29	Mutinies begin within French Army.
05/05	First use of Chars St. Chamond and Schneider tanks in action.
05/15	General Nivelle is sacked and replaced by General Petain who becomes Commander-in-Chief of French western front after large-scale mutiny at Aisne, which is not discovered by Germans.
05/16	Maria Bochkareva in Russia forms Women's Battalion.
05/19	General John Pershing takes over command of American Expeditionary Forces.
06/07	British attack at Messines Ridge uses detonation of 20 huge underground mines, decimating German defenses. General Allenby takes over British forces.
06/22	Pro-German King Constantine I of Greece forced to abdicate and pro–Allies Eleutherios Venizelos takes over leadership as premier.
06/25	United States troops first arrive in France.
07/02	Greece declares war against Germany and Austria-Hungary.
07/17	King George V changes last name to Windsor.
07/31	Third Battle of Ypres, known as Passchendaele, begins.
08/03	British begin their drive into Palestine but are repelled in the first and second Battles of Gaza.
08/14	After 320,000 Chinese were recruited to work as laborers and in medical units beginning in 1914, China finally declares war on Germany, although not participating in actual combat.
10/12	British Offensive at Passchendaele is restarted and ends in three weeks with 320,000 British casualties and 200,000 German casualties. The Bolshevik Revolution in Russia begins civil war and eventual total change in regime.
10/15	The standardized "Heavy Duty" Motor Truck is shown to Secretary of War Baker in Washington D.C. for the first time.
10/24	Beginning of Italian Caporetto Offensive, sometimes referred to as the twelfth Battle of Isonzo.
10/26	Brazil declares war on Germany as a result of the sinking of two of its ships by Germany in April and May, after a long-held neutrality.
11/06	Third Battle of Ypres ends as Canadian troops take Passchendaele Ridge. Bolsheviks seize power in Russia.

Opposite: **Romanticizing World War I on several different levels was the theme of this postcard from 1918 with the English and French inscriptions of "All for Victory."**

(1917)

11/07	Supreme Allied War Council is formed.
11/18	Sir Frederick Maude dies in Mesopotamia.
11/20	Mass tank attack at Cambrai using 381 tanks under General Haig. Initial success not exploited due to lack of reserves and mechanical breakdown of tanks.
11/21	Russian Women's Battalion is disbanded by new Bolshevik government.
12/03	German counterattacks at Cambrai result in recapture of terrain.
12/07	U.S. declares war on Austria-Hungary.
12/09	The British and Indian forces under new commander, General Archibald Murray, outflank the Turkish forces during the third Gaza Battle and General Allenby occupies Jerusalem. Also, Romania signs armistice with Germany on this date.
12/22	Trotsky begins peace negotiations with Germans at Brest Litovsk.

1918

01/08	President Wilson speaks about 14 Point Peace Program.
02/10	Trotsky stops negotiations and Germans resume hostilities against Russia.
03/03	Treaty of Brest-Litovsk ends World War I on the eastern front.
03/21	Beginning of German Spring Offensive known as Operation Michael.
03/23	German forces advance past Saint Quentin while Paris is shelled.
03/27	German troops advance within 32 miles of Paris, capturing Montdidier.
03/29	General Ferdinand Foch appointed Allied Coordinator in France and two weeks later as Supreme Allied Commander.
04/23	British Navy raids U-boat bases at Zeebrugge and Ostend.
04/24	First tank-versus-tank battle in an unexpected engagement of German A7V and British Mark IV at Villers-Bretonneux without clear outcome.
05/09	British scuttle cruiser *Vindictive* blocks the Zeebrugge canal.
05/27	Third Battle of Aisne begins with German troops at Marne in four days.
05/28	American troops capture Cantigny.
06/02	Battle of Chateau-Thierry.
06/06	Battle of Belleau Wood.
06/15	Battle of the Piave.
07/04	Battle of Le Hamel begins with tanks as a decisive part of the Allied plan.
07/15	Second Battle of the Marne as the final German offensive of the war begins with repulse by French troops and help from American Expeditionary Force.
07/16	Exiled Czar Nicholas II and family are executed.
07/20	German Army retreats from the Marne.
08/08	Amiens Battle Offensive by British begins and Ludendorff calls it "the black day of the German Army in the war."
08/21	Allies break through at Albert.
09/13	United States Expeditionary Forces begin offensive at St. Mihiel.
09/26	Meuse-Argonne Offensive begins.
09/27	Canal du Nord Offensive begins and Hindenburg Line is broken.
09/29	Bulgaria signs Armistice.
10/01	Damascus falls to the British under General Allenby.
10/03	Max von Baden becomes Chancellor of Germany.
10/05	Hindenburg Line is overwhelmed by Allied Forces.
10/24	Italian Vittorio Veneto Offensive begins.
10/27	General Erich Ludendorff resigns as German commander.
10/28	German Navy crews revolt at Wilhelmshaven with mutiny following among other German crews.
10/31	Turkey agrees to an armistice and Mosul is occupied by the Allies within a few days in November.
11/01	Serbs recapture Belgrade.
11/03	Armistice is signed by Austria-Hungary after defeat by Italian, French and British troops at Piave. German troops are driven from Meuse-Argonne.
11/04	Mutinies spread across Germany and mutineers control all crossings of the Rhine River.
11/07	Armistice Commission from Germany meets General Foch.

(1918)

11/09   Kaiser Wilhelm II of Germany abdicates and flees. New government in Berlin is set up after revolutionary provisional socialist forces take over.

11/11   Allies defeat Austria-Hungary in the Balkans with final Battle of Vardar River at Salonika. General Armistice is signed and on the 11th hour of the eleventh day of the 11th month a cease-fire endures.

11/21   German fleet sails to Scapa Flow and surrenders to British.

11/25   Under General Paul von Lettow-Vorbeck in East Africa, after skillful guerrilla war with Allies, German forces finally lay down arms, making it the last act of warfare by the German Army in World War I, due to a delay in communication.

12/14   Lloyd George wins British general election.

1919

01/12   Paris Peace Conference begins.

06/21   German Navy crews scuttle fleet at Scapa Flow.

06/28   Treaty of Versailles signed. Beginning of a short peace.

BIBLIOGRAPHY

Alexander, E. P. *Iron Horses*. New York: Bonanza Books, 1941.

American Armies & Battlefields in Europe. Washington D.C.: U.S. Government Printing Office, 1938.

The American City. Feb. 1917, pp. 175–76. July 1918, pp. 47–48.

Applegate, Susan. *North American Indians in the Great War*. Lincoln: University of Nebraska Press, 2007.

Arthur, Sir George. *Life of Lord Kirchener*. London: Macmillan, 1920.

Asprey, Robert B. *At Belleau Wood*. New York: G.P. Putnam, 1965.

_____. *The First Battle of the Marne*. New York: J.B. Lippincott, 1962.

Asquith, H. H. *The Genesis of the War*. London: Cassell, 1923.

Automobile Engineering: A General Reference Work. Vols. 1–5. Chicago: American Technical Society, 1917.

Automotive Industries. May 29, 1919, p. 1189.

Automobile Topics, Government Buys 54 Army Trucks. March 18, 1916.

Automobile Trade Journal. August 1916, p. 117. "U.S. Orders Large Number of Commercial Cars," June 1917. March 1918.

Ayers, Colonel Leonard P. *The War with Germany—A Statistical Summary*. Washington D.C.: U.S. Government Printing Office, 1919.

Baldwin, Hanson W. *World War I—An Outline History*. New Jersey: Hanover House, 1955.

Baldwin, Nick. *Classic Tractors A to Z*. Stillwater, MN: Voyageur Press, 1998.

Barres, Maurice. *The Faith of France*. New York: Houghton Mifflin, 1918.

Baumgarten-Crusius, Gen. Artur. *Die Marneschlacht 1914* . Leipzig, Germany: Lippold, 1919.

The Big Book of Harley-Davidson. Milwuakee: Harley-Davidson Centennial, 2003.

Bircher, Oberstleutnant Eugen. *Die Krisis in der Marneschlacht*. Bern, Germany: Berger-Levrault, 1921.

Bishop, Chris. *The Encyclopedia of Tanks & Ar-*

mored Fighting Vehicles. San Diego: Thunder Bay Press, 2006.

Blake, Robert. *The Private Papers of Douglas Haig*. London: Eyre and Spottiswoode, 1952.

Bloem, Walter. *The Advance from Mons 1914*. London: Peter Davies Press, 1923.

Bolton, Walter. *Petain*. London: Allen and Unwin, 1957.

Bourne, J. M. *Who's Who in World War One*. London: Routledge, 2001.

Bradley, W. F. *Automobile*. May 31, 1917, p. 1049.

Brownell, Tom. *A History of Mack Trucks*. Osceola, WI: MBI, 1994.

Buchan, John. *A History of the Great War*. London: Peter Davies, 1923.

Bulow, Field Marshal von. *Mein Bericht zur Marneschlacht*. Berlin: Scherl, 1919.

Cadillac Participation in the World War. Detroit: Cadillac Motor Car Co., 1919.

Campbell, Gerald. *Verdun to the Vosges*. London: Arnold Press, 1916.

Canadian General Staff, Army Headquarters. *The Western Front 1914*. Ottawa, Canada: 1957.

Carre, Commandant Henri. *La Veritable Historie des Taxis de la Marne*. Paris: Libraire Chapelot, 1921.

Carroll, John, and Gary Stuart. *The Classic Indian Motorcycle—A History of the Marque*. London: Salamander, 1999.

Chamberlain, Peter. *The Tank Mark VIII, "The International."* Surrey, England: Great Bookham, Armor in Profile, 1967.

_____, and Chris Ellis. *Pictorial History of Tanks of the World 1915–1945*. Harrisburg, PA: Stackpole Books, 1972.

Childress, David Hatcher. *The Fantastic Inventions of Nikola Tesla*. Stelle, IL: Adventures Unlimited Press, 1993.

Churchill, Winston. *Great Contemporaries*. London: Butterworth, 1937.

_____. *The Unknown War*. New York: Charles Scribner, 1932.

_____. *The World Crisis*. Vols. 1–4. London: Butterworth, 1923–1927.

Citino, Robert M. *Armored Forces: History & Source Book*. Westport, CT: Greenwood Press, 1994.

Clark, John Maurice. *The Costs of the World War to the American People*. New Haven, CT: Yale University Press, 1931.

Clarkson, Grosvenor, B. *Industrial America in the World War*. New York: Houghton Mifflin, 1923.

Cochenhausen, General von. *Von Scharnhorst zu Schlieffen*. Berlin: Mittler, 1933.

Coetzee, Frantz. *World War I: A History in Documents*. New York: Oxford University Press, 1993.

Coleman, Frederick. *From Mons to Ypres with General French*. New York: Dodd-Mead, 1916.

Collier, Peter, and David Horowitz. *The Fords: An American Epic*. New York: Summit Books, 1987.

Conner, Rick. *Harley-Davidson Data Book*. Osceola WI: MBI, 1996.

Cooper-Smith, A. *The Marne—And After*. London: Cassell, 1917.

Corcoran, Captain A. P. *Ladies Home Journal*, pp. 7–72, October 1918.

Cornebise, Alfred E. *The Stars & Stripes: Doughboy Journalism in World War I*. Westport, CT: Greenwood Press, 1984.

Crismon, Frederick W. *International Trucks*. Osceola, WI: Motorbooks International, 1995.

_____. *U.S. Military Wheeled Vehicles*. Osceola, WI: MBI, 1994.

Cruttwell, C. R. M. F. *The Great War 1914–1918*. London: Oxford University Press, 1964.

_____. *A History of the Great War*. New York: The Clarendon Press, 1934.

Doodly, Jr., William G. *Great Weapons of World War I*. New York: Walker, 1969.

Duhamel, Roger. *Canadian Expeditionary Force 1914–1919*. Official History of the Canadian Army in the First World War. Ottawa, Canada: Government Printing Office, 1962.

Dunham, Terry B., and Lawrence R. Gustin. *The Buick: A Complete History*. Kutztown, PA: Automobile Quarterly, 2005.

Dupuy, Col. Trevor Nevitt, and Wlodzimierz, Onacewicz, *Triumphs and Tragedies in the East 1915–1917*. London: Franklin Watts, 1967.

Dyke, A. L. *Dyke's Automobile and Gasoline Engine Encyclopedia*. Warrendale, PA: SAE, 1915.

Ellis, Chris. *Military Transport of World War I*. New York: Macmillan, 1970.

_____. *Vehicles at War*. Great Bookham, England: Armor in Profile, 1980.

Esher, Viscount Reginald. *The Tragedy of Lord Kitchener*. London: John Murray, 1921.

Esposito, David M. *The Legacy of Woodrow Wilson*. New York: Praeger, 1996.

Esposito, Vincent J. *A Concise History of World War I*. New York: Praeger, 1964.

Falls, Cyril. *The Great War*. New York: G.P. Putnam, 1959.

Farwell, Byron. *Over There: The United States in the Great War*. New York: W.W. Norton, 2000.

Fitzsimons, Bernard. *Tanks & Weapons of World War I*. London: Phoebus, 1973.

Ford at Fifty: An American Story, Ford Motor Co. New York: Simon & Schuster, 1953.

Foss, Christopher F. *The Encyclopedia of Tanks and Armored Vehicles—The Complete Guide*. San Diego: Thunder Bay Press, 2002.

Freidel, Frank. *Over There*. Boston: Little, Brown, 1964.

French, David. *The Strategy of the Lloyd George Coalition*. New York: Oxford University Press, 1995.

Fuller, J. F. C. *The Decisive Battles of the Western World*. Vols. 1–3. London: Eyre and Spottiswoode, 1956.

Gilbert, Adrian. *Illustrated History of World War I*. New York: Crown, 1988.

Gillie, M. H. *Forging the Thunderbolt, History of the U.S. Army's Armored Forces 1917–1945*. Harrisburg, PA: Stackpole Books, 1947.

GM: The First 75 Years of Transportation Products. Kutztown, PA: Automobile Quarterly, 1983.

Goodman, Bryan. *American Cars in Europe*. Jefferson, NC: McFarland, 2006.

Goodspeed, D. J. *Ludendorff*. London: Hart-Davis, 1966.

Gotlieb, W. W. *Studies in Secret Diplomacy during the First World War*. London: George Allen, 1957.

Gough, General Sir Huber. *The Fifth Army*. London: Hodder and Stoughton, 1931.

Graham, Frank D. *Audel's New Automobile Guide for Mechanics, Operators and Servicemen*. New York: Theo. Audel, 1943.

Grey, Viscount. *Twenty-Five Years*. Vols. 1 and 2. London: Hodder and Stoughton, 1925.

Groteleuschen, Mark E. *The AEF Way of War: The American Army & Combat in World War I*. New York: Cambridge University Press, 2007.

Guditt, Sharon. *Fighting Forces—Writing Women: Identity & Ideology in the First World War*. New York: Routledge Press, 1994.

Gudmundsson, Bruce I. *On Armor*. New York: Praeger, 1994.

Gunnell, John. *Standard Catalog of Light Duty Chevrolet Trucks*. Iola, WI: Krause, 1995.

_____. *Standard Catalog of Light Duty Dodge Trucks*. Iola, WI: Krause, 2002.

_____. *Standard Catalog of Light Duty Ford Trucks*. Iola, WI: Krause 2003.

Halberstadt, Hans. *Military Vehicles from World War I to the Present*. New York: Metrobooks, 1998.

Hallas, James H. *Doughboy War: The American Ex-*

peditionary Force in World War I. Boulder, CO: Lynne Rienner, 2000.

Halsey, Francis Whiting. *The Literary Digest History of World War I.* Vols. 1–10. New York : Funk & Wagnalls, 1919–1920.

Hankey, Lord. *The Supreme Command, 1914–1918.* Vols. 1 and 2. London: Allen and Unwin, 1961.

Hanley, George Philip, and Stacey Pankiw Hanley. *The Marmon Heritage.* Rochester, MI: Doyle Hyk, 1990.

Hatfield, Jerry, and Hans Halberstadt. *Indian Motorcycles.* Osceola, WI: MBI, 1996.

Henig, Ruth. *The Origins of the First World War.* New York: Routledge Press, 2002.

Henshaw, Peter. *The Encyclopedia of the Harley-Davidson.* London: Grange, 2001.

_____. *The Illustrated Directory of Tractors.* Osceola, WI: MBI, 2002.

Herman, Gerald. *The Pivotol Conflict.* Westport, CT: Greenwood Press, 1992.

Hoffmann, Ge. Max. *The War of Lost Opportunities.* New York: International, 1925.

Hogg, Ian V. *Armour in Conflict: The Design and Tactics of Armoured Fighting Vehicles.* London: Jane's Pub., 1980.

_____. *Tanks and Armored Vehicles.* New York: F. Watts, 1984.

_____, and John Weeks. *The Illustrated Encyclopedia of Military Vehicles.* New York: Prentice Hall, 1980.

_____, and _____. *The Illustrated History of Military Vehicles.* London: New Burlington Books, 1984.

Homans, James E. *Self-Propelled Vehicles—A Practical Treatise.* New York: Theo. Audel, 1907.

Horne, Alistaire. *The Price of Glory at Verdun.* New York: St. Martin's Press, 1963.

Jones, Arthur W. Automotive History Review, For Official Use Only: The Army Goes Shopping. Alexandria, VA: Society of Automotive Historians, 2004, pp. 28–36.

Josephy, Alvin. *The American Heritage History of World War I.* New York: American Heritage, 1964.

Kaegan, John. *The First World War.* New York: Vintage Books Random House, 1998.

Katz, Friederich. *The Life and Times of Pancho Villa.* Palo Alto, CA: Stanford University Press, 1980.

Kimes, Beverly. *Packard: A History of the Motor Car and the Company.* Kutztown, PA: Automobile Quarterly, 2002.

Kimes, Beverly. *Pioneers, Engineers and Scoundrels.* Warrendale, PA: SAE, 2005.

The Kissel Truck Sales Manual. Hartford, WI: Kissel, 1919.

Kowalke, Ron. *Standard Catalog of Buick.* Iola, WI: Krause, 2000.

_____, and John Chevedden. *Standard Catalog of Oldsmobile.* Iola, WI: Krause, 1997.

Lacey, Robert. *Ford: The Men and the Machine.* Boston: Little, Brown, 1986.

Lansford, William Douglas. *Pancho Villa.* Los Angeles: Author's Guild Back Imprints, 2003.

Leffingwell, Randy. *Caterpillar.* Osceola, WI: MBI, 1994.

Le Goffic, Charles. *General Foch at the Marne.* London: Dent, 1918.

Lenzke, T. *Standard Catalog of Cadillac.* Iola, WI: Krause, 2004.

Leslie's Illustrated. January 7, 1915; May 6, 1915. New York.

Liddell Hart, B. H. *A History of the World War 1914–1918.* London: Faber and Faber, 1934.

The Literary Digest. April 7, 1917, p. 1023. May 12, 1917, p. 1424. Nov. 17, 1917, p. 88. March 23, 1918, p. 3. August 17, 1918, p. 60. Nov. 23, 1918, pp. 59–60. Dec. 14, 1918, p. 55.

Lowry, Bullitt. *Armistice 1918.* Kent, OH: Kent State University Press, 1996.

Ludendorph, General Erich. *My War Memories 1914–1918.* Vols. 1 and 2. London: Hutchinson, 1919.

Lyons, Michael, J. *World War I: Short History.* New Jersey: Prentice Hall, 2000.

Marshall, George C. *Memoirs of My Service in the World War 1917–1918.* Boston: Houghton Mifflin, 1970.

Mason, Herbert Malloy. *The Great Pursuit.* New York: Random House, 1970.

Maxim, Hiram Percy. *Horseless Carriage Days.* New York: Harper and Brothers, 1937.

McCalley, Bruce. *Model T Ford: The Car That Changed the World.* Iola, WI: Krause, 1999.

McCarty, Jennifer Hooper. *What Really Sank the Titanic.* New York: Citadel, 2008.

McEntee, Girard. *Military History of the World War.* Boston: Little and Brown, 1930.

McLynn, Frank. *Villa and Zapata: A History of the Mexican Revolution.* New York: Carroll and Graf, 2000.

McMaster, John Black. *The United States in the World War.* New York: D. Appleton, 1918.

McPherson, Thomas A. *The Dodge Story.* McPherson, Osceola, WI: MBI, 1992.

McWilliams, James L. *Amiens 1918.* Stroud, Gloucestershire: Tempus, 2004.

Military Operations, France and Belgium 1918. HMSO, 1947.

Miller, David. *Directory of Tanks of the World.* London: Grenwich Editions, 2004.

_____. *The Illustrated Directory of Tanks & Fighting Vehicles.* Osceola, WI: MBI, 2000.

Misa, Thomas J. *A Nation of Steel.* Baltimore: Johns Hopkins Press, 1995.

Mitchel, Doug. *Standard Catalog of Harley-Davidson.* Iola, WI: Krause, 1996.

Montville, John B. *Bulldog.* Tucson, AZ: Aztex Press, 1979.

More, Charles. *Understanding the Industrial Rev-olution*. London: Kindle, 2000.

The Motor World, April 4, 1917. June 13, 1917. Page 38: "Makers Bid Low for Army Vehicles."

National Geographic. March 1917. April 1917. May 1917 (multiple articles). June 1918, p. 496. August 1917, inside back cover.

Nicholson, Col. G. W. L. Canadian Expeditionary Force 1914–1919, Official History of the Canadian Army in the First World War. Ottawa, Canada: Roger Duhamel, 1962.

Olsen, Byron, and Joseph Cabadas. The American Auto Factory, Osceola, MBI, 2002.

Orgill, Douglas. *Armored Onslaught 8th August 1918*. New York: Ballantine Books, 1972.

Ouditt, Sharon. Fighting Forces—Writing Women: Identity & Ideology in the First World War. New York: Routledge, 1994.

Palazzo, Albert. *Seeking Victory on the Western Front*. Lincoln: University of Nebraska Press, 2000.

Pershing, John. *My Experience in the First World War*. New York: Frederick Stokes, 1962.

Plana, Manuel. *Pancho Villa and the Mexican Revolution*. New York: Interlink, 2000.

Powell, Sinclair. *The Franklin Automobile Company*. Warrendale, PA: SAE, 1999.

Pripps, Robert N. *Illustrated Ford and Fordson Tractor Buyer's Guide*. Osceola, WI: MBI, 1994.

Rafferty, Tod. *The Illustrated Directory of Harley-Davidson Motorcycles*. Osceola, WI: MBI, 2001.
_____. *The Indian: The History of a Classic American Motorcycle*. Philadelphia: Courage Books, 1998.

Remak, Joachim. *Sarajevo*. New York: Criterion Books, 1939.

Ritter, Gerhard. *The Schlieffen Plan*. New York: Praeger, 1958.

Robbins, Keith. *The First World War*. New York: Oxford University Press, 1993.

Rollins, Peter C., and John C. O'Conner. *Hollywood World War I Motion Picture Images*. Bowling Green, OH: Bowling Green State University Popular Press, 1997.

Rolt, L. T. C. *A Picture History of Motoring*. New York: Macmillan, 1956.

Roosevelt, Theodore. *America & the World War*. New York: Charles Scribner, 1915.

Salas, Elizabeth. *Soldaderas in the Mexican Military*. Austin: University of Texas Press, 1990.

Seton-Watson, R. W. *Sarajevo*. London: Hutchinson, 1926.

Shotwell, James T. *Economic & Social History of the World War*. Washington D.C.: Carnegie Endowment for International Peace, 1924.

Sieber, Mary. *Standard Catalog of Cadillac*, Iola, WI: Krause, 1991.

Simonds, Frank. H. *A History of the World War*. Vols. 1–5. New York: Doubleday Page, 1917–1919.

Spears, Sir Edward. *Prelude to Victory*. London: Jonathan Cape, 1930.

Stallings, Lawrence. *The Doughboys*. New York: Harper and Row, 1963.

Stearns, Peter N. *The Industrial Revolution in World History*. Boulder, CO: Westview Press, 1998.

Stein, General von. *A War Minister and His Work*. London: Sheffington, 1930.

Stern, Sir Albert. *Tanks 1914–1918: The Log-Book of a Pioneer*. London: Hodder and Stoughton, 1919.

Stokebury, James L. *A Short History of World War I*. New York: HarperCollins, 1981.

Taylor, Edmond. *The Fall of the Dynasties*. New York: Doubleday, 1963.

Terraine, John. *Douglas Haig, the Educated Soldier*. London: Hutchinson, 1963.

Tesla, Nikola. *My Inventions: The Autobiography of Nikola Tesla*. Williston, VT: Hart Bros., 1982.

Thoumin, General Richard. *The First World War*. New York: G.P. Putnam, 1964.

Trewhitt, Philip. *Armored Fighting Vehicles*. New York: Barnes & Noble, 1999.

Truck Talk, GMC, Number Twenty. Pontiac, General Motors Truck Co., 1918.

Tuchman, Barbara. *Guns of August*. New York: Macmillan, 1962.

The United States Army in the World War, 1917–1919. Vol. 14. Washington D.C.: U.S. Government Printing Office, 1948.

War Department Annual Report, Report of the Quartermaster General. Washington D.C.: U.S. Government Printing Office, 1916.

Watt, Richard. *Dare Call It Treason*. New York: Simon and Schuster, 1963.

Welsome, Eileen. *The General and the Jaguar: Pershing's Hunt for the Mexican Revolutionary*. Boston: Little, Brown, 2006.

Wendell, C. H. *Standard Catalog of Farm Tractors*. Iola, WI: Krause, 1995.

The Western Front 1914, Canadian General Staff, Army Headquarters. Ottawa, Canada: 1957.

Wheeler, W. Reginald. *China & the World War*. New York: Macmillan, 1919.

White, B. T. *Tanks & Other Armored Fighting Vehicles 1900–1918*. New York: Macmillan, Blanford Press, 1970.

The White Service Record. Cleveland: White Company, 1919.

Willmott, H. *World War I*. New York: DK Press, 2007.

Wolff, Leon. *In Flanders Fields*. New York: Viking Press, 1958.

The World's Work. June 1914. July 1914. Doubleday, Page & Co. Garden City, Long Island.

Wynn, Neil A. *From Progressivism to Prosperity*. New York: Homes & Meier, 1986.

INDEX

*Numbers in **bold italics** indicate pages with photographs.*

ML   10/09